Lawyer Evaluation in Chinese Courtroom

Liping Zhang

Lawyer Evaluation in Chinese Courtroom

A Social-Semiotic Perspective

Springer

Liping Zhang
School of Foreign Languages
Southeast University
Nanjing, China

ISBN 978-981-97-1210-6 ISBN 978-981-97-1211-3 (eBook)
https://doi.org/10.1007/978-981-97-1211-3

This Springer imprint is published by the registered company Springer Nature Singapore Pte Ltd.
The registered company address is: 152 Beach Road, #21-01/04 Gateway East, Singapore 189721, Singapore

Paper in this product is recyclable.

Preface

The legal system in the millennia-long history of traditional China and its link with or (dis)continuity in the law and legal system of contemporary China in cultural and discursive dimensions have remained intriguing topics in the field of Chinese history, society, and law. Presumably, like other prominent legal systems in the world that have various philosophies in their tradition, the humanism-centered traditional law of China has offered particular patterns either in codified laws or legal procedures that embodied valuable experiences and wisdom compatible with the social practices and life in the past, despite drawbacks and limitations thereof that need to be overcome or eradicated by people situated in the changing context of the present time (Alford 1997). A proper assessment of the value and significance of the traditional law is beyond the scope of this research. Nevertheless, the legal culture may have certain implicit or explicit impacts on the institutionalization and practices of the legal system and legal language at present, for which it should not be dismissed as totally outdated or completely inefficient when we observe the communication of law and the processing of legal issues today.

The features of lawyer speech in China deserve panoramic portrayal and cultural interpretation. As is widely known, the socialist legal system of China, which belongs to the civil law system literally, has incorporated some adversarial features into its legal proceedings recently. The balance and compromise between ideology and actuality are situated at the core of intellectual and scholarly considerations. Lawyers, masters of the law, as the term suggests, who play crucial roles in the adversarial trial system, did not emerge as a legitimate profession until the early beginning of the twentieth century in Chinese legal history. It would be unfair to reckon that legal representation in the law had been absent in the imperial society (221 BC–1911AD). On the contrary, the 讼师 (*song shi* in pinyin), which means litigation masters, appeared as early as the end of the Spring and Autumn Period (501BC) and gradually evolved as a prosperous shadow (illegal) profession in later dynasties, who had managed to provide legal services to laypersons in that period (Dang 2005). As opposed to lawyers who began to officially engage in the legal system in England in the thirteenth and fourteenth centuries (Chroust 1960), Chinese lawyers have been very young in their standing. The linguistic practices of lawyers indeed come to the fore when discussing the practices of the law in legal procedures, although the language of the tribunal and ordinary litigants in law cannot be neglected.

Questions that may arise to scholars in the field of legal language may be more focused on the dynamic use of language in the court procedure because the trial talk vividly demonstrates the mechanism and operation of law in handling disputes to laypersons outside the law system. What does lawyer speech look like in the adversarial trials of China, where morality-centered Confucianism have been influential for centuries? Why does lawyer speech look less competitive and aggressive than that in Anglo-Saxon law countries? Is this speech style motivated by social and cultural factors? Is the speech style instrumentally adequate in enacting the force of the law in life? Bearing these in mind, the author began her voyage of inquiry on legal language research to explore the relationship between the identity of law, social order, and humanity. In this exploration, the cultural tradition of the law in China would be constantly referred to so as to grasp the characteristics of lawyer speech in court, which may show the similarities that lawyers share with their counterparts in the West and distinguish them from the latter in a certain way.

The main ideas of the work have undergone contemplation in two decades. The exploration into lawyer speech was initiated in 2003 when the researcher started her three-year Ph.D. project, and the study served as a theoretical description of lawyers' speech in the adversarial trial, following heated discussions among scholars at that time on the enactment of the revised Criminal Procedural Law (1996). In 20 years, the Criminal Procedural Law was further revised in 2012 and 2018, respectively, which has brought substantial changes to the trial practices in the institutionalization and instantiation of the law in life. The validity of the descriptions of lawyer speech outlined in the Ph.D. thesis, which was published with the Intellectual Property Publishing House (Beijing) in 2010, awaited scrutiny both in theory and in practice. Accordingly, with more trial data collected accumulatively over the years of research and more sophisticated abstraction and observation gathered from systematic discussions in research projects focusing on legal speech in China, we felt more at ease with some of the statements proposed in the work.

With the mindset to consolidate our perspective of lawyer speech in the Chinese context, we ventured to update some of the critical literature and then improve coherence in the theoretical propositions by providing cultural explanations regarding the speech patterns. Immature and inadequate as the work may be, it would serve as our attempt to sketch some regularities of legal communication in the Chinese context. The fruitful research findings reported in the literature as regards the lawyers' speech in the Western courts, which provided theoretical and material preparations in this exploration, were fairly credited but not over-relied. The lawyer speech in this study is systematically constructed and interpreted as a speech pattern of its own, which is supported by theoretical abstraction and substantial data in the Chinese context.

That said, this manuscript would be gladly presented not only to graduate students and researchers within the circle of language and the law but also to the broad community who are interested in language and culture in institutional settings, including but not limited to legal professionals.

Liping Zhang
Professor of Applied Linguistics
Southeast University
Nanjing, China

References

Alford, W.P. 1997. Law, law, what laws? Why western scholars of Chinese history and society have not had more to say about its law? *Modern China* 23(4): 398–419. http://www.jstor.org/stable/189393.

Dang, J. 2005. 古代讼师文化 [*Understanding the Culture of Litigation Masters in Imperial China*]. Beijing: Beijing University Press.

Chroust, A-Hermann. 1960. The ranks of the legal profession in England. *Western Reserve Law Review* 11: 561–601. https://scholarlycommons.law.case.edu/caselrev/vol11/iss4/5

Acknowledgments

I would like to acknowledge the contributions and help of many people, without whom the work could never take its shape.

First of all, my heartfelt gratitude would be extended to the teachers, instructors, and supervisors in the Ph.D. program of the Research Center of Linguistics and Applied Linguistics, Guangdong University of Foreign Studies, in particular, Prof. Jinbang Du, who patiently trained us to observe the mystery of legal language in its multifacetedness, which directed me onto the path of legal language research, and Prof. Xinhong Zhang, who generously shared his insightful ideas and valuable resources on legal language and the law.

I am much indebted to Prof. Zhenhua Wang at Shanghai Jiaotong University, who graciously offered suggestions concerning the functions of legal language, and Prof. Meizhen Liao at Central China Normal University and Prof. Guang Shi at Nanjing Normal University, for sharing with us their latest research findings. I also owe thanks to Associate Professor Xianwei Pu and Ms. Leina Lu from Nanjing University of Science and Technology, both of whom happily shared their practical experience in exploring data and selecting research tools.

I would like to express my sincere gratitude to the contributions and assistance from the many friends who kindly provided convenience as a research team. Their help enabled us to access data through official channels or personal connections. Among many, I would like to give special thanks to my former colleague, Prof. Xiaobai Jin, at Shanghai University of International Business and Economics. During our cooperation, he successfully helped to establish academic connections and cooperative projects with several courts where we could regularly observe the trials and obtain data; furthermore, as a professional lawyer and experienced researcher in cultural studies, he offered many of his inspirational ideas to enrich our exploration of the interdisciplinary study of legal language.

I would also like to extend my appreciations to my graduate students, Miss Chenxi Wu, Miss Shan Zong, Miss Chenying Guo, Miss Yan Zhang, and a few more, who actively participated in data collection and analysis and contributed their creativity to our research projects. Special thanks are to be given to Miss Fanglu Li for her precious time spent proofreading the manuscript.

Lastly, I am much grateful to the editors who assisted the production and publication of the work. The personnel in Intellectual Property Publishing House (Beijing) and People's Court Press (Beijing), whose names are not to be specified due to specific reasons, kindly responded to my queries with respect to the copyright issues in the preparation of the revised manuscript. Ms. Lydia Wang and Ms. Vinothini Elango at Springer provided assistance of various kinds to me throughout the publication process.

The remaining mistakes in the manuscript would be solely the researcher's responsibility.

Liping Zhang

Contents

List of Figures

List of Tables

Chapter 1
Introduction

Abstract This chapter introduces the research background, key terms, and research rationale of the study. Subsequently, it discusses the significance of the research, presents the research methodology employed, and concludes by outlining the structure of the manuscript.

1.1 Legal Speech in the Chinese Context

The speech style of lawyers in the adversarial trial system of China remains an intriguing issue in trial communication, which is what this study attempts to address. With the promulgation of the Criminal Procedural Law of the People's Republic of China in October 1996, the inquisitorial system, which had been employed in trials since the establishment of the People's Republic of China in 1949, was abolished. Instead, a new system with adversarial features in the trial proceedings was put in practice (see Zhang and Wu 2012) and continues to be used today. In the current trial system, lawyers are able to provide more defense services for a defendant than in the inquisitorial system. They are supposed to play a more active role on behalf of the defendant in the trial proceedings, presenting arguments before the judge, competing with their opposing counterparts and even challenging a judicial opinion sometimes. It should be noted here that the trial system is not a simple replicate of the adversary trials in an Anglo-American court. In order to emphasize the adversarial nature, the new trial system is designated as adversary trials or the adversary system for easy reference in this study.

The lack of lawyers with proficient lawyering skills in court has been a very urgent problem to solve in the practices of the adversarial system. In the revised editions of the Criminal Procedural Law in 2012 and 2018, additional protections for a defendant's lawful rights in the procedural aspect of the system design have been introduced to ensure that the representing lawyers can effectively and actively fulfill their roles in the trial. For instance, the lawyer retained by a defendant to handle their case is now allowed to provide defense representation at various stages of the case, including offering professional assistance to offenders even before the

L. Zhang, *Lawyer Evaluation in Chinese Courtroom*,
https://doi.org/10.1007/978-981-97-1211-3_1

formal prosecution of the case, reviewing the prosecution files when preparing the defense and offering professional advice to offenders regarding whether and how to voluntarily confess to their offenses at a public security office so as to potentially receive a lenient judgment concerning the alleged offense. However, in some cases, the cross-examination of evidence between the two opposing parties may not be fully and sufficiently conducted before judges due to obstacles related to social, political, cultural, linguistic, or cognitive factors. Time constraints during a trial, witnesses' reluctance to testify, and, more importantly, a lack of sufficient professional lawyers available to provide defense for every defendant all contribute to these challenges. As indicated in statistical figures, the lack of lawyers' participation or effective defense in criminal cases was prevalent in many parts of the country prior to 2010 (Qian 2009; Wu 2011), and the situation has not shown significant improvements recently due to various reasons (Zhang et al. 2020).

Meanwhile, rapid economic development and subsequent social changes have led to structural changes in the typology of both civil and criminal cases. Such newly-emerging offenses, crimes, or misconducts like cyberbullying, fraud, and infringement are rising in great numbers, while the traditional severe crimes like arson, robbery, and murder are decreasing. To cope with the judicial processing of a rapidly growing number of lawsuits, both in civil and criminal cases within the adversarial system, there is a dire need for more competent lawyering.

Among many factors, engaging in verbal competition with the opposing parties in a formal court may be impolite or face-threatening from a linguistic and cultural perspective of China, where the construction and maintenance of harmony in interpersonal relationships has long been regarded as essential due to the influence of Confucianism in China for centuries (Zhang 2014). As a result, how lawyers can behave more effectively in linguistic and discursive senses, in accordance with their legitimate roles in the adversary system, has received considerable attention from the media and legal scholars (see, for instance, Wu 2011).

In a well-documented critical review of the speech style of lawyers in some courts, particularly in underdeveloped areas, it was stated that some lawyers behaved "simplistically and inappropriately" and confronted the opposing party "radically, fiercely in every minute aspect throughout the trial process" (Zhang et al. 2001: 9–10, 23–27). The question arises as to what would be the "proper" speech style for a competent lawyer when they present arguments in a competitive trial within the Chinese legal system. During a high-level academic dialogue between three esteemed experts in the judicial circle, Zhang, Jiang, and Tian, a speech model characterized by being "rational" was proposed and advocated. In this model, skillful lawyers were described as behaving in a "polite, civilized manner" and responding in two ways: to unequivocally acknowledge arguments deemed logical and reasonable, and to offer convincing challenges to those perceived as illogical or unreasonable (p. 27). The proposal for such a rational speech style of lawyers is both illuminating and instructive from a metaphysical standpoint. After decades of judicial reforms and practices following the implementation of the adversarial system, this style has become the norm for lawyer speech in courts of many places, particularly the eastern part of the country, and in higher-level courts (p. 23).[1] Consequently, exploring the linguistic features of lawyers' speech style in court, regardless of whether the trial is criminal, civil, or administrative in nature, is of significance to scholars interested in legal language studies.

Theoretically, how lawyers objectively show their subjectivity in court awaits exploration. At present, dynamic studies on lawyer talk have documented diversified attempts, including the manipulation of witnesses or defendants in cross-examination (see, e.g., Aldridge and Luchjenbroers 2007; Baffy and Marsters 2015; Bennett and Feldman 1981; Drew 1990; Jacquemet 1996; Matoesian 1993; Walker 1987), the communication clash with witnesses (see, e.g., Cotterill 2010; Eades 1994, 2000; Heffer 2003; Walsh 1994), and the negotiation between professionals either in the bar (e.g., Maynard 1984; Pico i Junoy and López 2022) or at the bench (e.g. Gaines 2002; Kanner et al. 2019). Additionally, studies have explored the cognitive and linguistic processes involved in the negotiation of indeterminacy of meaning in law (see, e.g., Burton 1999; Cotterill 2003; Moore 1981; Stratman 2004; Tvrdíková 2023). An overarching theme that emerges from current research is the notion of power and control, which refers to the unequal distribution of power between interactants in legal communications.

However, an alternative question arises: Can lawyers go beyond relying solely on power and control and instead exercise their roles creatively? More specifically, is it possible for lawyers to engage in peaceful, less confrontational negotiations with each other while adhering to the boundaries set by the law? This theoretical inquiry serves as the focal point of the present study.

1.2 Lawyer Evaluation: Key Terms and Research Orientation

Since trial talk is composed of lawyers' expressions of their arguments, this research focuses on studying lawyers' evaluation of the case in a trial. In this study, the term "evaluation" follows the definition provided by Thompson and Hunston (2000: 5),

[1] The issue regarding the speech style of lawyers was initially raised in 2001 during a dialogue among three esteemed individuals in the legal field representing different participants in a trial. These individuals were Jun Zhang, who served as the chief judge in a criminal court of the Supreme People's Court at that time, Wei Jiang, the principal prosecutor in a state prosecution office, and Wen-chang Tian, a renowned lawyer specializing in criminal cases. Several decades later, when the revised criminal procedural law was enacted in 2012 and later modified in 2018, Zhang, Jiang, and Tian, holding positions as a prosecutor, a judge, and a lawyer respectively, engaged in further discussions and dialogues regarding the application of the revised law. In their discussions, Jiang, a chief judge, emphasized that peaceful exchanges of arguments between the prosecution, defense, and tribunal, as well as rational debates conducted within the legal framework and based on mutual understanding of each other, remained two fundamental manifestations of the trial system (Zhang et al. 2020: 17–18). As was observed in their discussion, the trial process began to "evolve towards a more cooperative mode, where the participants are engaged in more negotiating talk than in pure contestation" (p. 477). For more details, please refer to the implication section in Chap. 8.

which refers to the "expression of the speaker's attitude or stance towards, viewpoint on, or feelings about the entities or propositions that he or she is talking about." The attitude may encompass certainty, obligation, desirability, or other sets of values. Lawyer evaluation of the case in a trial, hereafter referred to as *lawyer evaluation*, denotes lawyers' expression of their attitudes or stances toward the various issues concerned in the case they represent or the propositions they put forward for the judges to consider in the resolution or disposition of a legal dispute.

The concept of *lawyer evaluation* has to be delimited at the outset. In essence, it refers to the kind of opinions, attitudes, or stances that lawyers have on the basis of legal reasoning within the framework of law. It should never be erroneously reduced to lawyers' personal preference or whatever, though the term is associated with opinions, stances, or attitudes. Admittedly, however, feelings or personal sentiments may inevitably sneak into the legal activity in a court (Yong et al. 2002: 280; Lynch 2009), which would indeed be excluded from this study.

Meanwhile, *lawyer evaluation* may also be conveyed nonverbally. For instance, nodding is a sign of agreement, and glaring at the opponent is an indication of strong dissatisfaction. Lawyer evaluation of this kind is not within the scope of discussion in this research.

In this study, the term *lawyer* serves as a comprehensive category that includes "agent ad litem" or legal representatives who appear in court on behalf of their clients. This category encompasses lawyers representing plaintiffs or defendants in civil cases, prosecuting lawyers in simple or private-prosecuting cases, and legal representatives for victims in criminal cases.[2] Unless explicitly stated otherwise, the term *lawyers* mentioned subsequently in this study will be used in this context.[3]

Lawyer evaluation permeates trial talk, encompassing the entirety of trial communication, including opening statements, the presentation of evidence, examination and cross-examination, and closing statements. In addition to its widespread occurrence throughout trial communication, both in terms of duration and volume, lawyer evaluation serves as a significant manifestation of legal agents' professional skills. This study aims to explore how lawyers engage in debates and express their subjectivity within legal settings, which typically emphasize objectivity as a normative requirement.

Lawyer evaluation is social and semiotic. It is social in the sense that opinions in court cannot be made on the basis of personal preferences but expressed within the bounds of the law, which is a norm-governed and socially organized activity constrained by the communicative routines in trial proceedings (see Levinson 1992). Meanwhile, it is social in the sense that it transcends mere verbal exchange and represents a performance of the legal activity that holds significance for the interests of the parties concerned and the broader public community.

---

[2] Actually, prosecutors may also be embraced within this category as they share with defense lawyers similar discourse skills in the court debate despite representing the state.

[3] In this study, the majority of the texts selected for illustration are defense lawyers' discourses. This decision is based on the assumption that the discourses of defense lawyers best exemplify the debating speech style in the court.

Lawyer evaluation in court is semiotic in that language itself is semiotic. Firstly, meanings in lawyer evaluation are determined in accordance with situations (Du 2001; Ludlow 2014). For one thing, lawyers' attitude toward the case is related to the interest of the party they stand for. To put it simply, the interests of the plaintiff or of the defense that lawyers set out to serve and defend compel them to position themselves differently. A lawyer may consider an act as an infringement if they represent the plaintiff, but hold a diametrically different position if they assume the role of a defense representative in the same case. For another thing, lawyers' opinions of the case are likely to be altered or modified to varying degrees during their interaction with other participants in court. Challenged by an opponent with more convincing evidence or reasoning, lawyers may re-adjust or re-consider their arguments. Secondly, lawyer evaluation is symbolic in nature since it serves a referential function. It establishes a relationship between the disputed act or behavior concerned in the case and the (potential) bearer of a claim/charge provided in the law. Through a discussion of the symbolic connection between the two, the legality of the said act and the legal duty or obligation of the party concerned are determined (Yong et al. 2002: 74; Lynch 2009). These two essential features of lawyer evaluation, contextualized meanings, and mediation in language, make evident the semiotic nature of it (see Littlejohn 1996: 159–160).

Of all linguistic theories that embrace social and semiotic views of language, Hallidayan Systemic Functional Linguistics (hereafter abbreviated as SFL) is the one that best accommodates the analysis in this study. SFL offers a robust framework for interpreting the functions of language and the connection between language and social structure. Particularly relevant to this investigation of lawyers' role in trial communication is the interpersonal metafunction of language within SFL. In brief, the interpersonal metafunction refers to

> the speaker's meaning potential as an intruder, the participatory function of language, the component through which the speaker intrudes himself into the context of a situation, both expressing their own attitudes and judgments and seeking to influence the attitudes and behavior of others. (Halliday 1978: 112–113)

Moreover, SFL provides an efficient tool for conducting discourse analysis. Its framework offers researchers a set of operational principles and techniques to analyze language usage in diverse contexts.[4] Thus, SFL serves as the theoretical guideline that will shape and inform the methodology employed in this research.

In short, this study aims to examine lawyer evaluation through the lens of the interpersonal metafunction of language within the Hallidayan tradition. By focusing on this particular aspect of language, the research seeks to shed light on how lawyers express their attitudes, opinions, and subjectivity during trial communication.

[4] For more reasons why SFG is chosen as a theoretical tool, see Chap. 2.

1.3 Research Questions

In order to explore the linguistic patterns of lawyer evaluation in adversary trials within the Chinese context, this study addresses four research questions as follows:

(1) What are the conceptual constituents of lawyer evaluation?
(2) How do the contextual constraints influence lawyer evaluation in the specialized setting of the courtroom?
    a. What role does the situational context play in the presentation of lawyer evaluation during the trial?
    b. What role does the legal context play in the presentation of lawyer evaluation during the trial?
(3) What stance do lawyers discursively construct via lawyer evaluation in the court, and how do they achieve this?
    The questions aim to investigate the stance of lawyers in their interaction with the opposing parties and trial judges, as well as the linguistic realizations of such positioning.
(4) What is the function of lawyer evaluation in the trial?
    This question pertains to how lawyer evaluation contributes to the ultimate purpose of legal dispute resolution or criminal case disposition in a trial.

1.4 Research Method and Data Collection

1.4.1 Research Method

This qualitative research is grounded in authentic data recorded, transcribed, or photocopied from trials in China. The texts of lawyer speech will undergo thorough discourse analysis, employing a methodology that combines deduction and induction, description and interpretation. This approach emphasizes depth over breadth, enabling a comprehensive understanding of the texts that may not be achievable through quantitative studies based on large corpora.

1.4.2 Data Collection and Description

The data collected in this study focused on the speech of lawyers during the stages of a trial, which encompassed opening statements, presentation, and examination of evidence, as well as closing statements. These stages were chosen because they allow lawyers to demonstrate their persuasive power and subjective roles through the use of language. Needless to say, topics related to the facts of a case, the determination of the facts in the law, and corresponding penalties or remedies were all covered in these two stages.

The data collection for this study was conducted in two distinct periods by the researcher and her team members. The first period took place between July 2003 and February 2005, while the second period occurred from September 2013 to October 2016. In instances where trial talks were directly recorded as audio files or trial records were accessed in photocopied form, prior approval or permission was obtained from the courts beforehand. This process ensured compliance with legal requirements and ethical considerations regarding data collection. For cases where data had to be indirectly collected, the materials used were publicly available, either in the form of video disks or online trial records. These sources were accessible to the public, thus allowing the researcher and her team members to utilize them for the study. By obtaining proper authorization or utilizing publicly accessible materials, the data collection process maintained integrity and followed appropriate procedures to ensure the legitimacy and validity of the data used in the study.

To ensure broad and comprehensive coverage of data, the data collection was primarily undertaken in courts at the local districts, and courts of the intermediate or supreme levels, specifically in cities located in the eastern or southern regions of China. Courts in these areas were chosen due to two factors. Firstly, since the eastern and southern parts of China have historically enjoyed more vigorous economic development and better educational resources compared with other regions, a higher concentration of lawyers with professional legal knowledge and skills in these areas may be guaranteed. As a result, laypersons in these regions may have better access to legal representation and benefit from the expertise of lawyers who possess a deeper understanding of the law. Secondly, targeting higher-level courts enabled researchers to observe more complex lawyering techniques in this study. These courts handle complex and diverse cases of significance in subject matter, involving intricate legal arguments and strategies. In this way, the researchers could ensure that the collected data included instances of sophisticated lawyer discourse and professional legal communication.

In total, 73 cases, encompassing criminal, civil, and administrative matters, were included in the datasets of the study. A wide range of materials, such as trial transcripts, lawyers' written statements, and legal opinions, were used for analysis. The total number of materials gathered amounted to 115.

The data consisted of texts in two clusters. The first one comprised audio-recorded or video-recorded trials and corresponding transcripts. To ensure consistency and accuracy in transcription, two researchers within the team, who received training in both language and the law, were responsible for the transcription work. Generally, in line with the assumptions with respect to the relationship between grammar and interaction (Ochs 2006; Ochs et al. 1996), we believe that the utterances produced by different speakers in a court are contingently bound to each other on a turn-taking basis and organized in adjacency pairs. The transcription followed the routine annotations in discourse analysis (Dressler and Kreuz 2000), with certain modifications made to suit the level of analytic delicacy of this study and to accommodate the characteristics of the Chinese language. Unlike utterances in judicial interactions that were transcribed in a refined manner by Atkinson and Drew (1990), due to the theoretical consideration and research purpose of the study, only the orthographic layer of the utterances in lawyer speech received careful transcription. The words or characters speakers produced in their interaction during the trial were honestly, consistently, and objectively transcribed. Few considerations were paid to paralinguistic features (such as pitch, rhythm, and volume), nonverbal elements (like facial expression, and posture), and interactive features (such as silence, breathing, and interruption) associated with the production of sounds, unless these features otherwise impacted the meanings represented through the words or characters. For detailed information on the transcription notations employed in this study, please refer to Appendix A.

The second dataset consisted of photocopied trial records, lawyers' written statements of defense (including opening and closing statements in court), and judgments. The second dataset was relevant to this study for two reasons. Firstly, it served as the sole accessible material when direct recording of trials was not possible due to factors such as the involvement of business secrecy or inconvenience of travel on the part of the research team. Secondly, the importance of these data cannot be understated. In fact, they were frequently referenced when the case was deliberated by the judiciary outside the courtroom. In the legal practices of China, which follow a Roman law system, documentary evidence holds significant importance, sometimes even surpassing the value of oral testimony. As parallel texts of lawyers' speech in a chain of genres (Swales 2004), the court's judgments were consulted wherever necessary, especially when we assessed the impact of lawyer evaluation in the study.

Although the discourse in this second set was in written form, it should not be disregarded as fundamentally different from lawyers' oral speech during trials. In the institutional setting of the courtroom, where professionalism is paramount, lawyers' written discourse retains similarities to their spoken discourse. Therefore, it is crucial not to dismiss the written discourse of lawyers as fundamentally distinct from their oral communication.

In order to protect the legitimate rights of the lawyers and individuals involved in the cases, all names and identification information of the cases were anonymized when cited in this study for publication.

1.5 Significance of This Study

Three points have led to the initiation of this study. Topping the list of the most cited reasons is the importance of institutional discourse analysis. As Makitalo and Saljo (2002: 57) point out, "It is hardly surprising [for institutional talk to be attractive to many scholars] since institutions may play a central role in the production and maintenance of social order." It is a fact, nevertheless, that the distribution of access to the institutional talk is very asymmetrical, with institutional organizers being in sole control of the talk (van Dijk 1996). Therefore, demystifying the routine constraints of institutions and exposing the patterns of how speakers respond to these constraints are of crucial significance to the study of institutional talk. The significance may explain the shift of academic interests over the past decade, with some conversational studies focusing more on institutional settings rather than ordinary interactions (see Heritage and Greatbatch 1991; Freed and Ehrlich 2009).

Compared with discourses in other institutional settings such as hospitals, schools, and governmental offices, courtroom discourse is notably more complex (Drew and Heritage 1992). Furthermore, the courtroom is a place where the use of language is closely tied to people's interests of various kinds, including matters as significant as life or death. Hence, the proper use of discourse holds tremendous importance in this context. However, it is crucial to recognize that participants in the courtroom do not have equal access to the communication code. Notably, even lawyers exhibit varying abilities in their engagement with courtroom communication, let alone laypeople within the larger population. Given this situation, it has become an urgent task for researchers interested in courtroom discourse analysis to demystify the constraints on lawyer evaluation, uncover the rules underlying lawyers' speech styles, and explore the language resources available for lawyer evaluation in court.

From the theoretical standpoint, an exploration of lawyer evaluation has the potential to enhance the holistic study of lawyers' language in communication, particularly within the Chinese context. This study seeks to anchor lawyer evaluation within the dimension of solidarity, offering an alternative perspective to the dimensions of power and status that have been examined predominantly in previous studies on legal language. By doing so, it provides a different lens through which to understand the work of lawyers in dispute resolution or disposition and their overall communication patterns. Through a solid theoretical foundation and comprehensive data analysis, this research aims to yield a novel understanding of lawyers' speech in the institutional context of the courtroom.

The second stimulus relates to the inadequacy of research on the interpersonal function of language. Comparatively speaking, the interpersonal function of language, i.e., the expressive function or subjective function of language, has been neglected in the history of linguistics (Lyons 1982: 102; Buhler 1934). Moreover, for quite a period, studies focusing on the subjective function of language have been limited to the grammar-based tradition, though the role of context has been recognized (Li 2002). Recently, however, scholars have realized that interpersonal resources are closely connected with genres and contexts (see, Li 2002: 65–67; Thompson 1996), and accordingly, they have made various explorations at the discourse level, such as Simpson (1993) on the points of view in narratives, Myers (1989) on hedging in scientific discourse, and Li (2000) on autobiography. More research in other fields, such as the courtroom, is desirable.

In the case of courtroom discourse, though numerous studies have highlighted subjectivity in lawyer talk, as is to be manifested in Chap. 2, specific works devoted to it have received comparatively scant attention so far. One possible explanation for this lack of study could be that scholars in forensic linguistics have been primarily focused on examining the functional aspects of language in specific cases. On the other hand, scholars in discourse studies and other related disciplines may have been hesitant to venture into the relatively unexplored field of courtroom discourse, possibly due to the formidable challenge of data collection. As a result, the question of how lawyers express their subjectivity within the institutional court setting remains unexplored and warrants further investigation.

Regarding the manifestation of the speaker's subjectivity in context, this study on lawyer evaluation can contribute to investigations into the relationship between evaluation resources and genres. Evaluation resources are influenced by the context or culture in which they are employed. Precht (2003: 240) asserts that although language provides individuals with a wide range of options for self-expression, many people are "culturally programmed" to utilize a limited and specific subset of these options. Therefore, the findings of this study, which examine the unique resources available to lawyers for expressing stance or attitude within the distinctive social setting of the courtroom, can serve as a valuable contribution to the field of evaluation studies.

The third reason that has emerged is the long-standing misconception regarding the magic role of lawyers' language in a trial. It is indeed true that lawyers' speech plays a significant part in the courtroom. Language not only facilitates the operation of the trial but, more importantly, it exerts an inconceivable impact on the ultimate outcome of the trial. The importance of language in the trial has been typically exemplified by transformational reconstructions of rape cases in court (see Ehrlich 2002; Matoesian 1993). Those examples create the impression that lawyers possess the ability to skillfully manipulate language to achieve their desired purposes in trial communication. The constructive function of language in law has been proved in numerous cases and research studies, for which the widely-quoted work of Goodwin and Goodwin (1997), serves as a compelling example. What was presented in that research is that the same incident, involving four police officers beating a black man, was linguistically constructed by the prosecution as a vicious use of force and an abuse of police power but was portrayed as a routine practice of police work by the defense party. These competing narratives were guided by different interpretive frameworks. However, it would be an exaggeration and an illusion to attribute trial success solely to verbal tricks employed by lawyers. To acknowledge the proper role of lawyer speech in a trial, this research explores how lawyer evaluation is expressed and negotiated in the courtroom debate.

Practically, the exploration of the speech patterns in lawyer evaluation can provide valuable insights into pedagogical issues related to legal education and training. Additionally, it can offer linguistic strategies that can be beneficial for practicing lawyers in their professional endeavors.

1.6 Organization of the Book

This study consists of eight chapters. This chapter serves as an introduction to the study, providing an introduction of the key terms, research orientation, and research questions. It also presents the research methods employed in this study and describes the process of data collection. Additionally, this chapter emphasizes the significance of the study and introduces the structure of the book. Chapter 2 critically reviews relevant studies in relation to lawyer evaluation. In Chap. 3, the theoretical framework of lawyer evaluation within the Chinese context is presented, followed by detailed data analysis in the subsequent four chapters.

Chapter 4 categorizes the constituents of lawyer evaluation in the textual form. In Chap. 5, the contextual features of the courtroom and their influence on lawyer evaluation, as observed in texts, are analyzed. Chapter 6 explores the patterns of lawyer evaluation within the Chinese courtroom, while Chap. 7 examines how lawyer evaluation achieves communicative goals during trials. Finally, Chap. 8 summarizes the significant findings of this study, acknowledges its contributions and limitations, and concludes with suggestions for future research.

References

Aldridge, M., and J. Luchjenbroers. 2007. Linguistic manipulations in legal discourse: Framing questions and "smuggling" information. *International Journal of Speech, Language and the Law* 14 (1): 85–107. https://doi.org/10.1558/ijsll.v14i1.85.

Atkinson, R.C., and P. Drew. 1990. *Order in court*. Hampshire & London: Macmillan Academic and Professional Ltd.

Baffy, M., and A. Marsters. 2015. The constructed voice in courtroom cross-examination. *International Journal of Speech, Language and the Law* 22 (2): 143–165. https://doi.org/10.1558/ijsll.v22i2.17895.

Bennett, W.L., and M.S. Feldman. 1981. *Reconstructing reality in the courtroom*. London: Tavistock.

Buhler, K. 1934. *Theory of translation: The representational function of language*. Amsterdam: John Benjamins.

Burton, S. 1999. *Introduction to law and law reasoning*. Translated by Zhiming Zhang and Xingquan Xie. Beijing: China University of Political Science and Law Press.

Cotterill, J. 2003. *Language and power in court: A linguistic analysis of the O.J Simpson trial*. Basingstoke: Palgrave.

Cotterill, J. 2010. Interpersonal issues in court: Rebellion, resistance, and other ways of behaving badly. In *Interpersonal pragmatics*, ed. Miriam A. Locher and Sage L. Graham, 353–380. Berlin, New York: De Gruyter Mouton. https://doi.org/10.1515/9783110214338.3.353.

Dressler, R.A., and R.J. Kreuz. 2000. Transcribing oral discourse: A survey and a model system. *Discourse Processes* 29 (1): 25–36. https://doi.org/10.1207/S15326950dp2901_2.

Drew, P. 1990. Strategies in the contest between lawyer and witness in cross-examination. In *Language in the judicial process*, ed. J.N. Levi and A.G. Walker, 39–64. New York & London: Plenum Press. https://doi.org/10.1007/978-1-4899-3719-3_2.

Drew, P., and J. Heritage. 1992. *Talk at work: Interaction in institutional settings*. Cambridge: Cambridge University Press.

Du, Jin-bang. 2001. 从法律语言的模糊性到司法结果的确定性 [From the vagueness of legal language to the definiteness of judicial outcomes]. 现代外语 [*Modern Foreign Languages*] (3): 305–310.

Eades, D. 1994. A case of communication clash. In *Language and the law*, ed. J. Gibbons, 234–264. London: Longman.

Eades, D. 2000. *I don't think it's an answer to the question*: Silencing Aboriginal witnesses in court. *Language in Society* 29: 191–195. https://doi.org/10.1017/S0047404500002013.

Ehrlich, S. 2002. (Re)contextualizing complainants' accounts of sexual assault. *Forensic Linguistics* 9 (2): 193–212. https://doi.org/10.1558/ijsll.v9i2.193.

Freed, A., and S. Ehrlich, eds. 2009. *Why do you ask? The function of questions in institutional discourse*. New York: Oxford University Press. https://doi.org/10.1093/acprof:oso/9780195306897.001.0001.

Gaines, P. 2002. Negotiating power at the bench. *Forensic Linguistics: The Journal of Speech, Language and Law* 9 (2): 199–230. https://doi.org/10.1558/sll.2002.9.2.213.
Goodwin, C., and M.H. Goodwin. 1997. Contested version: The discursive constitution of Rodney King. In *The construction of professional discourse*, ed. B.L. Gunnarsson, P. Linell, and B. Nordberg, 292–316. London & New York: Longman.
Halliday, M.A.K. 1978. *Language as social semiotic*. London: Edward Arnold.
Heffer, C. 2003. Making a case: Narrative and paradigmatic modes of legal-lay discourse in British jury trial. *Forensic Linguistics: Journal of Speech, Language and Law* 10 (1): 157–159. https://doi.org/10.1558/ijsll.v10i1.157.
Heritage, J., and D. Greatbatch. 1991. On the institutional character of institutional talk: The case of news interviews. In *Talk and social structure*, ed. D. Boden and H. Zimmerman, 93–137. Cambridge: Polity Press.
Jacquemet, M. 1996. *Credibility in court: Communicative practices in the Camorra trial*. Cambridge: Cambridge University.
Kanner, S., D.R. Luz, Y. Zohar, et al. 2019. Managerial judicial conflict resolution (JCR) of plea bargaining: Shadows of law and conflict resolution. *New Criminal Law Review* 22 (4): 494–541. https://doi.org/10.1525/nclr.2019.22.4.494.
Levinson, S. 1992. Activity types and language. In *Talk at work*, ed. P. Drew and J. Heritage, 66–100. Cambridge: Cambridge University Press.
Li, Zhan-zi. 2000. 语言的人际元功能新探—自传话语的人际意义研究 [*New exploration into the interpersonal meta-function of language: Interpersonal meanings of autobiographies*]. Beijing: Military Translation Press (军事译文出版社).
Li, Zhan-zi. 2002. 话语的人际意义研究 [*Interpersonal meanings of discourse*]. Shanghai: Shanghai Foreign Language Education Press.
Littlejohn, S.W. 1996. *Theories of human communication*. Belmont, Albany, Bonn: Humboldt University Press.
Ludlow, P. 2014. *Living words: Meaning underdetermination and the dynamic lexicon*. Oxford: Oxford University Press.
Lynch, M.P. 2009. *Truth as one and many*, online ed. Oxford: Academic. https://doi.org/10.1093/acprof:oso/9780199218738.001.0001. Accessed March 30, 2023.
Lyons, J. 1982. Deixis and subjectivity: Loquor, ergo sum. In *Speech, place and action: Studies in deixis and related topics*, ed. R.J. Jarvella and W. Klein, 101–124. Chichester: Wiley.
Makitalo, A., and R. Saljo. 2002. Talk in institutional context and institutional context in talk. *Text* 22 (1): 57–82. https://doi.org/10.1515/text.2002.005.
Matoesian, G.M. 1993. *Reproducing rape: Dominance through talk in the courtroom*. Oxford: Polity Press.
Maynard, D.W. 1984. *Inside plea bargaining*. New York: Plenum.
Moore, M. 1981. The semantics of judging. *Southern California Law Review* 54 (2): 151–294.
Myers, G. 1989. The pragmatics of politeness in scientific articles. *Applied Linguistics* 10 (1): 1–35. https://doi.org/10.1093/applin/10.1.1.
Ochs, E. 2006. Transcription as a theory. In *The discourse reader*, ed. A. Jaworski and N. Coupland, 166–178. New York: Routledge.
Ochs, E., E.A. Schegloff, and S. Thompson, eds. 1996. *Interaction and grammar*. Cambridge & New York: Cambridge University Press.
Pico i Junoy, J., and J.A. Andino López. 2022. Private communication between lawyers as evidence in a judicial process: A comparative journey. *International Journal of Evidence and Proof* 26 (1): 61–80. https://doi.org/10.1177/13657127211055232.
Precht, K. 2003. Stance moods in spoken English: Evidentiality and affect in British and American conversation. *Text* 23 (2): 239–257. https://doi.org/10.1515/text.2003.010.
Qian, Xue-min. 2009. 律师参与刑辩不过两成 [Lawyer participation and defense less than 20 percent of all cases in criminal trials]. 检察日报 (*Procuratorial Daily*), June 8: 7.
Simpson, P. 1993. *Language, ideology, and point of view*. London and New York: Routledge. https://doi.org/10.4324/9780203136867.

Stratman, J.F. 2004. How legal analysts negotiate indeterminacy of meaning in common law rules: Toward a synthesis of linguistic and cognitive approaches to investigation. *Language and Communication* 24: 23–57. https://doi.org/10.1016/S0271-5309(02)00041-1.

Swales, J.M. 2004. *Research genres: Exploration and applications*. Cambridge: Cambridge University Press.

Thompson, G. 1996. *Introducing functional grammar*. London: Arnold.

Thompson, G., and S. Hunston. 2000. Evaluation: An introduction. In *Evaluations in text*, ed. S. Hunston and G. Thompson, 1–27. Oxford: Oxford University Press.

Tvrdíková, L. 2023. Vagueness and indeterminateness in law: Are judges humpties dumpties? *International Journal for the Semiotics of Law* 36: 679–700. https://doi.org/10.1007/s11196-022-09935-0.

van Dijk, T.A. 1996. Discourse, power, and access. In *Texts and practices*, ed. Carmen R. Coulthard and Malcolm Coulthard, 84–105. London & New York: Routledge.

Walker, A.G. 1987. Linguistic manipulation, power, and the legal setting. In *Power through discourse*, ed. L. Kedar, 57–80. New Jersey: ABLEX.

Walsh, M. 1994. Interactional style in the courtroom. In *Language and the law*, ed. John Gibbons, 217–233. London: Longman.

Wu, Ji-kui. 2011. 对抗式刑事诉讼改革与有效辩护 [Adversarial criminal trial system reform and effective defense]. 中国刑事法杂志 [*Journal of China Criminal Law*] (5): 60–65.

Yong, Q., Cheng-guang Jin, and Rong-mao Yao. 2002. 法律适用中的逻辑 [*Logic in law application*]. Beijing: China University of Political Science and Law Press.

Zhang, Li.-ping. 2014. Linguistic politeness in lawyers' petitions under the Confucian ideal of no-litigation. *International Journal of Speech, Language and the Law* 21 (2): 317–342. https://doi.org/10.1558/ijsll.v21i2.317.

Zhang, Wu-sheng, and Ze-yong Wu. 2012. 对抗制诉讼与法官制度改革 [Adversarial litigation and judicial system reform]. *Qinghua Law Review* (2): 1–16.

Zhang, J., Wei Jiang, and Wen-chang Tian. 2001. 刑事诉讼: 控, 辩, 审三人谈 [*Criminal trials: A dialogue between the prosecution, defense and tribunal*]. Beijing: Law Press.

Zhang, J., Wei Jiang, and Wen-chang Tian. 2020. 新控辩审三人谈 (增补版) [*Further dialogues between the prosecution, defense and tribunal*] (Supplement version). Beijing: Law Press.

Chapter 2
Lawyer Evaluation in Text and Context

Abstract This chapter provides an overview of lawyer evaluation in three aspects: its conception, its realization as a linguistic activity, and its role as a legal activity, and explores the relevant studies on it into three strands of topics: the linguistic expression of it in text, the predominant roles that lawyers assume in the immediate context of the courtroom, and the prospective stances they may take under the mediating role of legal culture. The overview paves the way for the theoretical understanding of lawyer evaluation in the Chinese court.

2.1 Introduction

This chapter reviews relevant studies on lawyer evaluation in three aspects: its conceptions, its realization as a linguistic phenomenon, and its role as a legal activity, and explores lawyer evaluation in three streams of topics: its identification in text, the essential roles that lawyers assume in the immediate context of the court, and the prospective stances or positions they may choose in the mediating effect of the legal culture.

First of all, the term *lawyer evaluation* is introduced in its various senses, and the constituents it may encompass in text are discussed. Secondly, research on lawyer evaluation in the context of the court is thoroughly described. A linguistic survey highlights the essential roles that lawyers may assume in the context of the court and showcases how they manage their interpersonal relationships with the opposing party in court. Subsequently, a legal survey reveals the significant role of the legal culture, which refers to the Habermasian discourse theory, on lawyer speech in China. Finally, the chapter concludes by summarizing the implications and limitations of the existing studies.

L. Zhang, *Lawyer Evaluation in Chinese Courtroom*,
https://doi.org/10.1007/978-981-97-1211-3_2

2.2 The Construct of Lawyer Evaluation

This section presents conceptions related to the term *lawyer evaluation* and the various constituents it may encompass.

2.2.1 *The Conceptions of Lawyer Evaluation*

Defined as a linguistic concept in the present study, the term “lawyer evaluation” can be understood conceptually in both linguistic and legal senses.

Linguistically, expressions such as *speaker evaluation*, *speaker attitude*, or *speaker stance* all pertain to speakers’ expression of their attitudes (Thompson and Hunston 2000). Attitudes are widely employed in social activities, including academic communication (Biber and Finegan 1988; Hyland 2002, 2004; Hood 2004; etc.), mundane talks (Labov 2003; Page 2003; etc.), online interaction (Don 2003; Kristina 2006), political forum (Miller 2004), judicial reasoning (Kšrner 2000; Miller 2002), and media programs (Simon-Vandenbergen 2004; White 1998; etc.). Speakers’ appropriate expression of attitudes has thus become an integral and significant discursive means to achieve communicative goals in these activities.

With a specific focus on speaker attitude and evaluation, this study examines lawyers as the designated speakers within the courtroom context. The term *lawyer evaluation* is employed to conceptualize the expression of lawyers’ evaluative attitudes during legal debates or the linguistic representation of their viewpoints about a case under discussion in court. This term highlights the significance of the linguistic operations carried out by lawyers in the realm of judicial communication.

Furthermore, the concept of lawyer evaluation in this study is closely connected to the notion of “legal evaluation” within legal circles (Bai 2004; Yong et al. 2002). To legal scholars, legal evaluation is a cognitive process that involves determining the relationship between the factual aspects of a given case and the prescribed legal rules. It is primarily seen as an activity rooted in cognition rather than linguistics. Suppose the interpretation or understanding of the two foundational elements of judicial determination, namely the meanings of specific legal rules or regulations and the factual conditions of a given case, differ initially due to factors such as the guiding philosophy of law or the influence of legal traditions in a country. In that case, the eventual decision to be reached will also differ. The evaluation relies on “the appropriate selection of suitable legal rules or regulations and an accurate decoding or interpretation of them, as well as the cognitive reasoning of the judicial officer between the given facts and the prescriptive rules” (Yong et al. 2002: 280).

It is evident that the understanding of lawyer evaluation differs significantly between the linguistic and legal senses. In the linguistic sense, evaluation is seen as a linguistic behavior representing meaning-making in language as a semiotic process. In the legal sense, it is regarded as a cognitive activity that requires logical analysis. These two senses are considered complementary rather than contradictory to each other, as they provide different insights into the nature of lawyer evaluation.

With a focus on how lawyers express their evaluative attitudes regarding a case during trial proceedings, this study will conduct a linguistic analysis of how lawyers assess various aspects of the facts related to a given case, the relationship between the facts and the applicable rules, and the proposed solution(s) to the case in a court. Throughout the analysis, reference will be made to the legal sense of the term.

2.2.2 The Constituents of Lawyer Evaluation

The constituents of lawyer evaluation are classified with reference to current studies on speaker evaluation. Numerous works have been conducted on speaker evaluation, such as Labov and Waletzky (1997), Plum (1988) and Rothery (1990) on evaluative meanings in narratives, Biber and Finegan (1988, 1989) on evaluative meanings in different genres, Chafe (1986) on evidential markers in English, and Hood (2004) on students' stance in academic writing. Among these, the semantic-discourse theory of Systemic Functional Linguistics (SFL), i.e., Appraisal Theory, proves to be very illuminating in the analysis of speaker evaluation because it offers a framework that systematically organizes interpersonal meanings conveyed through language.

Appraisal Theory (Martin 2000; Martin and Rose 2003; Martin and White 2005; Zhang 2002; etc.) categorizes various kinds of speaker attitudes or opinions into three kinds, namely, AFFECT (the description of emotions and feelings), APPRECIATION (the esthetic evaluation of entities, reality, or the outside world), and JUDGEMENT (the evaluation of people's behavior or character) (Martin and Rose 2003: 24). The three evaluative attitudes are further analyzed according to different variables. The attitude AFFECT is examined in the variables of Dis/satisfaction, In/security, and Un/happiness. The APPRECIATION is analyzed in terms of Reaction, Composition, and Valuation. The JUDGEMENT is explored in terms of Social Esteem and Social Sanction. The first category, AFFECT, may be considered the fundamental evaluative meaning, while the other two, JUDGEMENT and APPRECIATION, are deemed as institutionalized feelings (Martin 2003).

Appraisal Theory proposes two general dimensions to explore speaker evaluation, positive/negative and direct/indirect (Martin and Rose 2003: 25). It is relatively important to note that the kind of evaluations speakers make is closely linked to Field (i.e., the activity taking place in the event) and that the manner in which evaluations are expressed is very sensitive to Tenor (i.e., the institutional positions of speakers) (p. 35). In other words, evaluations need to be analyzed within the context in which they are situated.

Appraisal Theory offers sufficiently detailed descriptions about how to identify speaker evaluation in text. Structurally, the expression of speaker evaluation comprises three elements: an evaluating item, an evaluator, and the evaluated topic. The evaluating item is the structure of language where the speakers' evaluative meaning is encoded. The evaluator is the speaker who expresses the evaluative attitude (Eggins and Slade 1997; Thompson 2005). The evaluated refers to topics to which the evaluative meaning applies. All three elements may be identified on the stratum of lexico-grammar.

Generally, there are two ways for an evaluative attitude to be realized in evaluating items: congruent and incongruent expressions. Opinions vary, however, regarding what can be considered congruent and incongruent. In earlier studies, some scholars distinguished between the two in terms of parts of speech. For instance, Eggins and Slade (1997: 126–134) unequivocally state that the use of an adjective constitutes a congruent expression of an attitude, while the derivatives of the adjectives, such as nouns, adverbs, and verbs, may be regarded as incongruent realizations. In later works, more researchers, such as Hood (2004), Martin and Rose (2003), and White (2003), have tended to differentiate between the two realizations using lexis versus non-lexis. According to them, lexis serves as congruent expressions of evaluative attitudes, whereas non-lexis features, including grammar, prosodic features in speech, and other discourse features, are incongruent expressions so long as they can be employed to encode evaluative meanings.

Similarly, the evaluator and the evaluated may also be identified in lexico-grammar. As the source of a voice from which evaluative opinions are derived, technically referred to as the "source of attitudes" (Martin and Rose 2003: 44), the evaluator may be either a voice represented in a clause or a voice that is concealed structurally but retrievable in the context (Eggins and Slade 1997; Martin and Rose 2003; White 1998). Likewise, the evaluated may be identified either locally, which means, in nominal phrases within a clause (Eggins and Slade 1997; Martin 2004a, b; White 2003; etc.) or more globally in units larger than a clause, depending on the practical needs of the researcher (for examples, see Hood 2004; Miller 2002).

The analysis of speaker evaluation using Appraisal Theory is fundamentally insightful. It offers a valuable framework for classifying and analyzing speakers' opinions or attitudes in text, providing an operational tool for the theoretical exploration of lawyer evaluation within the context of a Chinese court. However, it is important to acknowledge that lawyer talk, being a special site of evaluation, has to be understood in accordance with the communicative tasks and institutional roles of lawyers. Ultimately, the expression of speaker evaluation is mainly determined and shaped by the variable of Field in "context" in which it occurs (Martin and Rose 2003: 35).

2.3 Lawyer Evaluation and Context

Context is an umbrella term that may cover diversified arrays of factors related to the expression of meaning in language, including participants, topics, physical situations, goals of communication, cultural background, social background, and other elements (Hu 2002). Though it is widely accepted that context plays a vital role in the use and analysis of language and communication, divergent opinions are observed regarding what it means and what it covers.

In various perspectives, including the ethnographic approach (Gumperz 1982; Hymes 1972), the semantic approach (Lyons 1982, 1995), the pragmatic approach (Levinson 1987), and the functional approach (Firth 1957; Halliday 1994), the Hallidayan conception of context has often been employed in the analysis of legal language and legal communication (see, for instances, Gibbons 1994, 2003; Maley 1994, 1995). One of the fundamental reasons for its frequent application may be its socio-semiotic view of language deeply rooted in social context and the systemic mechanism it provides for discourse analysis (Xin 2002).

In Systemic Functional Linguistics (SFL) (Halliday 1978), *context* is understood as a semiotic construe of the situation types. It encompasses the *context of situation* and the *context of culture*. These terms originated from Firth in the Prague School, who, in turn, borrowed them from Malinowski (Halliday 1978: 5). Initially, when Malinowski, an ethnographer studying tribal languages, used these terms in his article (Malinowski 1923), they were limited to the pragmatic aspect of the text and did not yet possess a fully semiotic interpretation. Later, Firth, a linguist interested in the cultural background of language, provided linguistic definitions for these terms in 1935. It was at this point that context acquired functional interpretations. Halliday further developed a well-suited model of the context of situation, which comprises three variables: Field, Tenor, and Mode (Halliday 1978, 1985).

In SFL, the variable of *Field* pertains to the nature of an activity, what socially recognized action participants are engaged in, in which the exchange of verbal meanings has a part. The variable of *Tenor* relates to the role relationships between participants. The variable of *Mode* concerns the medium, either in written or spoken forms, the complex subvarieties derived from these media, and the distinct generic structure of the text that might be involved (Halliday 1978: 145). In functional terms, the *context of culture* refers to the much broader environment beyond the *context of situation*. It is used to denote something in "the ideological and material culture that serves as the source of speech situations and situation type" (Halliday 1978: 68). It includes many elements, such as ideology, social structure, and social order.

The SFL-based contextual analysis of the legal and judicial speech in terms of Field, Tenor, and Mode (Stygall 1994; Gibbons 2003; Maley 1994) enables researchers to systematically describe the context of the legal communication, where lawyer evaluation is embedded. As Maley (1994: 32) points out, the primary objective of courtroom discourse is to reach a determination or verdict regarding the legality of a social action, whether it be of a criminal or civil nature. Semiotically, two features of the role relationships, which are hierarchical power and confrontation, are unequivocally signified in the physical settings and linguistic behaviors of the participants in the courtroom. Firstly, the hierarchical power between the judiciary and the lawyers is semiotically represented through the physical, spatial form of the court. The physical arrangement of the room effectively represents and acknowledges the symbolic authority of the court, as it is designed to do (p. 32). Judges or magistrates typically occupy a dominant, focal position in adversarial trial courts following the Anglo-Saxon law system, indicating their role as representatives of sovereign justice. The opposing parties, represented by counsel, face the judges or magistrates from delimited areas at their respective tables. Secondly, the competition and confrontation between the two opposing parties in court are also evident in the physical layout. The counsel, advocating for their clients, are ready to compete fiercely before the judge (and the jury) so as to secure a decision in favor of their side. In addition, the arrangement of the interactive stages in the trial (such as the opening and closing statements by each party, the examination, and cross-examination) further highlights the oppositional roles assumed by the two parties throughout the trial proceeding. Textually, the court has strict rules, both written and oral, governing the sequence of the proceedings and the admission of evidence. For instance, it is the judge who holds the authority to rule on matters of evidence and procedure, and decides what statements can be presented.

The contextual features of an adversary trial in China align with Maley's (1994) description. Interpersonally, the confrontational and competitive nature of the relationship between lawyers is semiotically demonstrated through the allocation of roles and status in court. In China's current adversarial trial system, the prosecuting party (or the plaintiff) and the defense are granted equal rights and status to participate in the trial throughout the proceedings. The judges, positioned as impartial arbitrators, sit on an elevated platform, while the opposing parties sit on opposite sides of the court, facing each other. The dynamic relationship between the two parties can be metaphorically represented as an isosceles triangle, as illustrated in Fig. 2.1 (Chen 2002; Nan 2002). In this triangle, lawyers from opposing sides occupy the two endpoints of the baseline, each equidistant from the judge positioned at the top.

Fig. 2.1 Visual representation of the semiotic relationship between lawyers and judges in a Chinese court

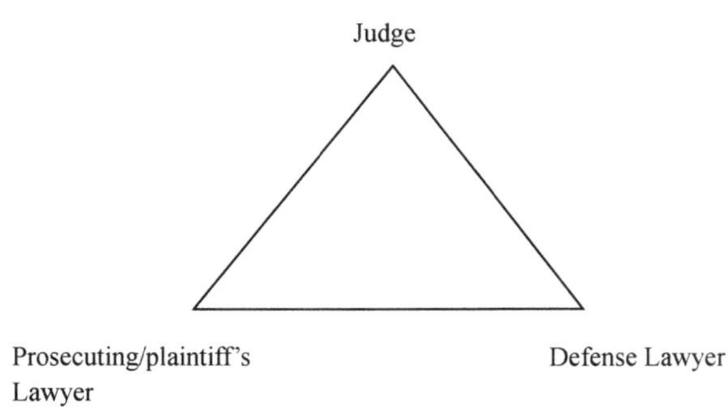

As is demonstrated in the figure, each of the three trial participants stands for their interests: the judge, who is primarily responsible for ensuring visible justice, represents state power, while the disputing lawyers represent conflicting interests.

In addition to drawing a depiction of the contextual features in the courtroom, Maley (1994) also emphasizes the impact of these contextual features on discourse in the courtroom interaction. "The adversarial nature of the trial process is the immediate determinant of its structural elements: the different stages which structure the proceedings" (Maley 1994: 35), and "the ideational, interpersonal, and textual meanings of the discourse type are strictly constrained" under these contextual features (Maley 1994: 33; see also Levinson 1992). Specifically focusing on trials in common law countries, Maley demonstrates that the interpersonal meanings conveyed during the interaction between the counsel in court revolve around confrontation and contestation demonstrated in their (counsel's) competition to establish "supremacy over each other" (Maley 1994: 33). Consequently, through the choice of "questioning" types in story-telling activity, they engage in a struggle for control over witnesses during the presentation of evidence. Obviously, such a competitive interpersonal relationship in counsel–counsel interaction is overwhelmingly oriented on the dimension of "power and status" (Brown and Gilman 1960).

Although it is convincing that the interpersonal relationship of confrontation between lawyers in an adversary trial is determined by the contextual feature of the trial system, it is still being determined whether orientation to power is the only dimension on which the confrontation is constructed. So far, the constraints of the context of situation in the courtroom on lawyer speech have been investigated thoroughly. Nevertheless, the role of the "context of legal culture" in the courtroom remains relatively unexplored. The broader social and cultural factors of a country and its legal traditions in resolving disputes may contribute to the context of legal culture in an adversarial trial. As a result, there is an equal possibility for the confrontation between lawyers to be constructed based on the dimension of solidarity. A discussion grounded in the Hallidayan socio-semiotic view of language and context would do justice to this argument.

The fundamental perspective of SFL posits that language is a form of social semiotics. It means that language should be interpreted within a sociocultural context, in which culture itself should be understood semiotically as an information system (Halliday 1978: 1–2). The context is itself a semiotic construct. Language serves as a means to represent the social system, metaphorically reflecting the diverse patterns of variation that exist within human cultures. In essence, this view establishes a dialectical relationship between language and context: context influences what can be expressed, and conversely, language usage contributes to the realization of the context in a mediating manner.

The relation between language, context and society is comprehensively elucidated by the stratification theory (Halliday 1978: 39). Drawing from the works of Hjelmslev in the Prague school, Firth in the London school, Lamb and Pike, Halliday conceptualizes language basically as a tri-stratal system comprising semantics, lexico-grammar and phonology, arranged from the top level down to the bottom level (Halliday 1978: 39). Each of these strata functions as a system of potential or a network of options or choices, encompassing a range of alternatives. Between strata, there is a process of realization. The lexicogrammar system is what the speaker can say structurally. What the speaker can say via the lexicogrammar system enables the speaker to realize the semantic system, which is what the speaker can mean—the "meaning potential". Thus, language works as a system of meaning potential. Following the upward progression, we may notice that what the speaker can mean through the system of semantics becomes a realization of what the speaker can do, the system of "behavioral potential", a stratum outside the language system and located at the social level.

Realization, which is of crucial importance to the stratification theory, denotes the inter-stratal relationship between ranks and strata. Each system realizes a higher system and is, in turn, realized by a lower system. Martin (2003: 5) provides a metaphorical explanation of the term. He compares it to the process of re-coding, similar to how hardware is mapped through software to display images and words on a computer screen. In summarizing the nature of the relationship, he suggests that it encompasses concepts such as symbolization, encoding, expression, manifestation, and more. According to Halliday (1978: 43), the relationship between strata in the process of realization is indirect and mediated by functions.

The functional approach to the linguistic system, considering the system as a potential for meaning, tends to categorize different types of meanings based on their functions. These functions are referred to as metafunctions, where the term "meta" denotes abstraction or primary significance rather than the microscopic level. In the triadic view of the metafunctions, the ideational (including experiential and logical), interpersonal, and textual functions coexist. The ideational function represents the speaker's capacity for meaning as an observer, encompassing the content aspect of language. The interpersonal function represents the speaker's potential for meaning as a participant, involving language as a means of action. This function allows the speaker to enter the context of situation, expressing their attitudes and judgments or attempting to influence the attitudes and behavior of others. The textual function pertains to the speaker's ability to construct text, ensuring that language remains relevant and connected. The textual function plays a crucial role in relation to the other two functions; it enables the actualization of ideational and interpersonal meanings within a text. Neither of the other two functions could fully manifest without the textual function.

The metafunctions of language are realized by the semantic system on the one hand and determine the latter on the other hand. In other words, the semantic system is responsible for implementing the metafunctions, while the metafunctions, in turn, shape and determine the characteristics of the semantic system. It is a reciprocal relationship where the metafunctions are realized by the semantic system and also play a role in determining how the latter functions in text. The ideational function determines the transitivity system, while the interpersonal function governs the mood and modality systems, as well as the newly-developed Appraisal System (Martin 2000). The textual function is responsible for the thematic system. These systems, located within the semantic stratum, are realized through the structural configurations found in the lexico-grammar system. Simultaneously, the metafunctions of language exhibit systematic relationships that extend upward to the situational context, which comprises three variables: Field, Tenor, and Mode. The ideational function is linked to the Field variable, the interpersonal function is associated with the Tenor variable, and the textual function corresponds to the Mode variable.

Alongside the realization between inter-stratal systems is *instantiation*, which signifies the intra-stratal relationship of a system as meaning potential at any given stratum and the manifestation of the potential in actual text (Martin 1999). Meaning is instantiated in the unfolding of text, and typical patterns of instantiations that occur in particular situation types are located somewhere on the continuum between the potential and the instance. System and instance have been described by Halliday (1992) as being really the same phenomenon viewed from two different angles: the former is the pattern formed by the latter, and each of the latter represents a case of the former.

With this stratal system of language, SFL has provided a very effective way to study language in relation to social context and social structure, despite the lack of sufficient empirical data to validate many of its propositions (Zhu and Yan 2001: 28–30). Since language evolves and is produced in environments or situations, a "dialectical determination" is observed between context and language use (Zhu and Yan 2001: 27; see Halliday 1978). Guided by sufficient information provided by a situation type, researchers can specify the semantic configurations that a speaker typically makes in the context of the given type. "Given an adequate specification of the semiotic properties of the context in terms of Field, Tenor, and Mode, we should be able to make sensible predictions about the semantic properties of texts associated with it" (Halliday 1978: 110).

Intervening in the determination is something fundamentally important—the context of culture. Actually, the context of situation is indirectly related to text through the intermediary level of register, which is influenced by factors such as the social structure or the coding orientation as defined by Bernstein (Halliday 1978: 11). In other words, the context of culture plays a mediating role in the utilization of language in text.

To exemplify the mediating role of the cultural context, the classroom discourse serves as a fitting example for discussion. As regards the teacher's talk in a classroom text, the context of situation can be broadly described to encompass the teaching objectives of the lesson, the teacher-student relationship, and the structure of the lecture. However, to interpret specific aspects such as how the teacher positions themselves in relation to knowledge within the context, whether as an authoritative and closed-minded expert or as an open-minded individual in pursuit of truth, researchers must consider the broader context—the culture of classroom teaching. The cultural context may include factors such as the nature of knowledge and truth and the role of teachers in education (Halliday 1985: 46).

Given such interpretative views of SFL regarding the relationship between language and context, it is justifiable to align with Maley's (1994) conclusive statement that the courtroom context, with its specific contextual features, leads to a characteristic feature of confrontation between opposing counsel during lawyer–lawyer interactions. Moreover, it is plausible to suggest that variations in the legal culture context within the courtroom can result in distinct patterns in which the interpersonal relationship between disputing lawyers is constructed in text.

In addition to its view on the intermediating role of the context of culture in the prediction of meanings in text, SFL notes with caution that social class may not relate to language variation in a fixed, systemic way and that the relationship between the interactants either in discursive roles or social roles can only be examined in the analysis of the interaction through language-as-exchange (Li 2002). Specifically, the social relationship between interactants predetermines what and how their discursive roles might be, a kind of meaning potential, and this potential has to be actualized in text/discursive production under the cooperative work of Field, Tenor, and Mode. Therefore, SFL can incorporate two distinct perspectives into the study of language and society: critical discourse analysis[1] for examining power and status, and "positive discourse analysis" for exploring solidarity (Martin and Rose 2003: 264). Consequently, as discussed by Maley (1994) and other scholars, the construction of confrontation as a manifestation of power represents just one possibility for realizing interpersonal meanings between lawyers. An alternative option, the dimension of solidarity, may be "at risk" in certain situations. This study is thus attempted to explore lawyer evaluation in such an alternative option.

As has been reviewed above, lawyer evaluation is constrained by the context and, therefore, needs to be closely examined in relation to context. The following sections will review current studies on lawyer evaluation from both linguistic and legal perspectives.

2.4 Lawyer Evaluation in Context: A Linguistic Perspective

This section delves into the examination of studies on lawyer evaluation as a linguistic behavior within the courtroom. It encompasses the identification of lawyer evaluation across different levels of the language system and the construction of it on two distinct dimensions: power and solidarity. However, the analysis places particular emphasis on the dimension of solidarity, exploring how it influences the manifestation of lawyer evaluation in courtroom discourse.

[1] This point explains why Critical Discourse Analysis takes SFL as its analytical tool (see also, Fowler 1996: 4–5).

2.4.1 Lawyer Evaluation Identified in Discourse

This subsection reviews the types of evaluative attitudes expressed by lawyers and their linguistic manifestations in text.

2.4.1.1 Presence of Lawyers' Evaluative Attitudes in Court

According to the findings of the current research, lawyers exhibit a wide range of evaluative attitudes in court, particularly when they construct the facts of a case. By consciously manipulating the "conceptual perspective" of a narrative or story through linguistic operation, lawyers indicate their evaluative attitudes toward the facts in the legal process. When the speaker communicates an object, relationship, or event to the addressee, the selection of words includes specific properties of the referent while excluding others with each choice (Clark 1997). In the terminology of Appraisal Theory, lawyers employ the elements of Affect or Judgement when expressing their evaluations in a trial.

The evaluative attitudes are frequently observed during the narration of case facts as a story in court. These attitudes encompass various aspects, such as the time a victim turns up and the place they frequent (Drew 1990, 1992), the defendant's motive and behavior (Cotterill 2003, 2004; Matoesian 1993, 2000; etc.), and the referring expressions associated with the victim (Danet 1980; Frohmann 1997). Meanwhile, it has been demonstrated that lawyers extensively employ these evaluative attitudes or Affect to convey their positions on a case. In a study based on corpora of data in the trial of O. J. Simpson, Cotterill (2001) reports that the prosecutor utilized connotative meanings within a single word, "control", to represent the distinct roles of the two parties, Simpson (the defendant/suspect) and Nichole (the wife/victim), within their marital relationship. By describing Simpson as an agent exerting direct *control* over Nichole or engaging in actions associated with *control*, the prosecution effectively constructed Simpson as a dangerous, aggressive, and outwardly violent individual, while portraying Nichole as a vulnerable and weak wife.

Lawyers indirectly display their Judgment on the characters of the parties involved in a case when they narrate the case facts in court. Drew's (1990, 1992) investigation into the manipulated scenarios implicatively associated with two references of the same place would serve as a compelling example for illustration here. In the trial of a rape case, the prosecutor described the place that the female victim frequently visited as a more respectable "bar", while the defense called it a "club" where people may seek casual relationships. The different connotative meanings attributed to the references of the same place reflect contrasting Judgements on the victim's character: one portraying her as a lady serious about sexual relations and the other depicting her as a woman who may engage in casual encounters. Accordingly, the opposing evaluative attitudes in the designation of the place reveal a fierce contest between the prosecution and the defense.

Appreciation of entities or objects is also evident when lawyers represent the entities, objects, or verbal statements that are involved in the facts of a case that may be admitted as factual evidence in legal proceedings. Lawyers demonstrate their attitudinal understanding of various factors, such as the disputed actions of an event (Goodwin and Goodwin 1997; Loftus and Palmer 1974), the entity/object (Danet 1980), the credibility of verbal statements by witnesses (Ehrlich 2002; Wang 2003), and even the roles or identities of legal professionals (Gaines 2002; Gibbons 2003). In a criminal case linked to abortion, Danet (1980) highlights that the use of "baby" versus "fetus" for something expelled or removed out of the uterus reveals different interpretations of the act of expulsion, either in its semantic or connotative senses. By framing the act as a purposeful behavior related to the life (and death) of a "baby", the prosecution sought to define the case as manslaughter, whereas the defense aimed to refute the charge by presenting the act as a technical removal of a "fetus" incapable of independent life.

Lawyers also showcase Appreciation on whether and how certain evidence is objective through the use of modality in questioning (Atkinson and Drew 1990; Goodrich 1988; Maley and Fahey 1991; etc.). According to Wang's (2003) comparison of modality used by lawyers in the cross-examination of the O. J. Simpson trial case, linguistic forms indicate to people, both explicitly and implicitly, how legal professionals exhibit their expertise and skill by means of evaluative judgments in legal activities.

In short, current studies on attitudes in lawyer evaluation are fruitful. However, the construction of lawyers' evaluative attitudes as a linguistic phenomenon in its own right and the systematical integration of these attitudes as a means to effectively realize legal communication tasks in court seem to be under-researched.

2.4.1.2 Loci of Lawyer Evaluation in Text

Currently, lawyer evaluation has been identified on different strata of the language system, including lexis, grammar, and discourse.[2]

Lawyer Evaluation in Lexis

To locate lawyers' evaluative attitudes in lexis, many researchers conducted a micro-linguistic analysis that focuses on lexical choices, as demonstrated in Cotterill (2001, 2003, 2004), Danet (1980), Ehrlich (2002), Frohmann (1997), and Matoesian (1993, 2000, 2001). Generally, in addition to adjectives, nouns, pronouns, and verbs can also convey evaluative meanings. Therefore, these different parts of speech are all capable of encoding evaluations and expressing attitudes.

[2] The division of strata of language here simply follows the tradition of structuralism. Of course, the categorization of lawyer evaluation on these levels, which is not a clear-cut division, is temporarily done for illustration.

Nouns can be used to convey lawyer evaluation if they have connotative or comparative meanings in the context where they occur. As a most obvious linguistic marker of power and prestige, terms of address in court serve as the locus for lawyers to express their evaluative judgments about their co-communicators. First of all, the use of address forms in the courtroom is indicative of the interpersonal relationship between participants in the legal setting. Generally, there is a hierarchical relationship between lawyers and judges, while lawyers from opposing sides are considered equal to each other, albeit with varying degrees of affinity or hostility, depending on the circumstances (Gibbons 2003: 82–83). Accordingly, all participants are called by their primary identities in the courtroom. Judges and clerks are universally addressed by their official titles, while opposing lawyers may be addressed as either "Attorney" followed by their surname or more general terms such as "my friend", "the defense party", "the prosecution party", and so on.

Secondly, a switch in the terms of address carries implications regarding the perceived relationship between the speaker and the addressee in a given context or the desired relationship the speaker intends to establish at that moment. As observed in Gaines' (2002) study, when lawyers used the formal address for the trial judge, such as *the Court*, *the Justice*, and *the Bench*, it signifies that the trial judge was perceived as an impartial third role; conversely, when lawyers used *Justice* or *Judge* plus the surname, it indicates that the judge was viewed as an individual person. Such a switch in the terms of address for the same person reveals subtle changes in the speakers' evaluative attitude towards the addressee. The same applies to lawyers' choices of address for their opponents. They usually refer to each other in the third person as *the Crown*, *Counsel for the Prosecution*, or *Counsel for the Defense*. However, when they switch to the second-person address, such as *my friend* or *my learned friend*, affective meanings, either mutuality or confrontation, may be conveyed.

Like terms of address, pronominal choices reveal lawyers' perceptions of their opponents. Studies conducted by Miller (2002), Kurzon (2001), and Harris (2003) all prove that legal professionals skillfully switch between *you* or *we* to signify the desired role relationship they wish to have with their addresses. In addition to nominal forms for addresses, evaluative attitudes become more pervasive when lawyers categorize certain elements of the case facts as narratives in court, for instance, the disputed entity in a criminal case (e.g., Danet 1980), the place of a disputed behavior (Drew 1990) and the personality of a witness (Atkinson and Drew 1990; Drew 1992).

Along with nouns, verbs may become another locus for lawyer evaluation if they are deployed to express ideational meanings in a disputed act. Loftus and Palmer (1974) provide an account of how different evaluative attitudes are conveyed through the choice of two verbs, "crash" versus "hit", in the depiction of a forensic event, specifically a car accident. The verb *crash* emphasizes the high speed of the moving car, while the verb *hit* mitigates the perception of the speed. Consequently, the two verbs present two contrasting evaluations regarding the driver's responsibility in the accident. Similarly, Goodwin and Goodwin (1997) demonstrate how the selection of verbs in police jargon and everyday vocabulary magically creates two distinct versions of the same event in the video. Meanwhile, the connotative meanings in verbs are also widely exploited when lawyers negotiate meanings, typically in cases involving rape (e.g., Matoesian 2001) or domestic violence where understanding the victims' real intentions are crucial.

In summary, lexical categories containing derivative meanings serve as very effective tools for lawyers to negotiate their positions in court. However, attitudes are not equally distributed across all types of lexis. Adjectives or adverbs are the most apparent carriers of speaker attitude in everyday settings (Martin and Rose 2003). In comparison, their usage for lawyer evaluation in legal settings seems less common. This observation may support the statement that speaker evaluation is conditioned by *Field* (Martin and Rose 2003). Moreover, it may suggest that due to the institutional character of the judicial settings, the analysis of lawyer evaluation in text should be made more thoroughly in large phases of text.

Lawyer Evaluation in Grammar

A significant body of research on courtroom discourse has revealed that lawyers possess the skill to manipulate grammatical, structural, and interactional resources as discourse tools in order to construct and reinforce their evaluative judgments about the case. These resources include turn-taking, topic selection, repetition, reformulation, and modality.

The main interactional resources available to lawyers are discursive control over the sequence of questions, question forms, and topics (Atkinson and Drew 1990; Walker 1987; etc.). These controls enable lawyers to construct and present in court the evidence the way they favor. In addition, for the purpose of winning a battle in the adversarial legal proceedings, questions are not used to fulfill their primary function: to gather information. Instead, they are used to construct through witnesses a reality of events, which allows the prosecution and the defense to make their own arguments and to destroy the opposition's arguments by discrediting their witnesses (Philips 1987; Walker 1987; etc.).

Gaines (1996) and Maley and Fahey (1991) provide direct evidence for the relationship between question forms and evaluative attitudes. Gaines (1996) demonstrates that the construction of evaluative stances could be achieved through grammar choice without overt control of questioning, while Maley and Fahey (1991) establish that opposing attorneys could construct similar evaluative stances by utilizing similar question forms. These two studies both reinforce and consolidate the proposition that grammatical forms can be employed to construct lawyer evaluation.

In summary, as reported in existing studies, lawyer evaluation could be conveyed through grammar. First, as a locus for lawyers' evaluative stance, grammar is regarded as a pervasive means for lawyers to express their evaluative attitudes. Second, the linguistic expression of lawyer evaluation is conditioned and constrained by the institutional character of the courtroom talk. Third, the organization of lawyer evaluation may also be sensitive to the trial system and the purpose of the trial.

Lawyer Evaluation in Discourse

Lawyers' evaluative attitudes are prominently conveyed at the discourse level, especially during the presentation of evidence in narrative form or in the process known as "discursive formation" (Fairclough 1992: 37–39).

Narratives or stories serve as the locus for lawyer evaluation because they involve accounts of events or experiences that are closely tied to personal views or subjective interpretations. Most of all, along with language, narratives have symbolic, iconic, and indexical functions (see Peirce 1932). The referential power of narratives gives them the quality of being a "metadiscursive practice" (Briggs 1996). In his studies on narratives, Labov explicitly concludes that stories invoke meta-discursive practices that allow participants to present their evaluations of past conflicts (Labov 2003; Labov and Waletzky 1997).

Since narratives may foreground the object of representation and the process of representation itself, they have been investigated thoroughly as a kind of speaker evaluation in the courtroom. Narratives play a central role in trials, serving as important means for disputing lawyers to reconstruct events and for judges and juries to interpret those events (Bennett and Feldman 1981; Heffer 2003; Maynard 1990). In the process of selecting and reformulating events, lawyers transfer events from one social context into another—the courtroom. Language plays a crucial role in this transfer, particularly in the lawyers' use of questions to obtain and shape these narratives. When leading questions are presented in court, the newly provided information is evaluated based on its consistency with the side of the story that the prosecution and the defense each have on their respective side and how the overall narrative aligns with the experiences of both the trial judges and jurors during the trial (see Jackson 1996). In other words, lawyers' evaluative attitudes regarding the case facts often emerge and are presented as evidence in a less conspicuous manner in all courts (Liao 2003a; Wodak 1980, 1984, 1985; Zhang 2005b).

Although narratives are a vital and powerful linguistic tool by which lawyers give their own evaluative judgment regarding case facts, the use of narratives in lawyer evaluation is constrained by institutional routines of the courtroom talk. The constraints expose the intertextual link between lawyer evaluation in court and the legal regulations governing it (e.g., Candlin and Maley 1997; Gao 2003; Philips 1998; Stygall 1994; Zhang 2005a).

Along with narratives, speech style could also be an indicator of lawyer evaluation. The choice of speech style is found to be in close association with speaker involvement and, hence, it influences the credibility of the speech in court. O'Barr and his team conducted specific research on the relationship between speech style and credibility judgment made by law students as mock audiences (e.g., O'Barr 1982; O'Barr and Conley 1990) and demonstrated that powerful language features, characterized by loudness, a large pitch change, fluency, and coherence, are perceived as more credible, compared with powerless speech features characterized by a small voice, low pitch, lack of fluency and incoherence.

In summary, lawyer evaluation could be identified more extensively within a larger text. It would broaden the horizon for identifying lawyers' evaluative attitudes and consequently highlight the importance of taking the courtroom context as a point of reference when we discuss lawyer evaluation in Chinese courts.

2.4.2 Two Dimensions for the Positioning of Lawyer Evaluation

In the realm of research on interpersonal relations, two overarching dimensions have been identified: power and solidarity (Brown and Gilman 1960). However, when it comes to lawyer speech, either in the Western courts or Chinese courts, there has been a noticeable disparity between the two dimensions. Studies focusing on the dimension of power have been more prevalent compared with those centered on solidarity.

On the dimension of power and control, the research literature reveals three central themes (Gibbons 2003; Wu 2002). The first theme pertains to the unequal distribution of power within the legal system, specifically between lawyers and judges on one hand, and between legal professionals and individuals outside the legal system, such as defendants, witnesses, or litigants on the other (see Atkinson and Drew 1990; Liao 2003a; Walker 1987; etc.). The second theme focuses on the presence of a mismatch or miscommunication between lawyers and laypeople (e.g. Eades 1994). Lastly, the third theme revolves around the manipulation of language, which contributes to the construction of reality in the courtroom (e.g., Drew 1992; Eades 2000; Ehrlich 2002; Goodwin and Goodwin 1997; Kedar 1987). These studies have been concerned with a wide variety of research topics ranging from question forms used by counsel (Gao 2003; Liao 2003a; Walker 1987), questioning strategies (Drew 1990; Liao 2003a, b; Zhang 2004), modality (Atkinson and Drew 1990; Han 2005; Wang 2003), reformulation (Atkinson and Drew 1990; Ehrlich 2002), lexical choices on crimes (Cotterill 2001; Danet 1980), to terms of address used by counsel for witnesses (Atkinson and Drew 1990; Gibbons 2003).

It seems that lawyer evaluation conducted on the dimension of power and control is primarily motivated by the characteristics of the jury trial system. In the adversary trial system, the determination of case facts rests with jurors, who are typically laymen with little knowledge of legal reasoning. These jurors, accustomed to the everyday narrative style, often make decisions on account of their perception of the credibility of the narrator (see, for example, Heffer 2003; O'Barr 1982). To sway the jury in their favor, lawyers usually rely on exerting power and control over the layperson witnesses or defendants, or engage in intense competition with opposing lawyers.

The situations for lawyer speech in China are quite different in a certain way. While disputing lawyers in Chinese courts exhibit a confrontational style in terms of interpersonal relationships, which is inherent to the institutional context of the court (Atkinson and Drew 1990; Zhang 2017), the courtroom environment in China does not foster as intense a competition for control as seen in Western courts. First of all, as a general rule in countries following the continental law system, emphasis laid on evidence in written form dramatically reduces the need for lawyers to assert control over the presentation of oral testimony. Secondly, unlike the trial proceedings in Western courts, there is no clear-cut division of labor between judges and jurors[3] in determining case facts and applying law. In practice, both of these responsibilities are undertaken exclusively by the tribunal (Yong et al. 2002: 87; Zhang 2017). It is unnecessary, therefore, for lawyers to try as many coercive means as possible to affect the decision-maker, the trial judges in this case. Accordingly, the main focus of a lawyer's argument in court is to debate with their contestants and justify their legal positions. It can be presumed that the dimension of solidarity or the negotiation of solidarity may emerge as a prominent aspect of trial communication in the Chinese context.

2.4.3 Lawyer Evaluation on the Dimension of Solidarity

In studies pertinent to lawyer evaluation conducted on the dimension of solidarity, research conducted by Gaines (2002), Kšrner (2000), and Miller (2002) is worth attention. According to them, the negotiation of solidarity may occur among legal professionals, primarily in fostering collegiality (i.e., the sense of belonging to the same legal group or team) and mutuality.

From an observation of the sidebar discussion that is outside the earshot of jurors, Gaines (2002) notices that the attorneys made use of a large amount of informal talk to achieve affective solidarity with the judge. By way of explanation, he argues very convincingly that, although we all hold the belief that a judge can make an entirely objective decision based solely on formal arguments, judges, like everyone else, are influenced by socialization and emotions.

Solidarity may be constructed through various means (Gaines 2002). First of all, lawyers may try to align judges and opposing lawyers by emphasizing shared values, common trade, and other professional skills, in particular, in less formal contexts such as a sidebar. Unlike the formal constraints of an open trial, the sidebar creates a quasi-private context where attorneys can leverage personal values, loyalties, and other aspects of identification to interact with judges in a more relaxed and open manner. This interaction aims to establish a sense of emotional connection and solidarity with the judge (Gaines 2002: 229).

---

[3] In the Chinese trial system, a tribunal typically consists of three to five persons, of whom, one or two persons are selected from the general public, technically referred to as "People's Jurors".

Many discursive acts related to the Judgement of personal characters or qualities such as self-confidence, integrity, and loyalty to the law can be understood as speakers' interactive moves intended to construct affective solidarity. On the one hand, since people tend to be impressed by those who are confident, righteous, and loyal, positively evaluating these traits may become one crucial step in aligning the judge and the opponents in terms of attitude. On the other hand, emphasizing common professional skills, such as expertise in judicial knowledge, can also be appealing to legal professionals. By making good use of the shared judicial knowledge or the "life-world" of the legal professionals (Phillips 2003), lawyers assume that they have meaningful and powerful connections with the judges and with each other. Therefore, acts that emphasize common values and shared judicial knowledge can be interpreted as efforts to influence and sway judges in terms of attitude and emotion, as they tap into the judges' impression of confidence, righteousness, and loyalty while also appealing to their appreciation of shared professional expertise.

Secondly, lawyers seek to align judges and opposing parties by demonstrating agreeability among the legal professionals. When lawyers behave in a pleasant and conciliatory manner, they create an image of themselves as kind and thoughtful individuals, possibly seen as those who are innocent and well-intentioned (Gaines 2002). They may exhibit a nuanced evaluation of the arguments put forth by the opposing side, thereby reducing confrontations between the two parties. By substantiating their agreeable behavior with sufficient reasoning, they essentially present their good intentions as a foundation for judges to lean toward their position.

Thirdly, lawyers may also attempt to align and disalign the legal professionals rhetorically through the use of rhetorical strategies like bald flattery or joking irony. While bald flattery can help associate judges in terms of attitude or emotion, the use of joking irony serves a dual function. Informal talks like jokes naturally bridge the gap between opposing lawyers, fostering a sense of camaraderie. Additionally, they may strengthen the connection between judges and the lawyers who are presenting their cases. In the adversary trial system of Western courts, opposing lawyers are compared to "gladiators" with positive attributes in the conflictual context of a trial. Engagement in intense competition is regarded as the right thing to do. In this situation, when lawyers use verbal means to (dis-)align themselves, it can lead to the establishment of two distinct teams: the team of US (including the judge) and the team of THEM (the opponents) (Kuo 2002). This dynamic can be made evident in discourse between multiple parties involved in legal proceedings (see Kangasharju 1996).

Gaines' (2002) analysis of lawyer speech during sidebar discussions provides some insights for this study. Firstly, it stresses the importance of solidarity in lawyer talk, offering an additional lens through which to examine lawyer evaluation in trial communication. It is crucial to recognize that the informal character of sidebar discussions does not necessarily confine solidarity to private contexts. Indeed, similar studies have demonstrated that solidarity can also be fostered in formal settings, such as the courtroom (Harris 2003; Kurzon 2001; Miller 2002), and lawyers' offices (Sarat and Felstiner 1986). As such, it is expected that the orientation toward solidarity in lawyer evaluation could be observed in the formal Chinese courts as well.

Secondly, despite the recognition of solidarity as a significant facet of lawyer attitudes in their discourse, Gaines (2002) perceives the establishment of solidarity with legal professionals solely as a power-gaining strategy, rather than an effective method for resolving judicial matters. Additionally, his analysis of the linguistic devices is somewhat disjointed. With more advanced research tools for investigating lawyers' evaluative attitudes, we might be able to identify more nuanced linguistic techniques.

Both Kšrner (2000) and Miller (2002) explore the complex interpersonal meanings that can arise in court opinions and verdicts. They note that multiple voices and viewpoints exist within the nuanced, potentially contentious environment of the trial proceedings. Two key findings emerge from their work. Firstly, evaluative attitudes of Judgement and Appreciation are prevalent in judicial discourse. While Affect is also present at times, it occurs less frequently than in everyday interactions, probably due to the value placed on objectivity in court. The choice of evaluative language appears to be constrained by the institutional context of the courtroom, where demonstrating impartiality is paramount.

Secondly, legal professionals have a variety of discursive means available to forge solidarity with each other when they construe their own evaluative stance amidst diverse opinions. Kšrner (2000) and Miller (2002) lucidly show that many linguistic devices and grammatical forms, such as hedging, intensifiers, quantifiers, conjunctions, modality, triadic structures, and projections, can be used to convey interpersonal meanings and negotiate evaluative attitudes. Through the use of these discursive means, judges engage in dialogic interaction with different viewpoints in court. They could open up various possibilities for distinct interpretations held by the lawyers and their peer judges to expand in text, thus drawing those viewpoints in dialogue. At the same time, they could close down those alternatives textually and make their own judgment stand upright. By engaging in dialogic argumentation, judges are able to effectively and convincingly establish the legitimacy of their final opinions on the case, without discrediting their fellow legal professionals. In this way, solidarity between legal professionals is maintained, and legal disputes are solved effectively.

Given that the two studies both have highlighted the significance of constructing solidarity as a means to handling legal disputes, what remains to be explored is the motivation for using such language in a less antagonistic manner and the justification for its effectiveness in legal dispute resolution or disposition.

The linguistic analyses presented by Kšrner (2000) and Miller (2002) could be more effectively framed within the interpersonal language resources outlined in Systemic Functional Linguistics (SFL). These resources, as defined by Martin (2000), include NEGOTIATION, INVOLVEMENT, and APPRAISAL.[4] Negotiation refers to how language enacts speech functions and conversational exchanges through the grammatical systems of mood and modality. Involvement deals with signs of social distance between interactants or the inclusion/exclusion of interlocutors in

[4] In SFL, all-capitals is typically used to indicate the functional categories. However, for the sake of brevity in this study, sometimes, only the initial letter of a functional category may be typed in uppercase.

discourse, which are manifested in choices of pronouns, address terms, vocatives, taboo language, swear words, slang, and technical/informal registers. The Appraisal System leverages the attitudinal meanings conveyed by lexical and grammatical choices like nouns, adjectives, adverbs, and syntactic constructions (Martin and Rose 2003; White 2003). Organizing judicial language within this SFL framework could provide deeper insight.

Appraisal, a system concerned with the expression of *evaluation*, includes three categories: ATTITUDE, which refers to the types of feelings or attitudes, GRADUATION, which describes the strength of the feelings or attitudes involved; and ENGAGEMENT, which means the attribution of values and alignment of readers (Martin and Rose 2003). ATTITUDE, as a sub-system for options of a person's attitudes, can be subcategorized into three basic kinds according to what is appraised, namely, AFFECT, JUDGEMENT, and APPRECIATION. AFFECT concerns the description of feelings or emotions, JUDGEMENT involves the description of characters of persons, and APPRECATION relates to the description of entities or objects. Within the sub-system of ENGAGEMENT, an attitude may be expressed in different ways. If it is voiced by or attributed to one person unanimously, it falls into the subcategory of MONOGLOSS; if it is represented through different voices, it is in HETEROGLOSS. At the same time, an attitude may be expressed with varying intensity, either in an intensified way (FORCE) or in a graded manner (FOCUS), within the sub-system of GRADUATION.

Incorporating Bakhtin's (1981) dialogical view of language, Appraisal Theory takes the expression of speakers' evaluative attitudes as a dynamic interaction with readers. On the one hand, evaluative attitudes encoded in language are meant to align readers interpersonally. On the other hand, putting the speakers' evaluative attitudes in interaction with the voices of others or modifying their evaluative attitudes is intended to elicit agreement from the readers. Therefore, Appraisal Theory is specifically dedicated to exploring how speakers negotiate their positions interpersonally. Its functional (sub-)categories are to be realized by different linguistic or rhetorical concepts. For instance, HETEROGLOSS is to be realized by projection, modality, concession, concessive, continuative, and other strategies, and FORCE is to be realized by intensifiers, attitudinal lexis, metaphor, swearing, or other linguistic means.

The semantic resources of Appraisal Theory are conceived as a further development of SFL in terms of interpersonal meaning. Speaking of the role of Appraisal Theory, Martin (2000: 144–145) points out, "What has tended to be elided in SFL is the semantics of evaluation—how the interlocutors are feeling, the judgments they make, and the values they place on various phenomena of their experience." It should be noted that the interpersonal resources organized in SFL are inherently related to those categorized in other studies (Simon-Vandenbergen 2004). NEGOTIATION has its equivalent with Speech Act Theory and INVOLVEMENT with Politeness theory (Brown and Gilman 1960). In Appraisal Theory, the realization of ATTITUDE in lexis is parallel to the work on Stance (Biber and Finegan 1988), ENGAGEMENT resource has its equivalent in the work of evidentiality by Chafe (1986), and GRADUATION in the work of vague language by Channell (1994). The appeal of Appraisal

Theory lies in its successful integration and systematization of various interpersonal meanings that were previously addressed in a fragmented manner. As a result, it has been widely applied to various genres such as literary works (Page 2003), media reports (White 2003), language learning (Painter 2003), history discourse (Hunston 2000), autobiography (Li 2002), and judiciary discourse (Kšrner 2000; Miller 2002, 2004).

A comprehensive review of the linguistic studies on lawyer evaluation in this section reveals insights that can be drawn. Firstly, Affect, Judgement, and Appreciation are all present in the courtroom, and they are realized in lexis, grammar, and discourse. However, constrained by the legal context, the distribution and expressions of these attitudes in the courtroom seem to be quite different from those in everyday settings. Comparatively speaking, in contrast to Affect, Judgement and Appreciation are more frequently employed by lawyers when dealing with case facts in the trial; lexical categories, such as nouns, adjectives, and verbs, which are usually associated with ideational meanings, may more readily serve as carriers of lawyers' attitudes than other parts of speech.

Secondly, regarding the positioning of lawyers' attitudes in court, lawyers may choose to construct their interpersonal relations on two dimensions: power or solidarity. If they wish to do so on the latter dimension, they have versatile linguistic resources at their disposal. Thirdly, methodologically, the framework of interpersonal meanings in SFL is a valuable tool for this study, with which the determinant role played by the legal context in relation to lawyers' choice and expression of attitudes may be fully explored.

In short, the critical review suggests that if we want to gain a comprehensive understanding of how lawyers express their evaluation in the Chinese courtroom, it is necessary to consider the social context in its entirety, encompassing both the situational context of the courtroom and the broader legal and cultural context.

2.5 Lawyer Evaluation in Context: A Legal Perspective

This section inquiries into the legal context in China, where lawyer evaluation is situated. First, the major topics or issues associated with lawyer evaluation will be discussed. Then, an overview of the legal culture in China will show that the prevailing theory to interpret or explain judicial communication in Chinese courts is rooted in the communicative action proposed by Habermas (1996). Finally, this section concludes by providing a concise summary of the legal context being discussed thus far.

2.5.1 Major Issues for Lawyer Evaluation

From the perspective of legal reasoning, scholars have generalized the major issues that lawyers evaluate in trial. With reference to situations in the Chinese context,

Yong et al. (2002: 39) point out that lawyer evaluation is mainly preoccupied with three primary activities: finding relevant case facts, selecting relevant legal rules, and deducing/finding a solution to the case. The first activity refers to verifying the presented evidence regarding the case facts. It entails determining which parts of the facts presented are relevant and whether they are supported by admissible evidence. This process is conducted based on the seven mandatory components of an event, often referred to as the "Seven Ws", which represent *when*, *where*, due to *what reason*, *who* (acts) to *whom*, in *what manner*, with *what instrument* and *what consequence* (result/effect), and presented in a narrative form (Yong et al. 2002: 179). The second activity entails selecting or identifying a specific legal rule with which to determine and judge whether the facts of a case may support or refute the claim or charge concerned. The third activity involves deducing a legal decision by applying the normative regulations of the legal rule to the case facts and determining the appropriate outcome. In fact, the three activities are the essential steps in the judicial application of law in all modern legal systems.

In the context of the adversarial trial system, which involves the interactive exchange of lawyer discourse in the courtroom, there is an additional issue (the fourth one) for lawyer evaluation: statements or opinions from the opposing party. Procedurally, both parties in court have the lawful right to express their legal viewpoints, as well as to accept, question, or challenge the opinions presented by the opposing side, so long as they adhere to legal rules. Consequently, lawyer evaluation in court is subject to continual contestation from opposing lawyers and judgment from the tribunal. In order to facilitate genuine discussions and debates, provisions are in place regarding the legal obligations of lawyers during trial proceedings. For instance, lawyers are required to "protect the procedural rights and other lawful rights and interests of a criminal suspect or defendant" and should "present materials and opinions regarding the innocence of a criminal suspect or defendant, the triviality of a crime, or the mitigation of or exemption from criminal liability … in accordance with the facts and the law" (see Article 37, the Criminal Procedure Law of the People's Republic of China [2018]; or Article 31 of the Lawyers Law of the PRC [2017]).

In summary, lawyer evaluation encompasses four topics or issues: case facts (which include the seven *W*s of a fact presented in the form of a narrative), relevant legal rules applicable (to determine whether the facts of a case support the alleged charge or claim), legal decisions to be reached, and the opposing party's legal opinions.

2.5.2 Legal Ideology on Legal Communication in China

This subsection explores the Habermasian perspective on law as a framework for understanding lawyer evaluation. Central to this perspective is Habermas' communicative action theory (Habermas 1986), which emphasizes rationality and proposes a procedural paradigm for law in his influential work, *Between Facts and Norms: A Discourse Theory of Law* (Habermas 1996). The significance of this perspective can be understood in two points. On the one hand, it aligns with the cultural values, legal reforms, and social changes taking place in China, as it underscores the importance of procedural justice and communicative discourse within the legal system. On the other hand, it recognizes the fundamental role of language in law and legal communication, highlighting its crucial role in facilitating understanding and effective legal interactions.

The alignment of Habermas' perspective with the specific situations in China can be comprehended in three aspects. Firstly, Habermas' (1996) perspective on rational dialogue in law corresponds to the longstanding Confucian value in China regarding the handling of differences in opinions in everyday life. According to Habermas (1996), law is not merely a set of rigid rules imposed by the governing body onto the populace but rather a process and outcome of communicative discourse within society. In essence, law should be grounded in rational dialogue, wherein individuals engage in open and honest discussions to reach mutually agreed-upon resolutions for disputes. A similar notion of rational discussion has been expressed by Confucius in the idiom "君子和而不同, 小人同而不和" (*junzi he er butong*, *xiaoren tong er buhe*, in pinyin) found in the Analects. This idiom juxtaposes two groups of people with contrasting characters. Literally translated, it conveys the idea that wise individuals find harmony amidst diversity, embracing divergent opinions and maintaining harmonious relationships. In contrast, foolish individuals seek uniformity by forcing others to conform to their views, disregarding unresolved differences and thus hindering collaboration.

While the Confucian perspective primarily pertains to the treatment of divergent viewpoints in daily life rather than the resolution of legal disputes, it underscores the significance of the Confucian value of "harmony" as a guiding principle and criterion for evaluating conflict resolution in everyday interactions. Given that harmony remains a central value within Confucian philosophy regarding human-nature and interpersonal relationships, the ability to engage in open and honest discussions, exchange viewpoints, and ultimately achieve mutual understanding and harmony is regarded as a distinctive attribute of wise individuals who serve as role models for proper social conduct. Conversely, the suppression or disregard of differences in order to superficially attain conformity is dismissed as bad behaviors associated with foolish individuals. Clearly, the emphasis on exchanging diverse views through discourse to ultimately attain harmony in Confucian-based Chinese culture closely parallels Habermas' concept of rational dialogue in social life and the law.

Secondly, the Habermasian conception of law resonates with the legal requirements of judicial reforms in China. Since the commencement of judicial reforms in 1997, China has implemented an adversary trial system, with necessary adaptations made to suit the specific circumstances of the country. A brief overview of some key features of the new trial system may be provided here. In contrast to the allocation of roles in the inquisitory system in the past, lawyers are granted the right to engage in arguments with their counterparts during legal proceedings, discussing the facts of a case and other relevant issues in it, while judges act as impartial arbitrators in an open hearing. Additionally, the inclusion of one or two individuals, selected from the public through a lawful process and referred to as people's jurors, allows them to participate in a trial as members of the five-member tribunal on the bench. The primary objective of the reform is to make the parties concerned to get involved more actively and the general public to participate more extensively, thereby empowering them to play respective roles in the practice of dispute resolution or disposition in court. This approach creates more opportunities for the audience and the public to assume increasingly significant roles in legal affairs. Alongside various other measures, which are not discussed here, emphasis has been placed on reinforcing procedural justice, granting it equal importance to substantive justice within the legal system (Zhang and Wu 2012). Given this context, the communicative approach to law, which seeks to achieve consensus and agreement between conflicting parties, takes center stage (Fan 2005b; Zhang 2005c).

Thirdly, the relevance of Habermasian procedural law extends to the social demands of the country in contemporary era. In the present stage, the construction of a harmonious society involves stimulating social vitality, advancing principles of justice and fairness, fostering a strong sense of law and integrity throughout society, and ensuring social stability and unity (Central Committee of CPC 2006). With the primary goal of coordinating interests and relationships among different societal spheres, there is a significant emphasis placed on the procedural involvement of citizens.

The Habermasian perspective on law holds relevance to the social landscape in China for two key reasons. To begin with, the discourse theory of law aligns philosophically with the current societal objective of establishing a harmonious society in China. The concept of a "harmonious society" as a strategic goal in China's social development is rooted in relevant social and political theories such as Marxism, Social System theory, and the theory of social equilibrium (Deng 2005). Habermas' discourse theory of law incorporates insights from both social theory and social democracy. By building upon the traditions of Kant, Enlightenment, and democratic socialism, Habermas emphasizes the transformative potential of reason in creating a more humane, just, and egalitarian society. Consequently, his social objectives are consistent with those of a "harmonious society".

Furthermore, Habermas' perspectives on law and democracy provide a suitable framework for understanding how lawful social integration can be achieved through discourse and communication, which is consistent with China's agenda since the economic and judicial reforms of the 1980s. China has aimed to establish a harmonious and prosperous society through the rule of law and active public participation. Habermas' procedural paradigm of law draws insights from various intellectual traditions, including the sociological theories of Weber, Durkheim, and Mead, linguistic philosophy and speech act theories of Wittgenstein, Austin, and Searle, the American pragmatist tradition of Peirce and Dewey, and the sociological systems theory of Parsons, in addition to the thoughts of Kant, Schelling, Hegel, and the Marxian tradition (Habermas 1981). His procedural paradigm emphasizes rational discourse as the central element for achieving consensus in social integration and democracy. China's objective of establishing a harmonious society, as stated unequivocally during the fourth session of the sixteenth Central Committee of the Communist Party of China in 2004, encompasses the rule of law and widespread public participation

(Fan 2005a; Fang 2005; Ji 2005). The effective combination of these two aspects can be understood and interpreted theoretically through the lens of Habermas' procedural paradigm of law, which highlights rational discourse and communication as the bridge between everyday discourse and society in the field of law.

In essence, Habermas' procedural understanding of law and democracy aligns well with the current circumstances of China. It serves as a potent guiding theory or ideology, particularly in legal discussions within Chinese courts. It is essential to highlight that the German origin of Habermas should not undermine the application of his theory, as the theory is not confined to the German legal system alone. It also draws from both the continental and the common law systems for contextual examples (Habermas 1996). This theory has been effectively applied across various scenarios, including the resolution of both international and domestic disputes. For detailed examples, refer to works by Fan (2005a), Ma (2002), O'Neill (2002), and Zhang (2005c), among others.

In addition to the relevance of the Habermasian theory to the situations of China in the three aspects presented above, the theory holds significance in the analysis of language within judicial contexts, thanks to its communicative or "dialogical" approach to legal argumentation (Feteris 1997; Jiao 2004). This dialogical aspect refers to Habermas' intersubjective perspective of law and legal communication. Unlike perspectives that view the law as solely objective or entirely subjective, Habermas posits that law has dual roles—acting as an enforceable set of rules and as a tool for facilitating social integration. The law, according to him, must be intersubjectively accepted by citizens, and the active participation of citizens is crucial in its creation and implementation. Indeed, only when citizens' views are incorporated into the law-making process can rational adherence to the law be assured during its enforcement.

By utilizing language as a medium, Habermas' theory of communicative action in law serves as a mechanism to guide participation and communication and establishes a foundation for coordinating actions among individuals. Grounded in rationality, communicative action involves speech acts that make claims to be justified in one of three ways: claims to propositional truth, claims to normative rightness, or claims to personal sincerity. These claims, although not explicitly stated, expose statements to criticism. Consequently, they necessitate the support of reasons. The interaction between criticism and reasoned justification plays a crucial role in enabling rationality and communicative action (Habermas 1996). This interplay is an inherent rule in the formulation and handling of legal matters, with citizens envisioned as a community of readers actively participating in the creation and enforcement of laws.

2.5.3 *Habermasian Interpretations of Judicial Communication*

In this subsection, the Habermasian interpretations of legal communication are presented, and their implications for lawyer evaluation are discussed.

2.5.3.1 Interpretations of Legal Communication

The theory of communicative action, hailed as revolutionary and influential in various fields of human sciences (Ou 1997: 2), offers a clear understanding of law and democracy through a discourse theory of law, which can be equated with the term "discourse". According to Habermas, communicative action can be defined simply as an action that relies on the listener's response to the speaker's validity claim, which can be a "yes" or "no" (Cooke 1998: 3). This definition implies that communicative action is a social interaction between two or more individuals using language as a means of communication and aiming for mutual understanding. In order to achieve this goal, specific validity criteria must be met for each claim, including truth, sincerity, and rightness.[5]

By highlighting the importance of raising and acknowledging validity claims in everyday linguistic interactions, Habermas presents a concept of social order as a network of relationships based on mutual recognition, which has two significant characteristics (Cooke 1998: 4). The first characteristic relates to the cooperative nature of obligation and accountability. Participants in communicative exchanges agree to act in specific ways, and the effectiveness of the interaction depends on both parties cooperating. The second characteristic is the inherent rational element in mutual recognition. Communicative participants take responsibility for the validity of their statements by providing reasons, and the other party can either accept those reasons or refute them with stronger arguments. It may be argued that everyday communicative action already involves a rudimentary practice of "argumentation", since it normally operates on the assumption that reasons supporting the validity claims are good ones. When the assumption is violated, which occurs more frequently in post-traditional societies, communicative action becomes hindered and ineffective. Participants then have three options: to break off the communicative action, switch to strategic actions, such as the use of violence or money, or recommence their communicative activity at a different, more reflective level, namely, the argumentative speech.

[5] This point serves as Habermas's interpretation of meaning, which is different from that of the speech-act theory by Austin (1962).

Habermas' intersubjective perspective on legal communication, as presented in his discourse theory of law and politics, also presents a legal world characterized by cooperation and rationality. While he agrees with legal positivism that legitimate law must be created through due process by an authoritative body, he argues for the participation of citizens in the entire process of lawmaking and application. Law is deemed legitimate to the extent that it aligns with the understandings of goals and norms reached in the public sphere through communicative action. It is through communicative action that people voice their opinions in lawmaking, thereby becoming both rational authors and recipients of the law (Phillips 2003). Above all, Habermas asserts that the legitimacy of law must satisfy two criteria: coercive binding force, and rational agreement and application by citizens.

Consistent with his overall perspective on law, Habermas unequivocally maintains that legal disputes should be resolved through intersubjective means. In order to resolve conflicts through communication, each statement made by the speaker is subject to potential criticism and must be justified with reasons to assess its validity. If the statement proves to be consistent with the routine activities of daily life, it can be considered a rational agreement among people and thus possesses the attribute of binding force for those affected. The necessity to provide reasoned justifications in the face of criticism promotes the rationality of communicative action.

2.5.3.2 Habermasian Law and Lawyer Evaluation

The discourse theory of law proposed by Habermas is insightful for this study on lawyer evaluation, as it offers valuable insights into legal argumentation and provides general principles that govern participants' discourse in communication. Within the framework of "idealizing presuppositions", there are six principles in total. Firstly, participants share a common objective of reaching a consensus on the validity of disputed claims. Secondly, the interests and opinions of those affected are given equal consideration and respect. Thirdly, no intellectually capable parties can be excluded from the discussion. Fourthly, no relevant arguments are intentionally withheld. Fifthly, the legal claims under deliberation must be justified with reasons to establish their truthfulness, sincerity, and legitimacy. Lastly, participants use language that is mutually comprehensible to facilitate communication (Habermas 1996: 230).

As normative regulations governing the role relationship between participants, these principles apply to both the process of argumentation and its outcome. In a court setting where procedural justice holds significant importance, these principles would influence how lawyer evaluation is presented in legal discussions.

This section provides an overview of lawyer evaluation in legal studies. It highlights two key points. Firstly, lawyer evaluation encompasses a range of topics and issues, including case facts, legal rules, legal decisions, and opposing party's arguments. Secondly, an influential ideology in Chinese courtrooms is the Habermasian discourse theory of law. This review sets the foundation for exploring the contextual constraints that impact lawyer evaluation within the legal context.

2.6 Summary

This chapter provides a comprehensive review of lawyer evaluation, its contextual constraints, and research conducted from both linguistic and legal perspectives. The review establishes the necessary background for studying lawyer evaluation in the Chinese context.

The discussion on the definition and components of lawyer evaluation directs this study toward a linguistic analysis of lawyers' evaluative attitudes within the context of legal activities conducted in the courtroom. Existing research on the contextual features of the courtroom suggests that language use in lawyer evaluation is influenced and shaped by the trial system, which can be semiotically described and explained from the perspectives of Systemic Functional Linguistics (SFL).

By combining studies on lawyer evaluation from linguistic and legal perspectives, this study offers a comprehensive overview of the progress made on lawyer evaluation within the context of trial proceedings. The linguistic investigation not only clarifies the types of evaluative attitudes expressed by lawyers and how they are conveyed and recognized in text but also examines how evaluations are manifested in dynamic interactions, particularly in terms of solidarity. The review of lawyer evaluation in the legal context highlights the key issues it addresses in trials and emphasizes the guiding legal ideology—the Habermasian communicative theory of law—as the cultural background for lawyer evaluation.

In conclusion, to conduct a linguistic analysis of how lawyer evaluation is organized to facilitate effective judicial communication within a Chinese courtroom, it is essential to integrate both the linguistic features of lawyer talk and the broader legal and social context.

References

Atkinson, R.C., and P. Drew. 1990. *Order in court*. Hampshire and London: Macmillan Academic and Professional Ltd.

Austin, J. 1962. *How to do things with words*. Oxford: Oxford University Press.

Bai, Jian-jun. 2004. 罪行均衡实证研究 [*Empirical study of proportionality in sentencing*]. Beijing: Law Press.

Bakhtin, M. 1981. *The dialogic imagination: four essays*. trans. C. Emerson and M. Holquist. London: University of Texas Press.

Bennett, W.L., and M.S. Feldman. 1981. *Reconstructing reality in the courtroom*. London: Tavistock. https://doi.org/10.1017/S0047404500010241.

Biber, D., and E. Finegan. 1988. Adverbial stance types in English. *Discourse Processes* 11: 1–34. https://doi.org/10.1080/01638538809544689.

Biber, D., and E. Finegan. 1989. Styles of stance in English: Lexical and grammatical marking of evidentiality and affect. *Text* 9 (1): 93–124. https://doi.org/10.1515/text.1.1989.9.1.93.

Briggs, C. 1996. Introduction. In *Disorderly discourse*, ed. C. Briggs, 3–40. New York, Oxford: Oxford University Press. https://doi.org/10.1525/jlin.1997.7.2.244.

Brown, R., and A. Gilman. 1960. The pronouns of power and solidarity. In *Style in language*, ed. T. Sebeok, 253–276. Cambridge, MA: MIT Press.

Candlin, C.N., and Y. Maley. 1997. Intertextuality and interdiscursivity in the discourse of alternative dispute resolution. In *The construction of professional discourse*, ed. Britt-Louise Gunnarsson, P. Linell, and B. Nordberg, 201–222. London & New York: Longman.
Central Committee of CPC. 2006. *Decision of the Central Committee of the Communist Party of China on some major issues concerning the building of a harmonious socialist society*. Beijing: People's Publishing House.
Chafe, W.L. 1986. Evidentiality in English conversation and academic writing. In *Evidentiality: The linguistic choice of epistemology*, ed. W.L. Chafe and J. Nichols, 261–272. Norwood: ABLEX.
Channell, J. 1994. *Vague language*. Oxford: Oxford University Press.
Chen, Wei-dong. 2002. 司法公正与律师辩护 [*Judicial justice and lawyer defense*]. Beijing: China Prosecutorial Publishing House.
Clark, E.V. 1997. Conceptual perspective and lexical choice in acquisition. *Cognition* 64: 1–37. https://doi.org/10.1016/S0010-0277(97)00010-3.
Cooke, M. 1998. Introduction. In *On the pragmatics of communication*, ed. M. Cooke, 1–20. Cambridge, MA: MIT Press.
Cotterill, J. 2001. Domestic discord, rocky relationships: Semantic prosodies in representations of marital violence in the courtroom. *Discourse & Society* 12 (3): 315–336. https://doi.org/10.1177/0957926501012003002.
Cotterill, J. 2003. *Language and power in court: A linguistic analysis of the O.J Simpson trial*. Basingstoke: Palgrave.
Cotterill, J. 2004. Collocation, connotation, and courtroom semantics: Lawyer's control of witness testimony through lexical negotiation. *Applied Linguistics* 25 (4): 513–537. https://doi.org/10.1093/applin/25.4.513.
Danet, B. 1980. "Baby" or "fetus": Language and the construction of reality in a manslaughter trial. *Semiotica* 32: 187–219. https://doi.org/10.1515/semi.1980.32.3-4.187.
Deng, Wei-zhi. 2005. 和谐社会笔记 [*Notes on harmonious society*]. Shanghai: Sanlian Bookstore Press.
Don, A. 2003. Attitude and email interaction. Unpublished dissertation, Sydney University, Sydney.
Drew, P. 1990. Strategies in the contest between lawyer and witness in cross-examination. In *Language in the judicial process*, ed. J.N. Levi and A.G. Walker, 39–64. New York and London: Plenum Press. https://doi.org/10.1007/978-1-4899-3719-3_2.
Drew, P. 1992. Contested evidence in courtroom examinations. In *Talk at work: Interaction in institutional settings*, ed. P. Drew and J. Heritage, 470–520. New York: Plenum Press.
Eades, D. 1994. A case of communication clash. In *Language and the law*, ed. J. Gibbons, 234–264. London: Longman.
Eades, D. 2000. I don't think it's an answer to the question: Silencing Aboriginal witnesses in court. *Language in Society* 29: 191–195. https://doi.org/10.1017/S0047404500002013.
Eggins, S., and D. Slade. 1997. *Analyzing casual conversation*. London & Washington: CASSWLL.
Ehrlich, S. 2002. (Re)contextualizing complainants' accounts of sexual assault. *Forensic Linguistics* 9 (2): 193–212. https://doi.org/10.1558/sll.2002.9.2.193.
Fairclough, N. 1992. *Discourse and social change*. Cambridge: Polity Press.
Fan, Hong-wei. 2005a. 民主法治是社会主义和谐社会的重要特征 [Democratic rule of law as an essential feature of the socialist harmonious society]. *Theoretic Observation* (4): 28–29.
Fan, Yu. 2005b. 以多元化纠纷解决机制保证社会的可持续性发展 [Ensuring sustainable social development through the mechanism of diversified dispute resolution]. *Journal of Law Application* 2: 2–8.
Fang, X. 2005. 加强法治建设, 构建和谐社会 [Strengthening the construction of the rule of law and building up a harmonious society]. 中国人大 [*The People's Congress of China*] (7): 27.
Feteris, E.T. 1997. A survey of 25 years of research on legal argumentation. *Argumentation* 11: 355–376. https://doi.org/10.1023/A:1007794830151.
Firth, J.R. 1957. *Papers in linguistics 1934–1952*. London: Oxford University Press.
Fowler, R. 1996. On critical linguistics. In *Readings in critical discourse analysis*, ed. C.R. Caldas-Coulthard and M. Coulthard, 2–15. London & New York: Routledge.

Frohmann, L. 1997. Convictability and discordant locales: Reproducing race, class, and gender ideologies in prosecutorial decision-making. *Law and Society Review* 31 (3): 531–555. https://doi.org/10.2307/3054045.
Gaines, P. 1996. The grammar of credibility assessment: A functional analysis of two legal questioning styles. *Social Semiotics* 6 (2): 199–230. https://doi.org/10.1080/10350339609384473.
Gaines, P. 2002. Negotiating power at the bench. *Forensic Linguistics: The International Journal of Speech, Language and Law* 9 (2): 213–234. https://doi.org/10.1558/sll.2002.9.2.213.
Gao, Hua. 2003. 刑事法庭调查中的填表式问句初探 [Form-filling questions in Chinese criminal court examinations]. 语言教学与研究 [*Language Teaching and Research*] (4): 37–44.
Gibbons, J. 1994. *Language and the law*. London & New York: Longman.
Gibbons, J. 2003. *Forensic linguistics*. Oxford: Blackwell.
Goodrich, P. 1988. Modalities of annunciation: An introduction to courtroom speech. In *Law and semiotics*, vol. 2, ed. R. Levelson, 143–165. New York: Plenum Press.
Goodwin, C., and M.H. Goodwin. 1997. Contested version: The discursive constitution of Rodney King. In *The construction of professional discourse*, ed. Britt-Louise Gunnarsson, P. Linell, et al., 292–316. London and New York: Longman.
Gumperz, J.J. 1982. *Discourse strategies*. Cambridge: Cambridge University Press. https://doi.org/10.1017/CBO9780511611834.
Habermas, J. 1981. *Kleine Politische Schrifen (I–IV)*. Berlin: Suhrkamp Verlag.
Habermas, J. 1986. Communicative rationality and the theories of meaning and action. In *On the pragmatics of communication*, ed. M. Cooke, 183–214. Cambridge, MA: MIT.
Habermas, J. 1996. *Between facts and norms*. Translated by William Rehg. Cambridge, MA: MIT.
Halliday, M.A.K. 1978. *Language as social semiotic*. London: Edward Arnold.
Halliday, M.A.K. 1985. Text, context, and learning. In *Language, context and text*, ed. M.A.K. Halliday and R. Hasan, 44–51. Oxford: Oxford University Press.
Halliday, M.A.K. 1992. Language as system and language as instance: The corpus as a theoretical construct. In *Directions in Corpus Linguistics: Proceedings of Nobel Symposium 82 Stockholm (TLSM65)*, ed. Jan Svartvik, 61–77. Berlin/New York: Mouton de Gruyter. https://doi.org/10.1515/9783110867275.61.
Halliday, M.A.K. 1994. *Introduction to functional grammar*. London: Edward Arnold.
Han, Zheng-rui. 2005. 律师辩论的人际意义研究 [Research on interpersonal meanings of lawyers' debate]. *Journal of Guangdong University of Foreign Studies* (3): 26–33.
Harris, S. 2003. Politeness and power. *Text & Talk* 23 (1): 27–52. https://doi.org/10.1515/text.2003.003.
Heffer, C. 2003. Making a case: Narrative and paradigmatic modes of legal-lay discourse in British jury trial. *Forensic Linguistics: Journal of Speech, Language, and Law* 10 (1): 157–159. https://doi.org/10.1558/ijsll.v10i1.157.
Hood, S. 2004. Managing attitude in undergraduate academic writing: A focus on the introductions to research reports. In *Analyzing academic writing*, ed. L. Ravelli and R. Ellis, 24–44. London & New York: Continuum.
Hu, Zhuang-lin. 2002. 语境研究的多元化 [A pluralistic approach to the study of context]. *Foreign Language Teaching and Research* (3): 161–166.
Hunston, S. 2000. Evaluation and the planes of discourse: Status and value in persuasive texts. In *Evaluation in text*, ed. S. Hunston and G. Thompson, 176–207. Oxford: Oxford University Press.
Hyland, K. 2002. Directives: Argument and engagement in academic writing. *Applied Linguistics* 23 (2): 215–239. https://doi.org/10.1093/applin/23.2.215.
Hyland, K. 2004. Patterns of engagement: Dialogical features and L2 undergraduate writing.
Hymes, D. 1972. Models of the interaction of language and social life. In *Directions in sociolinguistics*, ed. J. Gumperz and D. Hymes, 35–71. New York: Holt, Rinehart, and Winston.
Jackson, B.S. 1996. *Making sense in jurisprudence*. Liverpool, UK: Deborah Charles.

Ji, Jian-min. 2005. 人际关系的和谐是最基本的和谐 [Harmony in interpersonal relationship as a most fundamental one]. *People's Forum* (4): 52. https://doi.org/10.16619/j.cnki.rmlt.2005.04.018.

Jiao, Bao-qian. 2004. 当代法律方法论的转型 [From judicial syllogism to legal argumentation]. *Law and Social Development* (3): 97–103.

Kangasharju, H. 1996. Aligning as a team in multiparty conversation. *Journal of Pragmatics* 26: 291–319. https://doi.org/10.1016/0378-2166(95)00051-8.

Kedar, L., ed. 1987. *Power through discourse*. Norwood: Ablex.

Kristina, L. 2006. Appraisal in online discussions of literary texts. *Text & Talk* 26 (2): 217–244. https://doi.org/10.1515/TEXT.2006.010.

Kšrner, H. 2000. Negotiating authority: Logogenesis of dialogue in common law judgments. Unpublished doctoral dissertation, Sydney University, Sydney.

Kuo, Sai-hua. 2002. From solidarity to antagonism: The uses of the second-person singular pronoun in Chinese political discourse. *Text & Talk* 22 (1): 29–55. https://doi.org/10.1515/text.2002.004.

Kurzon, D. 2001. The politeness of judges: American and English judicial behavior. *Journal of Pragmatics* 33: 61–85. https://doi.org/10.1016/S0378-2166(99)00123-X.

Labov, W. 2003. Uncovering the event structure of narrative. In *Georgetown University roundtable 2001 on languages and linguistics: Linguistics, language, and the real world: Discourse and beyond*, ed. D. Tannen and J.E. Alatis, 63–90. Washington: Georgetown University Press.

Labov, W., and J. Waletzky. 1997. Narrative analysis: Oral versions of personal experience. *Narrative Inquiry* (7): 3–38. Orig. pub. in 1967. *Essays on the verbal and visual arts*, ed. June Helm, 12–24. Seattle, Washington: University of Washington Press.

Levinson, S. 1987. *Pragmatics*. Cambridge: Cambridge University Press.

Levinson, S. 1992. Activity types and language. In *Talk at work*, ed. P. Drew and J. Heritage, 66–100. Cambridge: Cambridge University Press.

Li, Zhan-zi. 2002. 话语的人际意义研究 [*Interpersonal meanings of discourse*]. Shanghai: Shanghai Foreign Language Education Press.

Liao, Mei-zhen. 2003a. 法庭问答及其互动研究 [*Question and answers in courtroom interactions*]. Beijing: Law Press.

Liao, Mei-zhen. 2003b. 法庭审判问答推理分析 [Argumentation in questions and answers of the courtroom]. In 语言与法律研究的新视野 [*New perspectives on language and the law*], ed. Qinsheng Zhou, Jie Wang, and Jinzhi Su, 202–212. Beijing: Law Press.

Loftus, E.F., and J.C. Palmer. 1974. Reconstruction of automobile destruction: An example of the interaction between language and memory. *Journal of Verbal Learning and Verbal Behavior* 13: 585–589. https://doi.org/10.1016/S0022-5371(74)80011-3.

Lyons, J. 1982. Deixis and subjectivity: Loquor, ergo sum. In *Speech, place and action: Studies in deixis and related topics*, ed. R.J. Jarvella and W. Klein, 101–124. Chichester: Wiley.

Lyons, J. 1995. *Linguistic semantics: An introduction*. Cambridge: Cambridge University Press.

Ma, Chang-shan. 2002. 哈贝马斯的交往理性法律观及其启示 [Habermasian communicative rationality in law and its implication]. *Chinese Journal of Law* (4): 101–106. https://doi.org/10.13858/j.cnki.cn32-1312/c.2002.04.017.

Maley, Y. 1994. The language of the law. In *Language and the law*, ed. J. Gibbons, 11–50. London: Longman.

Maley, Y. 1995. From adjudication to mediation: Third party discourse in conflict resolution. *Journal of Pragmatics* 23: 93–110. https://doi.org/10.1016/0378-2166(94)00030-I.

Maley, Y., and R. Fahey. 1991. Representing the evidence: Construction of reality in court. *International Journal for the Semiotics of Law* IV (10): 3–17. https://doi.org/10.1007/BF01303504.

Malinowski, B. 1923. The problem of meaning in primitive languages. Supplement 1. In *The meaning of meaning*, ed. C.K. Ogden and I.A. Richards, 296–336. London: Kegan Paul.

Martin, J. 1999. Modeling context: A crooked path of progress in contextual linguistics. In *Text and context in functional linguistics*, ed. M. Ghadessy, 25–61. Amsterdam: Benjamins.

Martin, J. 2000. Beyond exchange: Appraisal in English. In *Evaluation in text*, ed. S. Hunston and G. Thompson, 142–175. Oxford: Oxford University Press.
Martin, J. 2003. Introduction. *Text* 23 (2): 171–181. https://doi.org/10.1515/text.2003.007.
Martin, J. 2004a. Sense and sensibility: Texturing evaluation. In *New perspectives on education and discourse*, ed. J.A. Foley, 65–96. London and New York: Continuum.
Martin, J. 2004b. Mourning: How we get aligned. *Discourse & Society* 15 (2–3): 321–343. https://doi.org/10.1177/0957926504041022.
Martin, J., and D. Rose. 2003. *Working with discourse*. London, New York: Continuum.
Martin, J., and P. White. 2005. *Evaluation in text: Appraisal in English*. New York: Palgrave.
Matoesian, G.M. 1993. *Reproducing rape: Dominance through talk in the courtroom*. Oxford: Polity Press.
Matoesian, G.M. 2000. Intertextual authority in reported speech. *Journal of Pragmatics* 32: 879–914. https://doi.org/10.1016/S0378-2166(99)00080-6.
Matoesian, G.M. 2001. *Law and the language of identity: Discourse in the William Kennedy Smith rape trial*. London: Oxford University Press.
Maynard, D.W. 1990. Narrative and narrative structure in plea bargaining. In *Language in the judicial process*, ed. J.N. Levi and A.G. Walker, 65–95. New York & London: Plenum Press.
Miller, D. 2002. Multiple judicial opinions as specialized sites of engagement: Conflicting paradigms of valuation and legitimation in Bush v. Gore 2000. In *Conflict and negotiation in specialized texts*, ed. M. Gotti, D. Heller, et al., 119–141. Bern: Peter Lang.
Miller, D. 2004. "To meet our common challenge": ENGAGEMENT strategies of alignment and alienation in current US international discourse. *Textus* XVIII (1): 39–62.
Nan, Ying. 2002. 论辩护律师在刑事审判中的作用与地位 [The role and status of defense lawyers in criminal trials]. In 司法公正与律师辩护 [*Judicial justice and lawyer defense*], ed. Wenchang Tian and Yongzhong Gu. Beijing: China Prosecutorial Publishing House.
O'Barr, M. 1982. *Linguistic evidence: Language power and strategy in the courtroom*. New York: Academic Press.
O'Barr, W., and J. Conley. 1990. Litigant satisfaction versus legal adequacy in small claims narratives. In *Language in the judicial process*, ed. J.N. Levi and A.G. Walker, 97–132. New York and London: Plenum Press.
O'Neill, S. 2002. Are national conflicts reconcilable? Discourse theory and political accommodation in Northern Ireland. Workshop No. 5 of the Joint Sessions of the ECPR Political Accommodation in Ethnonationally Divided Societies, Turin, Italy, March. https://doi.org/10.1111/1467-8675.00314.
Ou, Li-tong. 1997. 哈贝马斯的 "批判理论" [*Habermas' "critical theory"*]. Chongqing: Chongqing Press.
Page, R.E. 2003. An analysis of appraisal in childbirth narratives. *Text & Talk* 23 (2): 211–237. https://doi.org/10.1515/text.2003.009.
Painter, C. 2003. Developing attitude. *Text & Talk* 23 (2): 183–209. https://doi.org/10.1515/text.2003.008.
Peirce, C.S. 1932. Elements of logic. In *Collected papers of Charles Sanders Peirce*, vol. 2, ed. C. Hartshorne, et al. Cambridge, MA: Harvard University Press.
Philips, S.U. 1987. On the use of WH questions in American courtroom discourse: A study of the relation between language form and language function. In *Power through discourse*, ed. L. Kedar, 83–111. New Jersey: ABLEX.
Philips, S.U. 1998. *Ideology in the language of the judge*. New York: Oxford University Press.
Phillips, A. 2003. *Lawyer's language: How and why legal language is different*. London & New York: Routledge.
Plum, G.A. 1988. Text and contextual conditioning in spoken English: A genre-based approach. Ph.D. thesis, University of Sydney.
Rothery, J. 1990. Story writing in primary school: Assessing narrative type genres. Ph.D. thesis, University of Sydney, Sydney.

Sarat, A., and W.L. Felstiner. 1986. Law and strategy in the divorce lawyer's office. *Law and Society Review* 20: 93–134. https://doi.org/10.2307/3053414.

Simon-Vandenbergen, A. 2004. Intersubjective positioning in talk shows: A case study from British TV. *Text & Talk* 24 (3): 399–422. https://doi.org/10.1515/text.2004.016.

Stygall, G. 1994. *Trial process: Differential discourse processing and discursive formation*. Amsterdam & Philadelphia: John Benjamins.

Thompson, G. 2005. Two levels of analysis on evaluative meanings. Discussion list of appraisal analysis. http://www.grammatics.com/appraisal. Accessed July 1, 2013.

Thompson, G., and S. Hunston. 2000. Evaluation: An introduction. In *Evaluation in text*, ed. S. Hunston and G. Thompson, 1–27. Oxford: Oxford University Press.

Walker, A.G. 1987. Linguistic manipulation, power, and the legal setting. In *Power through discourse*, ed. L. Kedar, 57–80. New Jersey: ABLEX.

Wang, Zhen-hua. 2003. 交叉询问双方的言语优势—辛普森案法庭语篇的"情态"分析 [Verbal advantages of both parties in cross-examination: A modality analysis of the O.J Simpson trial discourse]. In 语言与法律研究的新视野 [*New perspectives on language and the law*], ed. Qi-sheng Zhou, Jie Wang, and Jin-zhi Su, 225–238. Beijing: Law Press.

White, P. 1998. Telling media tales: The news as rhetoric. Ph.D. thesis, Sydney University, Sydney.

White, P. 2003. Beyond modality and hedging: A dialogic view of the language of intersubjective stance. *Text & Talk* 23 (2): 259–284. https://doi.org/10.1515/text.2003.011.

Wodak, R. 1980. Discourse analysis and courtroom interaction. *Discourse Processes* 3: 369–380. https://doi.org/10.1080/01638538009544498.

Wodak, R. 1984. Determination of guilt: Discourse in the courtroom. In *Language and power*, ed. C. Kramarae, M. Schulz, and W.M. O'Barr, 80–100. Beverly Hills: Sage.

Wodak, R. 1985. The interaction between judge and defendant. In *Handbook of discourse analysis*, vol. 4, ed. T.A. van Dijk, 181–192. New York: Academic Press.

Wu, Wei-ping. 2002. 语言与法律: 司法领域的语言学研究 [*Language and the law: Language in the judicial process*]. Shanghai: Shanghai Foreign Language Education Press.

Xin, Bin. 2002. 批判性语篇分析方法论 [Methodology in critical discourse analysis]. *Journal of Foreign Languages* (6): 34–41. CNKI:SUN:WYXY.0.2002-06-005.

Yong, Q., Cheng-guang Jin, and Rong-mao Yao. 2002. 法律适用中的逻辑 [*Logic in law application*]. Beijing: China University of Political Science and Law Press.

Zhang, Mei-fang. 2002. 语言的评价意义与译者的价值取向 [Evaluative significance of language and translators' value orientation]. 外语与外语教学 [*Foreign Languages and Their Teaching*] (7): 15–18.

Zhang, Li-ping. 2004. 控制与抗争: 法官与被告人法庭交际会话分析 [Control and contest: Discourse analysis of the judge-defendant interaction]. *School Journal of Nanjing University of Post and Telecommunication* (1): 21–24. https://doi.org/10.14132/j.cnki.nysk.2004.01.005.

Zhang, Li-ping. 2005a. 庭审叙事的对立与诉讼对抗: 话语分析对法官的启示 [Confrontation in courtroom narratives: Implications of discourse analysis to trial judges]. *Shandong Foreign Language Teaching* (5): 12–15. https://doi.org/10.16482/j.sdwy37-1026.2005.05.006.

Zhang, Li-ping. 2005b. 从庭审图式的话语理解论法官的言语反应 [A schema-based discourse comprehension of verbal responses from judges]. *Foreign Language Research* (5): 32–37. https://doi.org/10.16263/j.cnki.23-1071/h.2005.05.007.

Zhang, Wei-ping. 2005c. 我国替代性纠纷解决机制的重构 [Reconstructing alternative dispute resolution in China]. *Journal of Law Application* 2: 15–16.

Zhang, Fa-Lian. 2017. 中西法律语言与文化对比研究 [*A comparative study of legal language and culture between China and the west*]. Beijing: Beijing University Press.

Zhang, Wu-sheng, and Ze-yong Wu. 2012. 对抗制诉讼与法官制度改革 [Adversarial litigation and judicial system reform]. *Qinghua Law Review* (2): 1–16.

Zhu, Yong-sheng, and Shi-qing Yan. 2001. 系统功能语言学多维思考 [*Multi-dimensional thinking in systemic functional linguistics*]. Shanghai: Shanghai Foreign Language Education Press.

Chapter 3
Rational Discourse of Lawyer Evaluation

Abstract Following a classification of lawyer evaluation into three types, Affect, Judgment, and Appreciation, which are redefined in accordance with the legal context, this chapter systematically interprets lawyer evaluation in relation to the legal context and the communicative tasks of the trial. Subsequently, it presents the rational discourse of lawyer evaluation, which consists of three features, namely, equal role relationships, multi-voiced speech environment, and distinct discursive communities.

3.1 Introduction

To establish a theoretical framework concerning the speech pattern of lawyer evaluation in China, this chapter tries to integrate lawyer evaluation within the context in which it is used and analyze it from the perspective of the interpersonal metafunction of Systemic Functional Linguistics (SFL). Following a classification of lawyer evaluation into three types of evaluative attitudes, which are redefined in accordance with the legal context, this chapter offers a detailed discussion of how lawyer evaluation, the legal context, and the communicative tasks of the trial are integrated. Subsequently, this chapter presents a comprehensive framework for understanding the expression of lawyer evaluation in the Chinese court.

3.2 Lawyer Evaluation, Context, and Case Resolution

This section aims to explore the interrelationship between lawyer evaluation, the contextual situation in which it takes place, and the trial activities in which it is embedded. After a very brief introduction to the Hallidayan socio-semiotic perspective on language and context, the section categorizes lawyer evaluation into three distinct types and redefines them in the legal context, and then it examines the contextual characteristics of courtroom interactions and their influence on the expression

L. Zhang, *Lawyer Evaluation in Chinese Courtroom*,
https://doi.org/10.1007/978-981-97-1211-3_3

of lawyer evaluation. Furthermore, it investigates the discursive patterns of lawyer evaluation in texts, highlighting its functional role in serving the communicative objectives of the trial.

3.2.1 Socio-semiotic View of Language

Language is inherently social and semiotic, which means that "language should be interpreted within a sociocultural context, in which culture itself is interpreted in semiotic terms" (Halliday 1978: 1–2). By means of the stratification system, language, which comprises three meta-functions (ideational, interpersonal, and textual) across the strata/levels of phonology/graphology, lexico-grammar, and discourse, is related to society, which may be described in context, both the immediate situational context of a speech event and the broader social context (the context of culture) (Halliday 1978: 39). Accordingly, there should be a direct relationship of determination between the context of situation, which has three variables (Field, Tenor, and Mode), and the way people talk in a particular societal situation. Namely, Field determines the choice of ideational function, Tenor the interpersonal function, and Mode the textual function.

The relationship of determination, however, has been debated in the academic circle. For instance, Cheng (1989: 14) contended that "there is no such a direct one-to-one determination but a rough specification between variables of context and the functions of language in text". Specific functional studies on language use in different social settings, such as research conducted by Miller (2002, 2004) and Simon-Vandenbergen (2004), acknowledge that the relationship is in effect but the variables "appear to be working cooperatively to motivate the choice of linguistic forms" (Miller 2002: 138). These findings are consistent with the opinions held in SFL circles (Zhu and Yan 2001: 31–32).

Meanwhile, Halliday also emphasizes the importance of the context of culture in the interpretation of language use. The context of culture works as a mediator in determining how the context of situation influences the language used in a text (Halliday 1978). This point has been best illustrated with the example of the speech behavior in the classroom (Halliday 1985).

In accordance with the socio-semiotic perspective of language and context, a comprehensive analysis of language patterns in lawyer evaluation necessitates an initial focus on delineating the contextual characteristics inherent in the entirety of courtroom interactions. By delving into the contextual aspects of a courtroom, including its norms, roles, and communicative dynamics, we can establish a solid foundation for predicting and understanding the specific patterns of language employed in lawyer evaluation.

3.2.2 *Constituents of Lawyer Evaluation*

This subsection endeavors to categorize and delineate the constituents or components of lawyer evaluation and then provides a succinct overview of how these constitutes can be identified within textual data. Through this classification process, it becomes possible to discern and analyze the specific linguistic and discursive markers that signify instances of lawyer evaluation in text.

3.2.2.1 Three Constituents of Lawyer Evaluation

In line with Appraisal Theory (Martin and Rose 2003), the ATTITUDE system contains three distinct types of evaluative attitudes, namely, Affect, Judgment, and Appreciation. The first, Affect, pertains to a speaker's emotional and affective states; the second, Judgment, centers around assessments of a person's character or behavior; and the third, Appreciation, involves the aesthetic evaluation of entities or objects. Affect, being the fundamental type of attitude, represents the core emotional stance of a speaker, while Judgment and Appreciation, both of which are characterized as institutionalized sentiments, correspond to behavioral norms within the context of a proposal and value norms within the context of a proposition, respectively. The criteria for evaluations are significantly determined by the context where they are expressed, and the kinds of evaluations made by speakers are shaped by their institutional roles or positions (Martin 2000; Martin and Rose 2003: 63–64). Consequently, lawyers' evaluative attitudes can be categorized based on the topics under evaluation within a trial and the prescribed norm governing how evaluations on those topics are presented in the courtroom.

In the context of evaluative attitudes, which encompass three structural elements—namely, the evaluated, an evaluator, and an evaluating item—the initial step is identifying and categorizing the topics or issues to be evaluated. The evaluated topics can cover anything in relation to individuals, objects, or entities that are subject to evaluation. In previous Appraisal analyses found in published works (e.g., Eggins and Slade 1997; Martin 1997; Rothery and Stenglin 2000), the evaluated topics are typically identified as specific entities or phenomena at a micro-level within the text. For instance, in the phrase "a large sample", the *sample* itself is the evaluated element. However, in our study, we will adopt a macro-level approach and try to consider the evaluated topics in close relation to the specific discourse field in which they occur (Hunston 2000). As a result, we will refer to these evaluated topics or issues as macro-topics/issues of lawyer evaluation.

Four issues, which were identified as topics subject to evaluation by lawyers in a trial in Sect. 2.5.1, are case facts, legal rules applicable to a case, legal decisions to be made, and arguments put forward by the opposing party. It is important to note that these topics differ from each other in the nature of the activity or action they entail (see Hale and Gibbons 1999). As noted by Halliday (1978: 143), under the variable of Field, which refers to socially recognized actions that participants are engaged in through verbal exchanges, three sets of activities emerge in a continuum. At one end is a set of activities involving language in a subordinate or marginal role; at the other end is the set of activities where language plays a fundamentally important role, such as a seminar or a meeting, and in the middle between the two ends lie the set of activities where language is necessary but supplementary. For activities where language is inseparable, two orders of Field can be made, the first being the discussion or the talk itself and the second the "subject matter" of the verbal talk. In the context of a trial discourse, two orders of Field may be observed: lawyers' discussions as the *discussion* part in the first order and facts of a case as the *subject matter* in the second order.

Consequently, topics of lawyer evaluation may be coded in terms of Field so as to capture the distinctions between them. The topic, facts of a case, which is coded as the Field of domain (FD) due to its place in the second order of the Field, varies in context, encompassing scenarios such as trademark infringement in a civil court or causing physical injury in a criminal case. The other three topics are coded as FT, which designates these activities as part of the trial discussions in the first order of Field. To further distinguish between the three, the topic related to legal rules applicable to a case is coded as FT_R, legal decisions to be made as FT_A, and the opponents' arguments as FT_O. The categorization of these four topics under lawyer evaluation and their difference is demonstrated in Fig. 3.1. The bracket in the figure indicates inclusion, meaning that the four items on the right are all components of the "macro-topics", and lines indicate the layers of Field to which these items belong.

In addition to the topics under lawyer evaluation, established regulations stipulating how legal opinions shall be presented and what kinds of opinions are admissible in the institutional context of the courtroom also matter a lot to the classification of lawyer evaluation. According to procedural law, lawyers are required to provide evaluative opinions based on the factual evidence of a case and the relevant law, which would ensure that legal arguments and assessments are grounded in a solid foundation and conducive to the overall fairness and integrity of the trial process. Furthermore, as the principle of objectivity is highly valued within the legal profession, lawyers have to maintain a certain level of emotional detachment and impartiality in their communication during trial proceedings, so as to ensure that their legal arguments are based on rationality, evidence, and logical reasoning rather than personal biases or emotional influence (Yong et al. 2002).

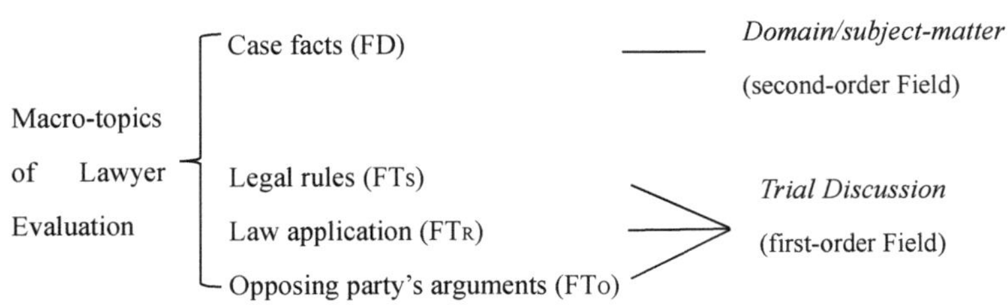

Fig. 3.1 Macro-topics of lawyer evaluation

Constrained by the two factors, the topics and the institutional regulations regarding lawyer speech, it is certain to claim that two evaluative attitudes, Judgment and Appreciation, are prevalent in lawyer evaluation in the trial talk concerning the legality of a disputed social act/behavior. Judgment may be expressed in the context of a proposal pertaining to the characters or behaviors of a person/party involved in a case, and it is therefore related to the topic of FD. Appreciation may be expressed in the context of a proposition pertaining to the nature of the disputed behaviors/acts of the said person/party and the respective decision on the behaviors/acts within the legal framework. It is mainly related to three topics of FT, namely, the relevant rules, the legal decisions to be made, and the arguments presented by the opposing party. Both Judgement and Appreciation can be further divided, of course.

In accordance with Appraisal Theory, Appreciation of the issues in court (FT) can be analyzed in terms of the three variables, Reaction, Composition, and Valuation, with the assistance of questions (see Martin and Rose 2003: 63). We may explain how these three variables can be explored with typical questions in the legal context. For Reaction, questions like "As a legal professional and/or an average person, how do lawyers feel about an allegedly illegal event?" may be asked; for Composition, questions like "Is the prosecuted or disputed act/action consistent with the scenario prospectively regulated in the law?" can be used for analysis; and questions such as "Is the prosecuted or disputed act a violation of the law?" "How serious is the prosecuted or disputed act in accordance with the regulations of the law?" or "What punishment or compensation can be made to the person involved in the prosecuted or disputed acts?" may be used to measure Valuation.

Judgment of a person's character has to be redefined in the legal context of the study. Evaluating the character aspects of a person/party involved in a given case is crucial in law, because the boundary between the three aspects of an individual's character, namely, personal capacity, moral quality, and legal quality, has a direct link to the legal nature of disputed acts related to the person/party and the corresponding legal decisions regarding punishment or compensation in the trial. The personal capacity of an individual has something to do with assessing their ability to fulfill their duties and obligations, or to enjoy their lawful rights, and estimating their genuine motive in a disputed action (see Atkinson and Drew 1990). So do the moral and legal aspects of quality, both of which apparently have a decisive role to play in determining the case in law. A morally condemned person may not be liable to punishment in law, and conversely, a person liable to punishment may not be morally wrong in their behaviors (Zhao 2004; Zhang 2003b). In other words, an appropriate division between the two aspects matters significantly in some cases, which is especially true in the context of Chinese law.

Judgment of a person's character has varied historically in the legal culture of China, where the Confucianized ethical value of filial piety was intertwined with legal norms in various ways (see Qu 1984). In the period of the traditional legal culture, which was operated under the feudal legal system mainly from the Qin (221 BC–206 BC), Han (206 BC–220 AD) throughout the Qing (1611–1912) dynasties, the rule known as "father-son mutual non-disclosure" was in effect. Subject to the rule, it was an accepted behavior, both morally and legally, for a son to shield his father from criminal liability, provided that the offense in which the father was involved was not one of treason or any other crimes committed against the government, and vice versa. What was reflected and protected by the rule is the familial duty and obligation between father and son as family members. However, although it would be a morally accepted behavior in that legal culture for a son to protect his father, who committed severe crimes, such as treason, by hiding the father from official investigations, it was not permitted by the law in that culture. On the contrary, the "protection" would incur punishment for both the son and the father, who both would be considered offenders under the law. In the case of severe crimes, then, the priority of protecting the state order or safety over filial piety means that the moral character of a person may conflict with their legal character. The Judgement of a person's moral and legal characters changed during the period of the democratic revolution (1919–1949), with new norms and values emerging in society and the law. Later, in the first several decades of the twentieth century, after the establishment of the People's Republic of China in 1949, filial piety, which had become a characteristic of the Chinese traditional culture for centuries, was no longer recognized in law as it had been in the traditional feudal legal system. Therefore, the act of a child protecting their father against any civil or criminal liabilities would be considered illegal, though it was morally justifiable. The change in judgment over the act remains the same even under the modernized legal system in China today. Regardless of the family ethics in traditional times, many actions or behaviors of a person in relation to their family members are redefined in the modern legal framework. Luckily, it is now legally acceptable for a person to refuse to testify about their family members in court, which has been regarded as an acknowledgment of the value of filial piety to families (Chai 2009). Generally speaking, the conflict between the moral and legal characters remains in many cases. It is important to note that the rule of "mutual non-disclosure" between family members, which was not an isolated case in Chinese legal history, has been reflected in the laws of many countries in Europe and East Asia as well (Fan 1997). Therefore, it would be worthwhile and necessary to delineate the moral and legal characters of a person in evaluation studies.

Given that a person's character may differ between the moral and legal considerations in law and that the difference may not be well captured through the present dichotomization of Judgement into Social Esteem and Social Sanction, modifications are proposed to be made to the subcategories. The definitions of the two variables, Social Esteem and Social Sanction, will be slightly altered, and a third variable, Social Punishment, will be tentatively added to this study.

In this study, the Judgement of a person's character or behaviors is to be analyzed in three variables: Social Esteem, Social Sanction, and Social Punishment. The first, Social Esteem, is defined as a means to investigate the qualities of a person as an individual, such as their normality, capacity, and tenacity. The second, Social Sanction, is used to evaluate the moral aspect of a person as a community member in the predominant ethical system. It contains two sub-variables: veracity and propriety. The third, Social Punishment, is employed to evaluate a person's character in terms of their behaviors within the legal value system.

The use of the term *social punishment* to metaphorically refer to the legal aspect of a person's character can be justified on two grounds. Firstly, compared with the term *sanction*, which implies a more general and voluntary adherence to norms associated with moral obligations, societal values, or principles in a general sense, *punishment*, which carries a stronger semantic force, is a more appropriate choice to describe the normative and mandatory force of an enforceable legal system. Secondly, with the influence of Confucianism, there was a long tradition of distinguishing between morality and law in China. The principle of "德主刑辅" (*de zhu xing fu*, in pinyin), which means that virtue or moral education took precedence over penal law in the maintenance of social order, governed legislative and judicial activities in imperial China from 202 BC to 1911 AD (Qu 1984). As a result, the blending of these two systems was emphasized in judicial practices and trial communication in traditional China (Shi 2006). Additionally, historical research on the legal system of early imperial China reveals that the coded laws, referred to as "刑" (*xing* in pinyin, and literally, *penal laws* in English), primarily focused on criminal aspects, with only a minor portion dedicated to civil or administrative matters (Zhang 2003a). As modern China has established a rule-based legal system to protect people's lawful rights and duties after the abolition of the imperial view of law as a means of social control, it is essential to note that the historical separation of morality and law still lingers unconsciously in some ways. Therefore, distinguishing the legal aspect of a person's character from their moral character remains an important conceptual distinction, and *social punishment* properly denotes the former associated with the mandatory force imposed by the legal system.

The three variables of Judgement can be illustrated with the help of relevant typical questions. For Social Esteem, we may ask whether the person is special (normality), whether they are capable (capacity), and whether they are determined (tenacity). For Social Sanction, we may check how honest a person is (veracity) and how good (propriety) they are in the moral and ethical sense. For Social Punishment, we may have five sub-categories, namely, honesty, reliability, loyalty, respectfulness, and culpability. The reason for the five sub-categories lies in the fact that the aim of evaluating a person's legal character is to assess how they behave within a legal relationship (see Carbonnier 1994), including their adherence to a legally binding obligation defined by the law and to the rules and regulations issued by the state or other law-enforcement bodies. Note that these questions may be expressed in the perfective or past tense due to the fact that the evaluation of a person's legal character primarily focuses on their past experiences or facts. Below are typical questions for exploring these sub-categories in Social Punishment.

Social Punishment:

Honesty: Has the person been truthful and consistent in their statements or behaviors?

Reliability: Has the person demonstrated any irresponsible or reckless behaviors? Has the person demonstrated any violent or aggressive behaviors?
Loyalty: Has the person shown commitment to fulfill their legal duties?
Respectfulness: Has the person shown any disregard for the law or the rights of others? Has the person shown any remorse for any wrongdoing in the past?
Culpability: Has the person been convicted/sued/charged in a case?

In contrast to Judgment and Appreciation, the use of Affect in court proceedings by lawyers may be less common, although its presence has been observed in judicial discourse (see Sect. 2.4.1.1). Yong et al. (2002: 314) acknowledge that, as human beings, lawyers may introduce personal emotions into their arguments. They further note that tactful management of personal emotions can be employed to elicit sympathy from the court. However, they caution against the contamination of legal evaluation by emotions, as it can transform the assessment into a purely subjective one, particularly when emotions are manipulated or excessively employed. It is reasonable to assert that personal emotions inevitably find their way into trial discussions, and that Affect can serve as an interpersonal resource for lawyers. Nevertheless, due to the emphasis on objectivity within the legal framework, Affect may occupy a peripheral role in lawyer evaluation.

In summary, lawyer evaluation is comprised of three constituents: Judgement, Appreciation, and Affect. Among the three, Judgement and Appreciation are more important than Affect. Judgment can be further analyzed in terms of Social Esteem, Social Sanction, and Social Punishment; Appreciation can be analyzed further in terms of Reaction, Composition, and Valuation. To differentiate between lawyer evaluation and speaker evaluation, this study uses title case, capitalizing the initial letter of the functional categories rather than all-capitals, when referring to the three types of evaluative attitudes. A schematic representation of lawyer evaluation in the three types is given in Fig. 3.2. The enclosing bracket indicates an inclusive relationship between the items within it and the item outside (on the left). The parenthesis under each item provides the sub-variables by which the item is to be analyzed.

3.2.2.2 Identification of Lawyer Evaluation in Text

Structurally, lawyer evaluation can be identified and described in terms of three parts, namely, an evaluator, the evaluated, and an evaluating item. An evaluator is the source of the evaluative attitude. The evaluated is the object or entity that the evaluative attitude applies to. An evaluating item is the locus of an evaluative attitude or the location where the attitude is encoded.

The term *evaluator* in this study refers to lawyers, including plaintiff's lawyers, defense lawyers, and prosecuting lawyers in some cases. It may be realized through nouns or nominal phrases as well as related pronouns that designate lawyers or the parties whom they represent, in some cases. How lawyers encode themselves in text as an evaluator, or the source of an evaluative attitude, is a process of selection. Generally, there are two options: to encode or represent their voice directly in a clause

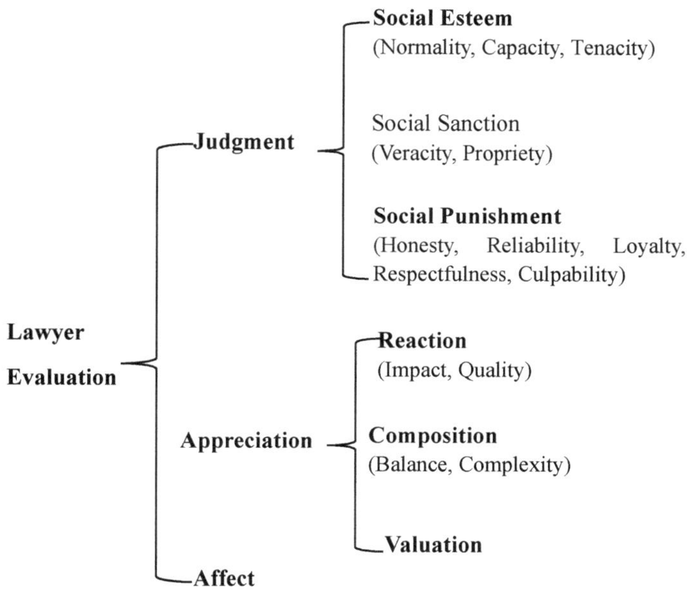

Fig. 3.2 Constituents of lawyer evaluation

or to conceal their voice and represent it indirectly. In the latter case, the evaluator may be retrievable in context. The term *evaluated* refers to objects or entities to which an evaluative attitude applies. It may be realized in nouns or nominal phrases and identified locally at the clause level or globally as part of a larger topic of lawyer evaluation.

Structurally, an evaluating item is the rudimentary element used to identify lawyer evaluation. As the locus of an evaluative attitude, it may have two different realizations, congruent and incongruent expressions (see Eggins and Slade 1997). In congruent expressions, a variety of lexical choices are typically employed as carriers of lawyers' attitudes. These choices include descriptive epithets, evaluative-laden adjectives, adverbs, and their derivatives. Verbs and nouns that convey comparative meanings in contrast to other words that precede or follow them can also carry evaluative meanings. In incongruent expressions, various structures in the language system, other than lexis, may become chief carriers of attitudes. At the grammatical level, metaphor, parallelism, lexical cohesion, and other rhetorical forms may be employed to convey evaluative meanings. At the phonological level, prosodic features, for instance, the unconventional use of stress, can also be attitudinally meaningful (Martin 2004a, b). At the textual level, the overarching generic structure, which is also referred to under the so-called "style", such as an argumentative essay or a narrative, also carries implications of evaluative meanings (see Hood 2004; Page 2003; White 1998).

In summary, lawyer evaluation can be expressed directly through lexis or indirectly through other means, such as grammar and style. It can be expressed in terms of polarity as either positive, negative, or neutral.

3.2.3 Legal Contexts as Determinants

The contextual features and their constraints on lawyer evaluation will be examined in two steps. As a first step, the context of situation in the Chinese court is semiotically construed, and its constraints on interpersonal relationships between lawyers will be discussed accordingly. In the second step, the context of legal culture in China will be introduced to investigate how lawyers orient their speech to the relationship.

3.2.3.1 The Context of Situation in the Courtroom

In the functional perspective, *situation*, which is a kind of scenario that involves background knowledge of people, actions, and events, shapes the production of meanings within this scenario. The *context of situation* is a term used to semiotically describe the relevant features in a scenario where language plays a part. It may encompass a wide range of factors, from very concrete and immediate aspects, such as the physical environment of a conversation, to more abstract or distant factors, such as the topics being discussed and the roles of the participants (Halliday 1978: 28–29). All the factors in it can be described by means of the three variables: Field, Tenor, and Mode.

The contextual features of the courtroom interaction in China are described as follows. Generally, what is going on in the court is a highly ritualized event or speech activity on the legality of a disputed act or behavior (Maley 1994). The event of the trial consists of two activities in the two orders of Field. In the second order, the disputed act or behavior is a narrative, verbally constructed based on verbal or written evidence, between the two or more parties involved in a given case. In the first order, the trial debate/discussion virtually comprises verbal exchanges of legal opinions between lawyers on both sides and the tribunal. It is conducted in a legal tone, with a mixture of jargon and bulk of ordinary language, and it typically follows a prescribed sequence of talk (Arena 1982; Mellinkoff 1963).

In light of the two orders of Tenor, the first order is related to the social status of participants, which is defined independently of language, despite being expressed through language as a form of behavior that projects their role. The second order pertains to the discourse roles of a participant, which are defined by and constructed by language (Halliday 1978: 144). In some social settings, there may be a systemic consistency between social status and discourse roles. For example, in the classroom, teachers typically assume a dominant role in both social status and discourse roles in front of students (see Sinclair and Coulthard 1975). Generally, however, there is no fixed correlation in roles between the first-order and second-order Tenor. The headmaster of a school may emerge as an information-seeker in a grocery store, to give a very simple case.

The relationship between opposing lawyers in China is competitive and confrontational in both orders of Tenor, similar to that in adversary trials of common law countries. In the current legal system, the plaintiff's lawyer and defense lawyer, who represent conflicting interests, are placed on equal footing in every aspect of the trial proceedings. With the judge standing as an arbitrator above them, their mutual relationship in terms of social status is combative, as metaphorically demonstrated in the isosceles triangle (see Fig. 2.1). Meanwhile, their discourse roles in trial communication are competitive with each other. In the proceedings of the trial system of China, the judge assumes a passive role, primarily listening and presiding over the sequential organization of the trial, while lawyers from opposing sides are given the floor to present arguments and engage in debate with each other. In other words, they are either arguers or counter-arguers, while the judge serves as an arbitrator, rule-checker as well as audience (Shen 2002: 81–91; Zhao 2005). From the above semiotic construal of the contextual features of the courtroom interaction, particularly the role relationship, it is clear that antagonism or confrontation are defining characteristics of the interpersonal dynamic between opposing lawyers (see Maley 1994).

Due to the antagonist nature of their roles, lawyers may orient their speech differently. They may choose to adopt a style that emphasizes power and control or a style that emphasizes solidarity (Gee 1996: 91). Both options of choices regarding how speakers inter-personally orient to conflict or confrontation are documented in social actions aimed at resolving differences or conflict. On the issue of differences and dialogism, Fairclough (2003: 41) highlights that "social event and interaction vary in the nature of their orientation to difference, as do texts as elements of social events" (see also Anderson et al. 2004). Five scenarios are provided below to illustrate these orientations:

(a) an openness to, acceptance of, and recognition of difference; an explanation of difference, as in "dialogue" in the richest sense of the terms;
(b) an accentuation of difference, conflict, polemic, a struggle over meaning, norms, power;
(c) an attempt to resolve or overcome differences;
(d) a bracketing of difference, a focus on commonality, solidarity;
(e) consensus, normalization, and acceptance of differences of power which brackets or suppresses differences of meaning and norms (Fairclough 2003: 41–42).

The discursive construction of confrontation along the dimension of power and control fits in social actions described in scenarios (b) and (e), while that along the dimension of solidarity resembles social actions in scenarios (a), (c), and (d). Similarly, the two options in discourse converge with de Beaugrande's (1997) elucidation of "discourse of power" and "discourse of solidarity", respectively. The former is explained as a speech that is meant "to promote authority … and pursue the goal of some participants at the expense of others", while the latter is "to promote negotiation and cooperation among participants and their goals" (de Beaugrande 1997: 2). The latter is thus known as a constructive resolution to differences of opinions or conflict (Stein et al. 1997: 235).

Can these two distinct orientations available to lawyers be understood and explained as two potential choices to speakers within the broad context of Tenor in SFL and the specific context of the courtroom? Certainly! Much fixed and stable as the relationship between participants is in terms of role relationships, it is nothing but a static description. Since speakers may construct their discourse roles dynamically in the process of conversation, they could flexibly manage their "ongoing interpersonal relationship" with their addressees as they perceive it necessary (Wang 2001; Li 2002; Martin 1992; Martin and Rose 2003; Thomas 1995). This would allow for the two options to emerge naturally. Now, the question is transformed into an examination of whether dynamic changes in discourse roles can be justified in the first place.

Two reasons may be provided to explain dynamic changes in discourse roles during the trial talk. First of all, participants are able to enact their roles in the social relationship through language as text unfolds, which reflects the dialectic relationship between language and society according to Halliday (1978: 14). Secondly, in addition to the competitive role relationship semiotically outlined above, the concept of "individual tenor" proposed by Miller (2002), which contrasts with the "institutional tenor" (Maley 1994), may be taken as a rescue. As the terms suggest, in contrast to the latter concept, which relates to participants' institutional identity in the court, the individual tenor (the former) may encompass personal relationships between lawyers or those between lawyers and judges in private, as well as similarities and differences between the legal professionals in terms of how they perceive and understand law and justice (Miller 2002; see also Zhang 2001). Judges' conception of law is a significant factor in legal practices, as studies by Philips (1998) and O'Barr and Conley (1990) demonstrate that a judge's preference for either procedure or substance in legal matters can significantly impact the outcome of a trial in countries with the case law system. Similarly, in China, personal beliefs or preferences of legal professionals are acknowledged as a very crucial aspect of trial practice (see Bi 2003), particularly in the current epic of legal reform where diversified or conflicting notions inevitably coexist (Gao et al. 2000). Moreover, ideological stances on the part of lawyers add to flexibility in the construction of interpersonal relations. Lastly, the choice of speech styles, persuasive or competitive, rational or coercive, are also a significant factor that affects the progression of trial communication. Given all these factors related to the construction of discourse roles in the courtroom, it is reasonable to maintain that two options of choices may be available to lawyers when they handle confrontation in court.

In summary, the context of the courtroom specifies confrontation as a striking characteristic of the interpersonal relationship between disputing lawyers, and the relationship can be constructed in two different styles, either the one that emphasizes power or the other one that emphasizes solidarity.

In light of Halliday's (1978) point of view, the context of situation determines, in a rough way, the choice of functions in text, and this determination is mediated through an intermediate factor—the register, which is in turn controlled by the coding orientations in social structure. To further locate how lawyer evaluation is discursively oriented to confrontation in the court, we would move on to explore the context of legal culture.

3.2.3.2 The Context of Legal Culture in China

As a broader environment of language, the term *culture* is used to refer to both ideological culture and material culture, which serve as the source of speech situations and situation types (Halliday 1978: 68). It may include many factors such as ideology (see Martin 1992: 495–496), social organizations (see Simon-Vandenbergen 2004) and social structure in the Bernstein's sense (see Halliday 1978: 67–68). Ideology, which is defined as a "cultural, cognitive and emotive subsystem of beliefs and attitudes that set priority among ideas, significances and so on" (de Beaugrande 1997: 532), is the focal point in this subsection. In close connection to lawyer speech are legal ideologies regarding the role relationships between participants in legal communication.

Currently, the predominant principles in the Chinese trial system are fairness and impartiality, which stress equal participation of all parties involved in a legal case and the fair judgment of the case based on facts and evidence. The Habermasian discourse theory of law, which adopts a dialogic approach to procedural justice, is highly relevant to this study due to its compatibility with legal practices, reform efforts, and the social and cultural conditions in China (see Sect. 2.5.2 for details).

In an intersubjective view of the law, Habermas argues for the participation of citizenship in the whole process of law-making and law enforcement. Law is legitimate to the extent that it reflects the collective understanding of societal goals and norms that are arrived at through communicative action among the people. Through communication, people could make their voices heard and understood in the field of law, thus becoming both rational authors of the law and addressees of it (Phillips 2003). It is fair to say that Habermas's theory of law has portrayed a legal system as a web of connections among individuals who recognize each other's rights and interests (Cooke 1998: 4).

Similarly, disputes in law should be solved intersubjectively through communicative action (Habermas 1996). When conflicting ideas arise, the validity of each claim must be tested through communication among the people. This requires that each claim be supported by justification and reasons so that it can be proven to be in line with the shared understanding. In other words, when a speaker makes and presents a claim, they have to provide justifications that are acceptable within the lifeworld so as to enable other participants to test and decide whether the claim is valid. The process of communication can thus confer binding force on claims that affect others, promoting people's perceptions of fairness in the legal system and their trust in the law. Obviously, it is the interplay between criticism and reasoned justifications that makes it possible for rationality in communicative action. All in all, both the making and application of laws are justified through open communication organized between the people.

Habermas' proposal of intersubjectively settling legal disputes is valid in the courtroom interaction between disputing lawyers and judges (Habermas 1996: 194–237). From the point of view of judges, a ruling to be made has to be, first of all, consistent with the body of the law; at the same time, it has to be rationally accepted by the disputing parties. It means that in order to ensure an impartial trial, a judge has to consider the legal arguments of both parties at the outset, assess the validity of each argument based on reasons in the legal sense, and then make judicial decisions accordingly. Such a process of decision-making reflects the communicative nature of the legal community and helps to ensure that legal decisions are fair and reflective of the diverse perspectives of people in the communication. From the perspective of lawyers, to gain the court's support and approval for the validity of their legal arguments, they have to adhere to norm-governing communicative principles that are intersubjectively shared by all parties. These include the procedures of hearing, rules on debating, and standards for assessing the legality of legal claims.

In light of the Habermasian conceptions of law and legal communication, for rational communication to be successful, lawyers are assumed to meet some requirements in their roles, which are proposed under the four "idealizing presuppositions" (Habermas 1996: 230). First of all, participants share the aim of checking the validity of disputed claims and reaching an agreement. Secondly, they give equal concern and respect to the interests and opinions of all parties who are concerned or affected, with no competent parties excluded from the discussion and no relevant argument deliberately suppressed in any way. Thirdly, they have to justify any legal claims under dispute and discussion with reasons so as to prove that the claims are valid and possess the attributes of truth, sincerity, and rightness. Fourthly, they use linguistic expressions in the same way and make their communication comprehensible to each other.

Given that these idealizing principles serve as normative regulations for both the process and outcomes of legal argumentation (Cooke 1998), this study will consider these four principles as guidelines within the cultural context and explore their impact on lawyer evaluation in the court. The core of these principles lies in mutual recognition and cooperation, emphasizing solidarity. Consequently, lawyer evaluation constructed within these ideological constraints can be seen as a discourse of solidarity, akin to de Beaugrande's concept (1997). Considering that rationality is an inherent feature in Habermas' theory of law, the discourse style of lawyer evaluation can be tentatively described as "rational discourse".[1]

[1] The term "rational debating" has been employed to designate legal communication in other works, such as Zhang's (2002) statement that law is a rational dialogue.

3.2.4 The Interactive Construction of Lawyer Evaluation

As discussed in the preceding subsection, within the contextual constraints of the legal culture in the courtroom, lawyers tend to adopt a discourse characterized by solidarity and rationality when engaging with opposing parties. In light of this observation, it becomes crucial to explore the specific stances that lawyers assume during trial proceedings. Furthermore, it is essential to understand how they navigate the seemingly contradictory objectives of engaging in legal communication based on mutual recognition while simultaneously working toward resolving the legal dispute. These questions form the basis of our upcoming discussion. In order to address them, we will examine both the impact of idealizing presuppositions on lawyers and the discourse resources available to lawyers within the realm of language.

The Habermasian idealizing presuppositions regarding the roles of speakers in communication provide guidelines for understanding how lawyer evaluation is presented in text. In the context of the court, lawyers are all competent legal professionals, so the presupposition related to language competence holds no particular implication here. Three requirements become significant. Firstly, participants are expected to approach the proceedings with a mindset of equality and freedom, aiming to reach an agreement rather than fostering hostility or antagonism. Secondly, they are expected to actively and sincerely engage in the trial dialogue, participating to the necessary extent dictated by the procedures. Thirdly, participants are required to support their arguments and counter-arguments with reasons and evidence within the regulated framework. Following the Hallidayan view that context determines the language use, when procedural justice is socially recognized as a guiding principle in a trial, these three points may serve as contextual constraints that shape the patterning of lawyer evaluation.

It is argued that lawyer evaluation constructed in a rational style encompasses three critical features in discourse: an equal relationship in roles, a multi-voiced discourse environment, and distinct discursive communities. The first feature, an equal relationship in roles, signifies that disputing lawyers are regarded as equals in their discourse roles. It implies that both parties are accorded equal respect and provided with equal opportunities to present their arguments. The second feature, a multi-voiced environment, pertains to the existence of diverse voices in the discourse when participants engage on an equal footing in trial communication. It enables the expression and consideration of different perspectives and viewpoints. The final feature, distinct discourse communities, suggests that as the discourse unfolds, arguments from each side are treated differently. Some arguments are supported and accepted, while others are rejected and marginalized based on reasons and facts. As a result, two distinct discursive communities with differing perspectives on the discussed issue emerge. These features collectively contribute to ensuring that lawyer evaluation is conducted reasonably and rationally. However, the discourse theory of law does not provide specific details regarding how these features interrelate in the practice of legal dispute resolution or disposition (Ma 2002). While it is beyond the scope of this study to offer sociological hypotheses, it is worthwhile to investigate how these features manifest in the language used within the courtroom, as social practices are constituted and realized through discourse (Fairclough 2003; Halliday 1978).

Discursively, lawyers could manage the expressions of evaluative attitudes, including Affect, Judgment, and Appreciation, in the course of their interactions with others during the trial. When evaluating a specific topic, they could express their opinions directly or indirectly, positively or negatively, in a softened or intensified way. They may also put their evaluations into interactions with other voices in various ways, such as comparing and competing with them directly or simply evading them.

Considering that disputing lawyers are inherently confrontational to each other in terms of the institutional Tenor (the first-order Tenor), as they both occupy roles subordinate to judges in the hierarchical power structure, it becomes essential to explore how they can establish a discursive environment that enhances the argumentation process. Meeting the normative requirement of a free and equal role relationship, lawyers can demonstrate positive attitudes toward the common ground shared by all participants and stress their professional skills or the shared lifeworld within the courtroom (see Gaines 2002). By doing so, they can contribute to creating an environment conducive to constructive argumentation.

Meanwhile, to adhere to the principle that participants shall give mutual respect and equal concern to all those affected and ensure that all relevant parties are able to participate extensively in the trial, lawyers from both sides must actively engage in verbal communication throughout the proceedings. They must acknowledge, or at the very least be aware of, the existence of alternative voices from others when presenting their views. Only by doing this can they foster a mutual understanding and decide which legal position warrants rational agreement. Therefore, the speaking lawyers find themselves immersed in a heteroglossic environment where diverse opinions coexist. The construction of such a multi-voiced environment involves using strategies like dialogical engagement through projection or conjunctive adjuncts (as outlined in Martin and Rose 2003) and aligning strategies such as the discourse marker *we think/believe* in the argumentation process.

However, since the main task of a trial is to solve the legality of a given social behavior, lawyer evaluation extends beyond constructing an equal role relationship and a multi-voiced environment. To fulfill their legal task, lawyers must construct their legal positions, argue against the opposite ones, and respond to any potential doubts that may arise from the audience. Normatively, they are required to present their arguments or counter-arguments in the regulated contest and support their views with justifications. Discursively, in the conflictual environment, lawyers strive to associate with the judges, the audience, and even their contestant(s) in the opposite party. They aim to construct a *we*-discourse shared with the judge and the audience (and sometimes the opposing side). At the same time, it is desirable for them to alienate the opposing side from the judge and the audience by devaluing their viewpoints. Thus, a *they*-discourse or *other*-discourse is constructed. Throughout the process of arguing and counter-arguing, the addressees are divided into two distinct groups: an ingroup of *us* versus an outgroup of *them*. For such groups that share the

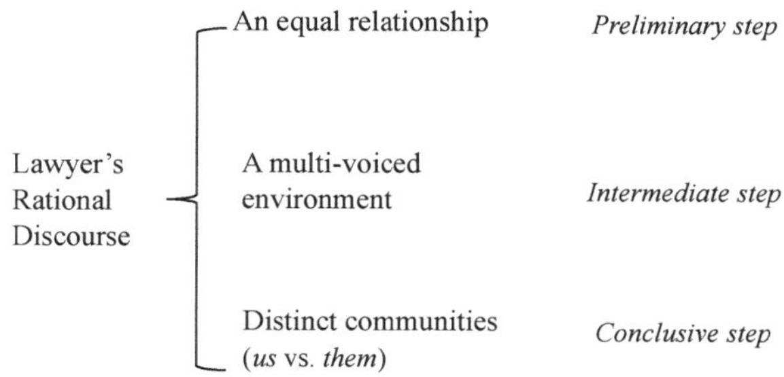

Fig. 3.3 The three features in the rational discourse of lawyer evaluation

same background knowledge and worldviews, many similar concepts are available in the literature, such as "groups or sub-cultures" (Holliday 1999), "network of interacting individuals" (Gumperz and Levinson 1996), "community of practice" (Eckert and McConnell-Ginet 1992), "discourse community" (Swale 1990) and "discursive community" (Pan et al. 1999), or *teams*, *affiliations*, *associations*, and *alliances* (Kangasharju 1996: 293–295; see also Gaines 2002; Kuo 2002). Since the teams, groups, or communities that hold similar opinions regarding various issues of a case are formed or constructed through lawyer evaluation in the sequential organization of the trial talk, the term "discursive community" is preferred here over other concepts accordingly. The two oppositional discursive communities, *us* versus *them*, are constructed and (re)established through the polarization of lawyer evaluation in three different ways: positive, negative, or graded evaluations (Duszak 2002: 5).

In summary, under the contextual constraints of the legal culture, namely the Habermasian interpretations of the role relationship between participants in legal communication, three principles shape how lawyer evaluation is organized and presented discursively in court. Generally, lawyer evaluation derived from the Habermasian principles turns out to be a rational discourse. It is demonstrated in three aspects: an equal interpersonal relationship, a multi-voiced environment, and distinct discursive communities (*us* vs. *them*) (see Fig. 3.3). These three features work together to help lawyers fulfill the communicative tasks in the trial.

By presenting their evaluations in different ways during the trial, lawyers manage to show their positions rationally, (dis-)aligning the audiences rhetorically and exerting influence on the social relationship as rational debaters. The evolving role relationship between participants can be traced and substantiated by examining the ongoing interactions and dynamics among them as the text unfolds.

3.2.5 The Functions of Lawyer Evaluation in the Trial

This subsection explores how the rational discourse of lawyer evaluation contributes to the general goal of trial communication—legal dispute resolution or criminal case disposition. Text, which is realized in the lower levels of the linguistics system, is itself the realization of higher-level semiotic structures with their modes of interpretation (Halliday 1978: 138). Accordingly, lawyers' interpersonal positioning in the court is meant to realize the social activity of legal dispute resolution or disposition.

Legal dispute resolution or disposition is a complex social activity primarily conducted verbally in the trial. According to Hymes (1972), verbal communication in the trial may serve two distinct purposes: achieving a common goal and pursuing personal goals. The common goal aims to discover an objective resolution to the case at hand, whereas personal goals involve advocating for the interests of the parties involved. The question is whether both of these goals can be achieved through rational discourse and lawyer evaluation.

The common goal and personal goals in the trial are interrelated and simultaneously realized through lawyer evaluation, discursively. Viewed from the legal perspective, the common purpose, an objective resolution of the dispute, or "the cooperative search for truth in the case", is always the most fundamental task to participants in court (Habermas 1996: 228). However, it does not mean that personal goals can be ignored or sacrificed. Habermas emphasizes that personal goals cannot be overlooked but should be integrated within the pursuit of the mutual goal shared by the participants (Habermas 1996: 228–230; see also Ma 2002; Wang 2002). In essence, the personal goals of defending the interests of the party involved must be harmonized with the search for a fair solution to the case and the pursuit of justice within the legal framework.

As a vague, dynamic, and multi-faceted concept, justice contains contesting values of what is good and evil. It thus is open to interpretation (Nussbaum 2006: 3). To begin with, law itself is a meaning-making process. By its very nature, the law, particularly its interpretation and application, is virtually a social-semiotic activity (Gibbons 1994). On the one hand, the lack of sufficiency in the coverage of the law makes interpretation necessary. Conditions described speculatively in a normative legal regulation are merely situations or possible contextualized events that may be foreseeable in the near future and thus cannot be claimed to be exhaustive of all conflicting situations in life. However, all citizens have the potential to become the potential bearers of the force of the regulation (Yong et al. 2002: 74–75). For instance, subject to the legislative text, "no murder is allowed and any person who commits a murder shall receive a penalty of …", all citizens are potential bearers of this proposition; and if a person does deliberately and directly cause a person to die, they may become the actual bearer of the regulation once proved guilty. To determine whether they are the actual bearer, one must compare the specific situations of their behavior with the conditions provided in the rule. The process of comparison entails both verbal and semiotic processing of information. Since language plays a vital role in determining how a person is going to be related to the law, legal interpretation and application remain largely a semiotic phenomenon. On the other hand, in a well-accepted post-positivist contention, as a conventional linguistic practice, law shares the impression of the "messiness" of social life (Hutchinson 1995: 799) to the extent that even legal judgments are, at best, related to "truth" on a probabilistic basis. The messiness is reflected in the dynamic and contingent nature of social (and institutional) life, as well as in the structurally indeterminate nature of language itself. In fact, applying the same criteria to all similar cases may mean injustice to specific parties concerned because no two cases are so identical in their circumstances that identical regulations could be applied to them without variation. Given these two considerations, it seems sufficient to state that *justice*, or an objective solution to disputes, may fall hostage to the indeterminacy of language and social life (Posner 1990; see also Rawls 1999). Meanwhile, there is room for lawyers to strive for the best interests of their clients. Nevertheless, discussions of any topic in pursuit of personal interest or settlement of indeterminacy must be made in accordance with law as a commonly-agreed "lifeworld", which enacts its dual function: to enable lawyers to work for their personal goal and to provide them with the "manual" to search for justice at the same time. As a result, law and its application being such complicated matters, justice would be a vague standard with no fixed meaning and become a negotiable issue in court. Consequently, both goals, the strive for personal goals and the search for the objective resolution to the said case, or the search for justice, are to be handled interpersonally.

The rational discourse of lawyer evaluation becomes a linguistic and discursive activity of negotiation in the trial. By presenting their evaluations interpersonally, lawyers align and alienate the audiences to various degrees, which manifests their endeavors to negotiate meanings regarding the main topics/issues of the trial in the court. In other words, the interpersonal positioning of lawyers contributes to and realizes the social practice of dispute resolution or disposition.

The process of negotiation is unfolded in three inter-woven aspects of the judicial process in the court: constructing the case facts through testimonies, determining the legal nature of the case, and making a legal decision to the case (Yong et al. 2002). Through interactive expressions of evaluative attitudes, lawyers negotiate justice in various ways. They may choose to intensify or weaken certain aspects of the facts when presenting them based on testimonies or evidence. When it comes to the legal nature of the case, they may present evaluations on how distinct the said case is from the prototypical conditions associated with an alleged charge or complaint. Finally, when making a legal decision, they may negotiate the balance between the typical conditions required for the alleged charge/complaint and the proposed liability for their party to bear.

3.3 The Theoretical Framework: Rational Discourse

This section presents the theoretical framework for understanding lawyer evaluation in the Chinese court. Adopting the Hallidayan functional perspective, this study views lawyer evaluation as social semiotic and attaches great importance to the legal practice and ideology when analyzing lawyer speech.

In accordance with Appraisal Theory and the specific situations of the trial talk, three constituents of lawyer evaluation are classified, namely, Judgment, Appreciation, and Affect. Judgment refers to evaluations of the character of witnesses or concerned parties. Appreciation involves evaluations of various issues in the trial, and Affect pertains to evaluative descriptions of feelings related to facts, persons, or events. Judgment may be further analyzed in terms of three variables: Social Esteem, Social Sanction, and Social Punishment. Similarly, Appreciation can be further analyzed in terms of three variables: Reaction, Composition, and Valuation. It is worth noting that all variables, among which Social Punishment is proposed to be placed alongside Social Esteem and Social Punishment under Judgement, have been redefined in this study. Lawyer evaluation can be identified by examining evaluating items either in the lexical or grammatical form or in a large discourse structure (Eggins and Slade 1997; Martin and Rose 2003).

Since text is mainly determined by context (Halliday 1978, 1994), by thoroughly investigating the contextual features of the courtroom interaction and their impact exerted on lawyer evaluation, this study identifies confrontation as a primary characteristic of the interpersonal relationship between disputing lawyers, which is a claim consistent with the viewpoints regarding lawyer speech in the existing literature. To further examine how lawyers orient themselves to the confrontational relationship in text in the Chinese court, this research draws upon the insightful statements in the theory of Habermas on law and legal communication, which has been found to be compatible with the reforms in the trial system of China and the social, cultural, and political conditions of the country. Following the Habermasian interpretations of participants' role relationships in legal communication, the study proposes that lawyers may opt to speak and contest on the dimension of solidarity (Brown and Gilman 1960; Gee 1996) and that they may position themselves as provided in the three normative requirements regarding role relationships in a rational discussion: to mutually recognize each other, to give equal concern to claims of all participants, and to seek a resolution to disputes through justification based on reasons (Habermas 1996; see also Cooke 1998).

Under the influence of the three normative requirements concerning speech roles, lawyers may display three features when they present their evaluations in court: equal relationships in roles, multi-voiced speech environments, and distinct communities of *us* versus *them* (see Gaines 2002; Kangasharju 1996, 2002; Kuo 2002). The first feature is usually employed as the preliminary step of the trial talk, the second the intermediate step, and the third the conclusive step. Regardless of the order in which they appear, these three features or aspects may be used coordinately or simultaneously in a module to help lawyers fulfill the task of dispute resolution or disposition in court.

The three features are all realized through lawyer evaluation in the semantic system of language. To fulfill the first feature, an equal role relationship, lawyers can highlight the common ground shared between opposing parties and emphasize the shared lifeworld in the judiciary discipline (Gaines 2002). To construct the second one, a multi-voiced speech environment, lawyers may dialogically engage in the trial talk through the use of projection or conjunctive adjuncts (Martin and Rose 2003) and the employment of aligning strategies conveyed by the interpersonal metaphor (or discourse marker) *we think/believe*. To realize the last one, two distinct communities, lawyers may polarize their attitudes by presenting positive, negative, or graded evaluations of the diversified issues in the trial (Gaines 2002; Kangasharju 1996, 2002).

The three features, which are developed under insightful statements of the three normative requirements concerning role relationship in the theory of Habermas and linguistically realized in discourse, are the salient features of lawyer speech constructed on the dimension of solidarity in trial interaction. Because the Habermasian law is characterized by rationality on the one hand and is consistent with the political ideal and cultural notion of achieving "harmony" in society through dialogue and discussions, the discourse of lawyer evaluation that encompasses these features is referred to as the "rational discourse of lawyer evaluation" or "lawyers' rational discourse" (Zhang et al. 2015; Zhang 2011).

Finally, to explore how the discourse of lawyer evaluation is used to fulfill the task of trial communication as a social and legal activity, this study discusses lawyer evaluation in relation to justice and legal dispute resolution or disposition functionally. As both the concept of justice and the law itself have the attribute of indeterminacy, the search for justice or fair judgment in a legal dispute is viewed as a process of negotiating meanings. In this process, lawyers behave as rational debaters and manage the meaning-making process by interpersonally positioning themselves in flexible ways in front of others.

In a word, the systemic and detailed analysis of the legal context in China and the language of lawyers from the Hallidayan social semiotic perspective has enabled us to theorize the rational discourse of lawyer evaluation, which is diagrammatically demonstrated in Fig. 3.4.

In Fig. 3.4, the italicized phrase typed in the vertical direction and placed on the right side, *SOCIAL SEMIOTIC PERSPECTIVE*, indicates the general perspective this study adopts. The word CONTEXT typed in the vertical direction and placed on the left side, contains the two levels, the context of situation (or situational context) and context of culture (or the legal culture) in the courtroom, which are placed on the two sides of the dovetail, respectively. As both levels of context serve as the contextual backgrounds for the positioning of lawyer speech in the text of the trial talk, the situational context (in the lower side) yields "contest" or confrontation as the primary feature in roles between disputing lawyers; the context of culture (situated in the upside of the dovetail), mediates the contextual determination and makes solidarity (rationality in the Habermasian sense) to be the particular style in which lawyers orient their speech to contest and confrontation. The effect of the contextual determination on lawyer evaluation is demonstrated by the dovetail pointing to the right.

Placed in the middle part of the figure are the four blocks indicating texts in the trial talk. Arranged from the bottom to the top, they are loosely parallel to the strata of the language system and the social structure in the Hallidayan sense. At the bottom, lawyer evaluation (L.E.) encompasses three types/constituents in text, and L.E. is then constructed as RATIONAL DISCOURSE (in the third block from the bottom), capitalized for emphasis. Functionally, the speech of RATIONAL DISCOURSE

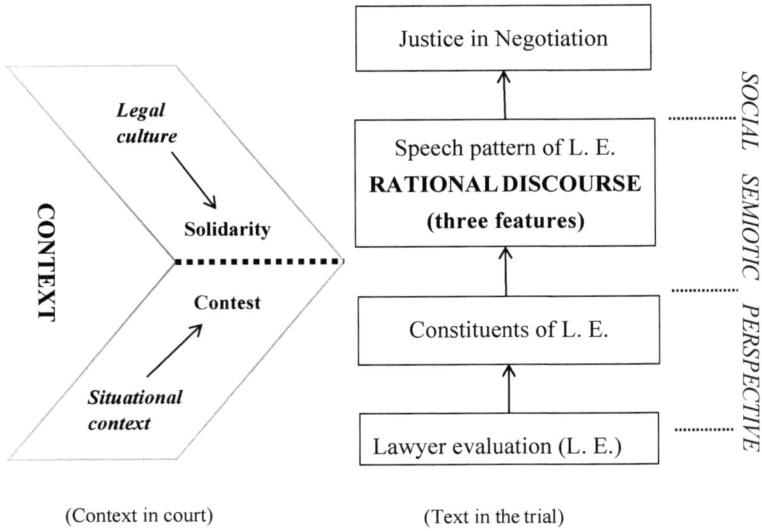

Fig. 3.4 A synthetic view of the rational discourse of lawyer evaluation

serves to realize the goals of the trial communication, to negotiate Justice (in the block on the top). The upward arrows between these blocks reveal the logical connections of realization between items in the blocks.

The RATIONAL DISCOURSE of lawyer evaluation is expanded in Fig. 3.5. In Fig. 3.5, the enclosing brackets indicate a relationship of inclusion between the items inside and those outside the brackets. For instance, the "RATIONAL DISCOURSE of L.E." includes three features: an equal role relationship, a multi-voiced environment, and distinct communities of *us* versus *them*. In turn, the first feature, "an equal role relationship", is realized by two strategies: evaluating the common ground and emphasizing the shared lifeworld.

The system of the rational discourse is to be illustrated with a nuanced analysis of data in the chapters to follow. Take the strategy "evaluating the common ground" as an example. By showing appropriate evaluations of a particular topic in the same way the opposing party may view it, lawyers could show that they share common ground with their opponents and can thus construct the impression that they are equal in roles and stances in the court. For instance, in a trial on bribery, if the defense lawyer utters the sentence unequivocally, "We agree that anti-corruption is of crucial importance to the country", they present a positive Appreciation toward "anti-corruption", the evaluated topic, which happens to be the social and political goal of the trial. This positive attitude is identified in the lexical phrase of the projected clause, "crucial significance". Another layer of evaluation, identified in the speech act verb "agree" of the projecting clause, is the defense lawyer's positive Appreciation in terms of Reaction toward the proposition on "anti-corruption". Textually, the speech act verb "agree" is used as a response to the proposition on anti-corruption, which is

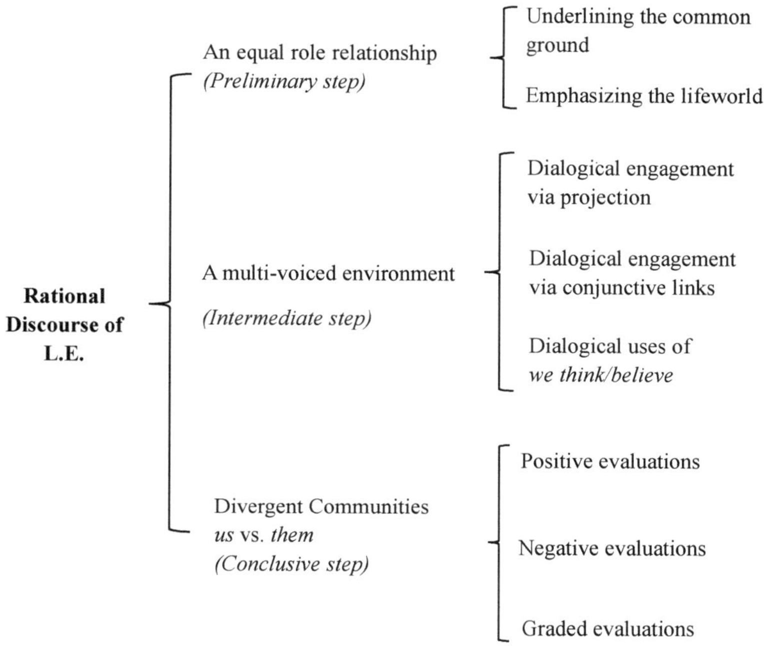

Fig. 3.5 The rational discourse of L.E.: features and discursive strategies

assumed to be made by the prosecution who represents the state interest in this case. When demonstrating that their view converges with that of the prosecuting party on that topic, the defense lawyer would discursively indicate that they are equal to the prosecution and thus create a common ground with them. It helps to undermine the tension between the opposing parties. Of course, more often than not, evaluations in the two orders may conflate with each other.

Resources and strategies that are used to realize the Rational Discourse are listed in Table 3.1.

3.4 Summary

This chapter has presented a theoretical framework for the speech pattern of lawyer evaluation in the Chinese courtroom. Firstly, it classifies the constituents of lawyer evaluation and explores the two levels of context in the Chinese courtroom and their contextual constraints on language use from the functional perspective. Based on the analysis, the pattern of lawyer evaluation is proposed as the Rational Discourse

Table 3.1 Resources and strategies employed in rational discourse

Main features	Realizations		
	Resources involved	Typical discursive strategies	Examples (lexico-grammar)
Equal role relationship	Attitude, modality	Underlining the common ground, highlighting judicial knowledge	Consensus, shared understanding
Multi-voiced environment	Attitude, engagement	Projection, conjunctive adjuncts, and so on	Testify, state, mention, … not … but
Distinct communities	Attitude, graduation, modality	Positive/negative/graded evaluations	Hold no objection, basically true, inadequately supported

of lawyer evaluation, which consists of three features that are further realized in the language system. Finally, the discourse of lawyers is interpreted as a process of negotiating justice in the activity of legal dispute resolution or disposition.

With the theoretical framework in place, this study will move on to conduct detailed data analysis in the four chapters to follow so as to carefully examine how lawyer evaluation works in text and context.

References

Anderson, R., L.A. Baxter, and K.N. Cissna. 2004. *Dialogue: Theorizing difference in communication studies*. London: Sage. https://doi.org/10.4135/9781483328683.

Arena, L.A. 1982. The language of corporate attorneys. In *Linguistics and the profession*, ed. R.J. Di Pietro, 143–157. Norwood, NJ: ABLEX.

Atkinson, R.C., and P. Drew. 1990. *Order in court*. Hampshire and London: Macmillan Academic and Professional Ltd.

Bi, Yu-qian. 2003. 自由心证主义与法定证据主义在中国之实行 [The practice of discretionary evaluation of evidence and the system of statutory evidence in China]. 律师文摘 [*Lawyers' Digest*] (1): 21–24.

Brown, R., and A. Gilman. 1960. The pronouns of power and solidarity. In *Style in language*, ed. T. Sebeok, 253–276. Cambridge, MA: MIT Press.

Carbonnier, J. 1994. Legal relationships. In *Introduction to civil law*, vol. 1, ed. Jean Carbonnier and Jean-Louis Halpérin, 79–109. Translated by John H. Merryman. London and New York: Routledge.

Chai, Rong. 2009. 论中西 "容隐制度" 与当下中国相关法律的完善 [The rule of mutual non-disclosure between relatives in China and the West and its implication for the reconstruction of relevant laws in China]. 江汉论坛 [*Jianghan Forum*] (9): 112–118.

Cheng, Yu-ming. 1989. 英语语体学 [*English stylistics*], 66–104. Shanghai: Shanghai Foreign Languages Education Press.

Cooke, M. 1998. Introduction. In *On the pragmatics of communication*, ed. M. Cooke, 1–20. Cambridge: MIT Press.

de Beaugrande, R. 1997. *New foundations for a science of text and discourse : Cognition , communication and the freedom of access to knowledge and society*. Norwood: ABLEX.

Duszak, A. 2002. Us and others: An introduction. In *Us and others : Social identities across languages , discourses and cultures*, ed. A. Duszak, 1–28. Amsterdam/Philadelphia: John Benjamins.

Eckert, P., and S. McConnell-Ginet. 1992. Think practically and look locally: Language and gender as community-based practice. *Annual Review of Anthropology* 21: 461–490. https://doi.org/10.1146/annurev.an.21.100192.002333.

Eggins, S., and D. Slade. 1997. *Analyzing casual conversation*. London & Washington: CASSWLL.

Fairclough, N. 2003. *Analyzing discourse*. London: Routledge.

Fan, Zhong-xin. 1997. 亲亲相为隐: 中外法律的共同传统—兼论其根源及其与法治的关系 [Mutual non-disclosure and convergence between Chinese law and foreign laws: Tradition, origin and relationship with the rule of law]. 比较法研究 [*Research on Comparative Law*] (2): 113–134.

Gaines, P. 2002. Negotiating power at the bench. *Forensic Linguistics: The International Journal of Speech, Language and Law* 9 (2): 213–234. https://doi.org/10.1558/sll.2002.9.2.213.

Gao, Qi-cai, Chen-guang Wang, and Ze-zhou Feng. 2000. 程序, 法官与审判公正 [Procedure, judges and fair trial]. 法学 [*Journal of Law*] (8): 6–13.

Gee, J.P. 1996. *Social linguistics and literacy: Ideology in discourse*, 2nd ed. London: Taylor & Francis.

Gibbons, J. 1994. *Language and the law*. London & New York: Longman.

Gumperz, J.J., and S. Levinson. 1996. Introduction: Linguistic relativity re-examined. In *Rethinking linguistic relativity*, ed. J. Gumperz and S. Levinson, 1–20. Cambridge: Cambridge University Press.

Habermas, J. 1996. *Between facts and norms*. Translated by William Rehg. Cambridge, MA: MIT.

Hale, S., and J. Gibbons. 1999. Varying realities: Patterned changes in the interpreter's representation of courtroom and external realities. *Applied Linguistics* 20 (2): 203–220. https://doi.org/10.1093/applin/20.2.203.

Halliday, M.A.K. 1978. *Language as social semiotic*. London: Edward Arnold.

Halliday, M.A.K. 1985. Text, context, and learning. In *Language, context and text*, ed. M.A.K. Halliday and R. Hasan, 44–51. Oxford: Oxford University Press.

Halliday, M.A.K. 1994. *Introduction to functional grammar*. London: Edward Arnold.

Holliday, A. 1999. Small culture. *Applied Linguistics* 20 (2): 237–264. https://doi.org/10.1093/applin/20.2.237.

Hood, S. 2004. Managing attitude in undergraduate academic writing: A focus on the introductions to research reports. In *Analyzing academic writing*, ed. L. Ravelli and R. Ellis, 24–44. London & New York: Continuum.

Hunston, S. 2000. Evaluation and the planes of discourse: Status and value in persuasive texts. In *Evaluation in text*, ed. S. Hunston and G. Thompson, 176–207. Oxford: Oxford University Press.

Hutchinson, A.C. 1995. A post-modern's hart: Taking rules skeptically. *The Modern Law Review* 58 (6): 788–810. https://doi.org/10.1111/j.1468-2230.1995.tb02053.x.

Hymes, D. 1972. Models of the interaction of language and social life. In *Directions in sociolinguistics*, ed. J. Gumperz and D. Hymes, 35–71. New York: Holt, Rinehart, and Winston.

Kangasharju, H. 1996. Aligning as a team in multiparty conversation. *Journal of Pragmatics* 26: 291–319. https://doi.org/10.1016/0378-2166(95)00051-8.

Kangasharju, H. 2002. Aligning in disagreement: Forming oppositional alliances in committee meetings. *Journal of Pragmatics* 34: 1447–1471. https://doi.org/10.1016/S0378-2166(02)00073-5.

Kuo, Sai-hua. 2002. From solidarity to antagonism: The uses of the second-person singular pronoun in Chinese political discourse. *Text & Talk* 22 (1): 29–55. https://doi.org/10.1515/text.2002.004.

Li, Zhan-zi. 2002. 话语的人际意义研究 [*Interpersonal meanings of discourse*]. Shanghai: Shanghai Foreign Languages Education Press.

Ma, Chang-shan. 2002. 哈贝马斯的交往理性法律观及其启示 [Habermas' discourse theory of law and its implication]. 法学研究 [*Journal of Legal Studies*] (4): 101–106. https://doi.org/10.13858/j.cnki.cn32-1312/c.2002.04.017.
Maley, Y. 1994. The language of the law. In *Language and the law*, ed. J. Gibbons, 11–50. London: Longman.
Martin, J. 1992. *English text : System and structure*. Philadelphia/Amsterdam: John Benjamin.
Martin, J. 1997. Analyzing genre: Functional parameters. In *Genres and institutions: Social processes in the workplace and school*, ed. F. Christie and J.R. Martin, 3–39. London: CASSELL.
Martin, J. 2000. Beyond exchange: Appraisal in English. In *Evaluation in text*, ed. S. Hunston and G. Thompson, 142–175. Oxford: Oxford University Press.
Martin, J. 2004a. Sense and sensibility: Texturing evaluation. In *New perspectives on education and discourse*, ed. J.A. Foley, 65–96. London and New York: Continuum.
Martin, J. 2004b. Mourning: How we get aligned. *Discourse & Society* 15 (2–3): 321–343. https://doi.org/10.1177/0957926504041022.
Martin, J., and D. Rose. 2003. *Working with discourse*. London, New York: Continuum.
Mellinkoff, D. 1963. *Language of the law*. Boston, MA: Little Brown.
Miller, D. 2002. Multiple judicial opinions as specialized sites of engagement: Conflicting paradigms of valuation and legitimation in Bush v. Gore 2000. In *Conflict and negotiation in specialized texts*, ed. M. Gotti, D. Heller, et al., 119–141. Bern: Peter Lang.
Miller, D. 2004. "To meet our common challenge": ENGAGEMENT strategies of alignment and alienation in current US international discourse. *Textus* XVIII (1): 39–62.
Nussbaum, M. 2006. *Frontiers of justice: Disability, nationality and species membership*. (Belknap Press of) Harvard University Press.
O'Barr, W., and J. Conley. 1990. Litigant satisfaction versus legal adequacy in small claims narratives. In *Language in the judicial process*, ed. J.N. Levi and A.G. Walker, 97–132. New York and London: Plenum Press.
Page, R.E. 2003. An analysis of appraisal in childbirth narratives. *Text & Talk* 23 (2): 211–237. https://doi.org/10.1515/text.2003.009.
Pan, Zhong-dang, Chin-chuan Lee, J. Man Chan, et al. 1999. One event, three stories: Media narrative from cultural China of the handover of Hong Kong. *International Communication Gazette* 61 (2): 99–112. https://doi.org/10.1177/0016549299061002001.
Philips, S.U. 1998. *Ideology in the language of the judge*. New York: Oxford University Press.
Phillips, A. 2003. *Lawyer's language: How and why legal language is different*. London and New York: Routledge.
Posner, R.A. 1990. *The problems of jurisprudence*. Cambridge, MA: Harvard University Press.
Qu, Tong-zu. 1984. 中国法律与中国社会 [*Law and society in traditional China*]. Beijing: San Lian Bookstore. 三联书店.
Rawls, J. 1999. *A theory of justice*. Cambridge, MA: The Belknap Press of Harvard University Press.
Rothery, J., and M. Stenglin. 2000. Interpreting literature: The role of appraisal. In *Researching language in schools and communities*, ed. L. Unsworth, 222–244. London: Cassell.
Shen, Bing-you. 2002. 质证规则研究 [Research on rules of evidence]. 律师文摘 [*Lawyers' Digest*] (4): 78–105.
Shi, Guangquan. 2006. *The comprise of Li and law and historical changes of Chinese traditional legal culture*. Beijing: Law Press.
Simon-Vandenbergen, A. 2004. Intersubjective positioning in talk shows: A case study from British TV. *Text & Talk* 24 (3): 399–422. https://doi.org/10.1515/text.2004.016.
Sinclair, J., and M. Coulthard. 1975. *Towards an analysis of discourse: The English used by teachers and pupils*. London: Oxford University Press.
Stein, N., R. Bernas, and D. Calicchia. 1997. Conflict talk: Understanding and resolving arguments. In *Conversation: Cognitive, communicative and social perspectives*, ed. T. Givon, 233–267. Amsterdam/Philadelphia: John Benjamins Publishing.
Swale, J. 1990. *Genre analysis*. Cambridge: Cambridge University Press.

Thomas, J. 1995. *Meaning in interaction: An introduction to pragmatics*. London: Longman.
Wang, Jian-hua. 2001. 话语礼貌与语用距离 [Discursive politeness and pragmatic distance]. 外国语 [*Journal of Foreign Languages*] (5): 25–31.
Wang, Xiao-sheng. 2002. 合法化与可辩护性 [Legitimacy and defensibility]. 福建论坛 [*Fujian Tribune*] (4): 42–47.
White, P. 1998. Telling media tales: The news as rhetoric. Ph.D. thesis, Sydney University, Sydney.
Yong, Q., Cheng-guang Jin, and Rong-mao Yao. 2002. 法律适用中的逻辑 [*Logic in law application*]. Beijing: China University of Political Science and Law.
Zhang, Wei-ping. 2001. 律师与法官: 不同与相同 [Lawyers and judges: Similarities and differences]. 中国律师 [*Chinese Lawyers*] (8): 59–62.
Zhang, Qian-fan. 2002. 法律是一种理性对话 [Law as a rational dialogue]. 北大法律评论 [*Law Review of Beijing University*] 5 (1): 69–100.
Zhang, Jinfan. 2003a. 中国法制史 [*History of Chinese legal systems*]. Beijing: Higher Education Press.
Zhang, Jun. 2003b. 法与德的冲突及其法理思考 [Conflict between law and ethics and a legal interpretation]. 现代法学 [*Modern Law Science*] (4): 93–99.
Zhang, Li-ping. 2011. Arguing with otherness: Intertextual construction of the attorney stance in the Chinese courtroom. *Text & Talk* (6): 753–769. https://doi.org/10.1515/TEXT.2011.036.
Zhang, H., Liping Zhang, and Wangzhen Zhan. 2015. 和而不同: 哈贝马斯主体间性关照下的法庭理性辩论 [Harmonizing differences: The discourse of rational debates in court through the lens of the Habermasian intersubjectivity]. *School Journal of Lanzhou University* (5): 103–109.
Zhao, Li (赵利). 2004. 道德与法律关系的理性思考 [Rational reflections on morality and law]. 齐鲁学刊 [*Journal of Social Sciences in Qilu*] (4): 67–70.
Zhao, Ai-nong. 2005. 神圣与市场的统一: 我看律师的本质属性 [The unity between the sacred and the market: Views on the attributes of lawyers]. 中国律师 [*Chinese Lawyers*] (6): 55–56.
Zhu, Yong-sheng, and Shi-qing Yan. 2001. 系统功能语言学多维思考 [*Multidimensional thinkings on systemic functional linguistics*]. Shanghai: Shanghai Foreign Languages Education Press.

Chapter 4
Lawyer Evaluation in Texts: Three Constituents

Abstract This chapter analyzes the three constituents of lawyer evaluation in text: Affect, Judgement, and Appreciation. Influenced by the context of a trial, two prominent features emerge in the use of the three constituents. Firstly, compared with Affect, Judgement and Appreciation both play a more significant role in the trial talk. Secondly, the three constituents are usually realized by congruent and incongruent expressions in integration.

4.1 Introduction

This chapter is intended to analyze the three constituents of lawyer evaluation in text: Affect, Judgement, and Appreciation. Redefined in accordance with the legal context of a trial, Affect refers to descriptions of participants' emotions or feelings in trial communication; Judgment focuses on evaluations of characters or behaviors of persons or parties involved in a case; and Appreciation means evaluations of evidence, entities, objects, events, or characteristics of others issues in the trial.

The three constituents occupy quite different places in lawyer evaluation. Although Affect is deemed as the fundamental element of speaker attitude in everyday life, it is the least common in the court debate, subject to restrictions in the trial proceedings. Judgment and Appreciation both play a more prominent role in lawyer evaluation. Appreciation, in particular, permeates the evaluations of various topics in the trial, including facts of a case, legal issues, and the opposing party's viewpoints.

Consequently, the three constituents will be analyzed with varying degrees of delicacy in accordance with their significance in lawyer speech. Unlike Affect, which is to be discussed briefly, Judgement and Appreciation will receive much detailed analysis. Both of them are to be analyzed further in terms of three variables. Judgment is to be studied in terms of Social Esteem, Social Sanction, and Social Punishment, and Appreciation is to be investigated in terms of Reaction, Composition, and Valuation.

Lawyer evaluation may be identified and analyzed in text by tracing how it is structured. Generally, it can be realized through lexis, which includes adjectives, nouns, verbs, or adverbs, or through grammar, which includes the choice of tense,

L. Zhang, *Lawyer Evaluation in Chinese Courtroom*,
https://doi.org/10.1007/978-981-97-1211-3_4

sentence structures, or even larger units of the text, such as the generic structure. When it is realized through lexis, it is called a congruent expression, and when it is done through non-lexis means, it is called an incongruent expression. Lawyer evaluation may be conveyed either positively, negatively, or neutrally, in direct or indirect manners. Above all, how it is realized and expressed in text is closely related to Field (i.e., the activity in which it is involved) (Martin and Rose 2003).

4.2 Lawyer Evaluation as Affect

In the trial talk, the use of Affect is less pervasive since emotions or feelings are usually dismissed as sentimental and subjective. However, Affect may inevitably occur when lawyers describe the severity of a disputed act or its consequence or when they advance their arguments sometimes. See Excerpt (1) for illustration. Note that two different notational conventions, bolding and underlining, are used to represent two different ways in which lawyer evaluation is realized. The bolding indicates a congruent expression, and the underlining indicates an indirect/incongruent expression.

Excerpt (1) No. X-D-008

被害人代理: 这种犯罪给被害人带来的巨大的悲剧后果, 使这种犯罪为整个人类社会所不齿, 所痛恨, 即使<u>罪犯也极少有人敢</u>采用这种犯罪手段	LV: Due to the **immensely tragic** consequences it incurs to victims, such a violent offense is bitterly **detested** and **condemned** by humanity to the extent that <u>few criminals would dare</u> to resort to it

In this excerpt, the lawyer highlights the destructive nature of the criminal act, which in this case involves disfigurement with chemical liquids. Technically, the lawyer makes an evaluation here, with themselves as the speaker/evaluator, the act (of disfigurement) as the topic of their evaluation, and the consequence as a sub-topic. What is involved are three evaluating items, two in lexis and one in a clause.

Advancing their position on the result of the violent act, the lawyer employs the adjective "悲剧" (tragic) first and then intensifies it with a graded adjective "巨大的" (immensely), to evaluate the act negatively in terms of how the act is related to or received by the victim whom they represent in court. Then, to illustrate how serious the consequence of the said act is and to prove how appropriate their negative evaluation of it is, the lawyer uses two descriptions of emotional reactions. One is the feeling from the average person expressed in two predicated phrases, "不齿, 所痛恨" (bitterly detested and condemned), and the other is a criminal's reaction expressed in a modalized negation, "罪犯也极少有人敢" (few criminals would dare to …). The negated modal expression of inclination intensifies the devastating result. Contextually, the co-coordinating use of two affective attitudes accelerates the enormous injury caused by the act and provides support to their evaluation of it. In other words, the lawyer's congruent expression made through the first two adjectives is expanded textually and illustrated by the two adverse evaluative reactions from other persons, which include the ordinary people's feelings in the congruent expression and the criminals' feelings in the incongruent one.

In cases where the disadvantaged in law, such as children and women, are involved, lawyers may display their personal feelings very straightforwardly, which is a very acceptable verbal practice in the culture of China that stresses familial obligations parents have towards their young children in the ethical sense. In a case that relates to the willful desertion of a newly-born baby, when analyzing the severity of the male defendant's motive, the prosecutor employs (in)congruent expressions of Affect, including feelings and emotions associated with the victim and defendant. See Excerpt (2).

Excerpt (2) No. X-S-Z-25

公诉人: 每一次公诉人看到弃婴的无助而充满哀怨的照片, 心里都受到严重的震撼, 被告人难道还能够安心平静地看待自己亲生儿子在山坡上树丛中等待死亡吗?	Prosecutor: Whenever the prosecutor saw the **helpless, pitiful looks** of the abandoned baby in the photo, he [I] would be deeply shaken in his heart. How could the defendant have remained calm and tranquil, knowing that his flesh and blood son was left to die in the bushes on a hill?

To convey the severity of the defendant's behavior of abandoning his baby, the prosecutor makes pervasive uses of the emotive Affect. On the whole, three evaluative attitudes, including the baby's Affect and that from the prosecutor and the defendant, are placed in contrast. To the baby who is described as being "无助而充满哀怨" (helpless, pitiful) from its looks and its fate of "等待死亡" ([being] left to die), the prosecutor and the defendant have different reactions. The prosecutor feels "受到严重的震撼" (deeply shaken), which is a natural, positive reaction to the sufferings of the vulnerable, while the defendant is negatively described as indifferent, as is indirectly revealed in his behaviors "安心平静地看待" (remain[ing] calm and tranquil, knowing …).

Meanwhile, an evoked feeling of anger may be implicitly conveyed not only in the contrasted reactions but in the different packaging of the two reactions in ideational meanings. The prosecutor's reaction is packed in a mental process, "震撼" (shaken), which is intensified by the adverb "严重的" (deeply) as a modifier, thereby signifying the prosecutor's heartfelt sympathy. By contrast, the defendant's reaction is described in the relational process with a durative verb of cognition, "看待" (know) (Halliday 1994: 120). The grammatical encoding of the defendant as the subject in the relational process of duration augments the deliberate, if not willful, intention of the defendant.

The use of Affect can also be observed when the motive of an act in civil cases is described, as is shown in Excerpt (3).

Excerpt (3) No. M-D-019

被代: 人们都以参加了该剧的制作为自豪, 为荣耀, 为事业上的一个闪光点, 甚至成为自己增值的砝码。A女士就是在这样一种热浪中 失去平衡的。回想请她为该三首歌配唱录音之时, 她那种高兴, 感激, 诚恳合作的态度, 使我们不敢相信, 这份如此虚假的诉状是出自她的手	DL: Feeling **proud and honored**, most staff members viewed their engagement in the film as a **highlight** in their careers. Some even considered it **a worthwhile experience that could lead to greater rewards**. It was such **an unrealistic mindset** that caused Miss A to lose herself. Recalling her **happiness, gratitude, and sincere cooperation** as she was invited to work as a background singer for the three songs involved in the case, we could hardly believe that she was the one who filed such a fake lawsuit against us

In this excerpt, which is related to a copyright infringement case, the defense lawyer describes the plaintiff's motive in the lawsuit. There are a couple of evaluative attitudes conveyed, as summarized in Table 4.1.

Compared with the staff members who are described as having positive reactions to their engagement in the film, the plaintiff is evaluated implicitly in the phrase "失去平衡的" (lose herself), which implies that she is insane and greedy, in particular when it is read in the background "在这样一种热浪" (unrealistic mindset). The negative portrayal of the plaintiff, Miss A, is also evident in the description of the Affect from the defense party, "我们不敢相信" (we could hardly believe), at the sudden change of attitude from the previous positive reaction "高兴, 感激, 诚恳合作的态

Table 4.1 Coded Affects in Excerpt (3)

Evaluator		Evaluated (topic)	Evaluating item(s)	Polarity of evaluation
First-order	Second-order			
N/A	人们 (Staff members)	参与制作 Engagement in the film	自豪, 荣耀 (proud, honored); 闪光点 (a highlight)	Positive
N/A	Some people [Retrievable in context]	参与制作 Engagement in the film	增值的砝码 (worthwhile experience leading to greater rewards); 热浪 (unrealistic mindset)	Negative
N/A	A女士 (Miss A)	Work as a singer	高兴, 感激, 诚恳合作的态度 (happiness, gratitude, and sincere cooperation)	Positive
Speaker	N/A	Miss A's reaction	失去平衡 (lose herself)	Negative
Speaker	N/A	Miss A's filing a case	我们不敢相信 (could hardly believe); 虚假的诉状 (a fake lawsuit against us)	Negative

度" (happiness, gratitude, and sincere cooperation) to her insincerity evidenced by her behavior of filing "虚假的诉状" (a fake lawsuit against us). All the evaluations are made to serve the defense's communicative purpose: to de-construct the plaintiff's motive and to refute the legality of her complaint.

Similarly, Affect may be employed when lawyers analyze the motives and consequences of an alleged action or other issues in criminal cases. In addition, it is also used when they interactively evaluate the opposing party's arguments.

Excerpt (4) No. X-D-026

被代: 令人不能理解的是,《起诉书》不仅将上述W某出于朋友关系送给H某的钱认定为H某受贿, 而且将两人换戴手表也认定为行贿受贿。这里我们不禁要问: H某在收受W某送钱时在哪方面利用了职务上的便利?......至于互戴手表, 如果是行贿受贿怎能发生在大庭广众面前, 这合乎情理吗?	DL: What is **confusing** to us is that in the Indictment, the money that W gave to H out of friendship was determined as a bribe. So was the exchange of watches between them. We cannot help but ask: In what way did H take advantage of his position when accepting money from W … As to the exchange of watches, if it is bribery, how can it happen in public? Is it reasonable?

In Excerpt (4), the defense lawyer expresses their doubtful attitude regarding the prosecution's opinion of taking some of the evidence as bribes. Their feeling of doubt, unequivocally expressed in "令人不能理解" (confusing to us), is placed at the initial position of the speech as the Hyper-theme, which highlights their doubt. The thematized feeling of confusion and doubt is accelerated by the provocative questions that follow. Furthermore, the encoding of questions is perceived as intensely emotive. Firstly, the two questions are introduced by a straight-forward challenge in the modalized expression "不禁要问" (cannot help but ask). Secondly, the way questions are managed conveys attitudinal meanings. After contextualizing the exchange of watches "大庭广众面前" (in public), the defense lawyer establishes a bizarre association between "行贿" (bribery) and an act conducted "发生在大庭广众面前" (in public) because as a crime, bribery is usually assumed to be conducted in secret. By recasting the association of the two in a counterfactual condition, "如果是行贿受贿怎能发生在大庭广众面前" (if it is bribery, how can it [the exchange of watches] happen in public), the lawyer implicitly downplays or undermines the credibility of the prosecutor's opinion regarding the evidence. At last, with the emotive rhetorical question, "这合乎情理吗?" (Is it reasonable?), directed at the prosecutorial position, the defense's dissatisfaction with the accusation in the bill of indictment has been brought to a climax.

In all the trials, instances of Affect are distributed in a scattered fashion. Affect can be found in various stages of the trial talk, including the presentation of the facts of a case (for instance, the motives, severity, and process of the act), the legal discussion on the attribute of the facts, or debates with the opposing side.

Finally, it should be clarified that the use of Affect cannot be dismissed as a "fallacy" in legal speech even though the use of feelings or emotions is less permissible in the trial than legal opinions based on facts and reason. Our investigation of the data shows that skillful lawyers could make effective use of emotions or feelings to achieve unexpected effects in persuading others and winning the court over.

4.3 Lawyer Evaluation as Judgment

Judgment is the description of people's characters or behaviors. In the court, lawyers' Judgment focuses specifically on the characters or behaviors of the parties concerned in a case, which include witnesses on both parties, defendants and plaintiffs. For behaviors or characters under evaluation, it is crucial to tell whether they are positive or negative, acceptable or unacceptable in the ethical or legal senses, owing to the fact that the personal, moral, or legal attributes of a person might be related to the assessment of their motive or intent in a disputed behavior or act. As a result, Judgement has to be analyzed in detail so as to capture these subtle differences in the court.

Judgment may be analyzed in terms of three variables: Social Esteem, Social Sanction, and Social Punishment, which have been redefined and explained in Chap. 3. The first variable, Social Esteem, relates to a person's character in terms of Capacity, Normality, and Tenacity. It is made to refer to the qualities of a person as an individual. Examples to be given are "lucky, fortunate, capable, determined, powerful, and brave" (Martin and Rose 2003: 62). The second, Social Sanction, is concerned with the ethical or moral qualities of a person as a public member of the community, which may be investigated in terms of Veracity and Propriety. Typical examples are "truthful, credible, authentic, frank, fair, just, kind" (Martin and Rose 2003: 62–63). The third, Social Punishment, which is proposed as a new variable in this study, refers to the qualities of a person as the bearer of the law. It may be further analyzed in terms of Honesty, Reliability, Loyalty, Respectfulness, and Culpability. Typical examples available are trustworthy, cautious, loyal, legally accountable, and so on.

The realization of Judgment is determined by the context of the courtroom. As objectivity is given priority over pure personal opinions in law (Rogers and Erez 1999), Judgment is more likely to be conveyed in congruent expressions accompanied by or embedded in incongruent expressions, mainly when case facts are presented in court.

4.3.1 Social Esteem

Social Esteem is the variable to investigate the qualities of a person as an individual, in particular, their capacity, tenacity, and normality. We may explore it with questions such as how special, capable, or resolved a person is (Martin and Rose 2003: 62).

Lawyers present their Judgements straightforwardly and frequently when they evaluate the personal qualities of the parties they represent, as in Excerpts (5) and (6).

Excerpt (5) No. X-D-008

被害人代理: 被害人的品质是众人皆夸的: 其自小学至中学年年被评为三好学生; 读大学时又被评为 "优秀团员", 奖学金获得者, 校学生会文娱委员。踏上工作岗位一年后即被评为助理经济师, 单位证明其表现很好	LV: The victim has a **well-acclaimed** personality: she was awarded the title of "**student with merits**" every year from elementary school to middle school; when she was in university, she received the award "**Excellent League Member**", won **scholarships**, and served as a **member of the student union** in charge of entertainment activities; one year after she started working, she was promoted to **an assistant economist**, and received a good evaluation from her employer

The lawyer shows a positive evaluation of the capacity of "被害人" (the victim), whom they represent in the court. Initially, there comes a favorable Judgement in the adjective "众人皆夸" (well-acclaimed). As the praise is predicated in the clause, which serves as the Hyper-theme of the paragraph, the favorable Judgement is topicalized and emphasized. Then, the attitude of Judgement is supported by an account of prizes and awards the victim once earned in the past: "三好学生" (student with merit), "优秀团员" (excellent league member), "奖学金获得者" (scholarship winner), and "助理经济师" (an assistant economist). The series of complimentary words depict the victim as highly capable.

Excerpt (6) No X-D-027

被代: 被告人H某在工作期间, 思想解放, 工作大胆, 对某市的改革开放, 经济建设做了大量的工作。H在案发前, 中央以及省有关组织和领导对此也是给予了肯定和积极评价的。某市群众对其工作成就也给予了较高的评价	DL: When he was in office, defendant H was **open-minded** and **innovative** in his work and made tremendous contributions to the reform and economic development of the city X, where he worked. As a result, he received **positive and affirmative comments** from organizations and leaders both at the central and provincial levels before he was charged. People in that city also gave much **high praise** for his achievements in work

In Excerpt (6), the defense lawyer expresses favorable Judgments of the defendant in terms of capacity, as is summarized in Table 4.2.

Table 4.2 Positive Judgements of the defendant in Excerpt (6)

Evaluator		Evaluating items	Manner of realization
First-order	Second-order		
The speaking lawyer	N/A	思想解放, 工作大胆 (open-minded and innovative in his work); 做了大量的工作 (made tremendous contributions)	Congruent, incongruent
	中央以及省有关组织和领导 (organizations and leaders both at the central and provincial levels)	肯定和积极评价 (positive and affirmative comments)	Congruent
	某市群众 (people in the city X)	较高的评价 (much high praise)	Congruent

In addition to evaluating their party favorably, lawyers also make negative Judgements of the opposing party, as is illustrated in Excerpt (7).

Excerpt (7) No. M-D-019

被代: ……她因此有了向国内外自荐为 "H 公主" 剧主题歌主唱或原唱的资本。至于人家对此事表示质疑, 那也是因为她不能正确对待自己, 夸大其词地向他人自荐造成的	DL: She [plaintiff] thus had the **capital** to nominate herself as the lead singer or original singer of the theme song of the drama "Princess H" at home and abroad. As for some doubts arising from people concerning the matter, it is also due to her inability to present herself accurately and her tendency to embellish her accomplishments when introducing herself to others

In this excerpt, when describing the female plaintiff's motive in filing the case of copyright infringement, the defense lawyer evaluates the tenacity of the plaintiff in pursuit of fame. As is observed, the lawyer begins by introducing the plaintiff's attitude toward her work in the play, which is framed in the noun phrase with a neutral connotation, "资本" (capital), using the formula "she (the evaluator) takes her work as a kind of 'capital'" (evaluating item). Of course, in the cultural context of China, where self-cultivation and modesty in the face of fame are valued, the text can be read as an indirect, negative Judgement of the plaintiff made by the lawyer, who is the first-order evaluator. After this, the lawyer moves on to critically judge the plaintiff for her lack of control in relation to her achievements in work, using two phrases with negative connotations: "不能正确对待自己" (her inability to present herself accurately) and "夸大其词地向他人自荐" (her tendency to embellish her accomplishments …). Of course, the criticism is made more apparent if readers notice the evaluative Affect conveyed in people's adverse mental reactions to the plaintiff's behaviors in "质疑" (doubts).

As has been demonstrated in the excerpts mentioned above, lawyers covey their evaluations on the characters or behaviors of the parties involved in a case through lexical or grammatical choices. The combined use of both expressions is a distinctive feature of lawyer evaluation as Judgement.

4.3.2 Social Sanction

Social Sanction is the variable related to the moral aspect of the character of a person as a community member. With a focus on the character of a person in public relations, it may be further analyzed in terms of Veracity or Propriety. Typical questions to be asked may include how honest/truthful a person is or how acceptable or suitable a person's behavior is in the moral sense (Martin and Rose 2003: 62).

Lawyers may make contrastive Judgments about the characters of the two opposing parties in the same case. See Excerpt (8).

Excerpt (8) No X-D-008

被害人代理: 与被告人先后发生两次大的风波以及被告人身上所存在的缺点 (如爱说谎, 图虚荣, 无事业心, 心胸狭窄, 脾气暴躁等), 她都及时向父母做了汇报, 认真听取父母的意见。被害人曾分别于3月与8月郑重向被告人提出分手, 皆因被告人再三保证改正而表示愿意给其机会, 遗憾的是被告人自己不争气	LV: She [victim] reported to her parents in time the two conflicts with the defendant and the defendant's shortcomings (**such as lying , vanity , lack of motivation in a job, narrow-mindedness, and hot temper**) and sincerely listened to their suggestions. The victim once sincerely proposed a breakup with the defendant in March and August but eventually agreed to give him time to mend his ways because the defendant repeatedly swore that he would rectify his behaviors. **Unfortunately**, the defendant failed to do that as he promised

In this excerpt, the lawyer makes favorable Judgments of the victim and negative ones toward the defendant. In terms of Propriety, the victim is indirectly judged as responsible, cautious, and sincere, which is implied in the descriptions of how she behaved when conflicts occurred with the defendant. Her actions in "及时向父母做了汇报" (report[ing] to her parents in time) and "认真听取父母的意见" (sincerely listen[ing] to their suggestions), conform to the ethical standards in the Chinese culture for a responsible person and a respectful daughter when dealing with interpersonal conflicts in a romantic relationship. Meanwhile, the victim is judged positively for the way she handled her relationship with the defendant when she "郑重......提出分手" (proposed a breakup sincerely) and for her willingness to generously and lovingly forgive the defendant by "愿意给其机会" (agree[ing] to give him time). On the contrary, the defendant's character is judged negatively and directly, in terms of Tenacity, in these descriptive phrases "爱说谎, 图虚荣, 无事业心, 心胸狭窄, 脾气暴躁" (lying, vanity, lack of motivation in a job, narrow-mindedness, hot temper).

Another layer of evaluative attitudes toward the two individuals is discerned in the distinct ways their characters or behaviors are encoded. The defendant's shortcomings, which are expressed directly, are accompanied by an adjunct of comment, "遗憾的是" (unfortunately), thereby highlighting the lawyer's negative evaluation and intensifying their evaluative tone. In contrast, the victim's moral qualities are all depicted indirectly in ideational meanings. Metaphorically, the contrast in the linguistic expressions helps to convey that the victim's merits are tangibly and observably based on facts and witness statements.

Meanwhile, lawyers also make negative Judgments of the moral characters of defendants in criminal cases, as in Excerpt (9).

Excerpt (9) No X-D-026

被代: 从被告人的家庭出身, 个人成长经历来看, 他的本质上并不坏, 之所以走上犯罪道路, 与<u>他放松世界观改造</u>, <u>个人主义膨胀</u>是分不开的	DL: Viewed from his family background and his personal growth, the defendant [a male] is **not a bad person in nature**. His engagement in criminal activities is inseparable from his <u>decreasing attention to improving his worldview</u> and <u>his growing egoism</u>

To analyze the motive of the defendant in illegally taking money in the above excerpt, the defense lawyer first judges the personal quality of the defendant with a negation, "他的本质上并不坏" (not a bad person in nature), which may downplay the severity of the disputed act to a certain degree. This evaluative Judgement is reinforced by the emphasis on the Propriety of the defendant as a member of the community. Instead of using a static attribute, the lawyer employs phrases indicating a dynamic process or action to construct the said behaviors, such as "放松世界观改造, 个人主义膨胀" (decreasing attention to improving his worldview, and growing egoism). It implies that the defendant commits the offense due to contingent reasons related to his cognitive state. Meanwhile, in Chinese culture, which stresses self-cultivation, showing repentance and self-reflection are regarded as positive qualities of a person who has made mistakes. By attributing the defendant's criminal offense to his mental corruption, the lawyer attempts to mitigate the severity of the defendant's motive in the case.

As has been demonstrated in the above excerpts, Judgments are widespread in the court. Generally, lawyers make favorable Judgments of the party they represent and negative evaluations toward the individuals from the opposing party. Interestingly, in criminal cases, defense lawyers may take negative Judgments of the defendants' moral character as an effective means to reduce the severity of the motive in the disputed act.

4.3.3 *Social Punishment*

Social Punishment is the variable related to a person's character or behavior within the legal framework. It may be further analyzed in terms of the five sub-categories: Honesty, Reliability, Loyalty, Respectfulness, and Culpability. Typical inquisitory questions to be asked are listed in the following:

Honesty: Has the person been truthful and consistent in their statements or behaviors?
Reliability: Has the person demonstrated any irresponsible or reckless behaviors? Has the person demonstrated any violent or aggressive behaviors?
Loyalty: Has the person shown commitment to fulfill their legal duties?
Respectfulness: Has the person shown any disregard for the law or the rights of others? Has the person shown any remorse for any wrongdoing in the past?
Culpability: Has the person been convicted/sued/charged in a case?

It is important to note that the perfective tense is used in the inquisitory questions because evaluations of a person's character in the legal sense are primarily based on past experiences or facts rather than on speculative reasoning.

The variable of Social Punishment is particularly relevant to lawyers when they discuss the characters or behaviors of a party involved in a case, since it has a direct link to the legality of the disputed act. Negative Judgments of the characters of a specific person or party in terms of Honesty and Loyalty in Social Punishment are frequent in civil cases, as is shown in Excerpt (10) below.

Excerpt (10) No. M-D-010

被代: (但是)时隔不久, 被告便一反其先诺, 提出其对事故毫无责任的观点, 拒绝赔偿	DL: (However) just a short time later, the defendant [a male] broke the promise he had made earlier. He argued that he should not be held responsible for the event, and he refused to pay the damage

This excerpt is from a civil trial related to an injury. The defense lawyer judges the quality of the defendant by describing his abnormal actions in "一反其先诺" (break[ing] the promise he had made earlier) and in "拒绝赔偿" (refus[ing] to pay the damage), which evokes a Judgement of his unreliability and dishonesty in his civil behavior. This negative evaluation is detrimental to the defendant in the civil case, where honesty and integrity are valued as the basic principles in civil law.

The Judgement of how blameworthy or faulty a person may be or how much legal obligation or responsibility a person should bear in terms of Social Punishment is significant to a trial regarding the legal nature of the case to be determined and the corresponding penalty/punishment to be decided. For illustrations, see Excerpt (11), which provides an example of the situations in criminal cases.

Excerpt (11) No X-D-001

被代: 被告人Z某虽然罪大却并非恶极, 表现之一是如前所述, 其杀人并非事先预谋, 而是为"情"所困, 一时冲动所致; 表现之二是, 杀人后, 并无逃跑和破坏现场, 毁灭罪证等行为, 他离开犯罪现场并非是为了逃避法律的惩罚, 而是对自己的杀人行为极其后悔, 想一个人去山上"把自己饿死"	DL: Although defendant Z committed a serious crime, he is not **extremely evil**. As was stated previously, one indication of this is that the murder was not planned in advance but was committed on an impulse when he was obsessed with "love". Another indication is that he did not do such behaviors as fleeing, destroying the crime scene, or eliminating the evidence after the murder. He left the scene not because he attempted to evade punishment but because he felt highly regretful for his actions and wanted to "starve himself to death" on a hill

In the text extracted from a murder trial, the defense lawyer judges the defendant's character or behaviors in legal terms. First of all, the defendant (a criminal suspect in this case) is given a mitigated evaluation in terms of the sub-variable, Reliability, through a negation, "并非恶极" (not extremely evil), despite his "罪大" (having commit[ed] a serious crime). Secondly, the Judgement is justified with two pieces of evidence, the cause of the crime and the defendant's subsequent behavior of remorse, both of which are constructed in contrast to typical behaviors of a merciless murderer. Compared with the circumstance of "事先预谋" (plan[ing] in advance), the cause for the killing is constructed less negatively as emotional and contingent, most probably related to the defendant's romantic relationship with the victim, as stated in "为 '情' 所困, 一时冲动所致" (on the impulse when he was obsessed with love). The negative Judgement of the mental state of the defendant in terms of Honesty means that the emotional disorder is attributed as the main reason for the murder. Of course, this Judgment is attempted to redress the potential accusation against the defendant being a cruel killer. Meanwhile, the lawyer gives a favorable Judgement of the defendant's regret for his offense, as stated in "极其后悔" (feeling highly regretful). The favorable evaluation is intensified by the defendant's own testimonial statement "把自己饿死" (to starve … to death), which is quoted and inserted in the lawyer's speech. Furthermore, the favorable Judgments of the defendant's repentance are highlighted by contrasting them to the markedly destructive and irresponsible behaviors that cruel killers usually engage in, such as "逃跑和破坏现场, 毁灭罪证" (flee[ing] or destroy[ing] the crime scene and eliminat[ing] the evidence). In this way, the lawyer has employed Judgments of the defendant's mental disorder in terms of Honesty and his remorse in terms of Respectfulness to the law to justify the understated evaluation of the defendant as not being so "evil".

Negative Judgments of the defendant's character in Social Punishment may be presented in different scales or degrees. See Excerpt (12).

Excerpt (12) No X-D-027

被代: 作为市委书记, 不论为领导还是为个人在工作上给予一些支持帮助, 而收受其财物, 是党纪国法所不允许的。但是, 上述事实表明, 他毕竟不同于那些利用职权对有关单位或个人实行管, 卡, 压, 借此索取或收受他人财物的行为, 更不同于那些索取他人财物或收受贿赂之后, 违反原则, 滥用职权为他人谋取不正当利益的受贿行为	DL: As a party secretary of the municipal government, accepting property from individuals or organizations, regardless of whether it is for personal or leadership support, is not allowed by the disciplines of the Party and the national law. However, as has been shown in the facts presented above, he [defendant] is fundamentally different from those who use their power to command, control, or suppress relevant organizations or individuals for the purpose of soliciting or accepting others' property, and even more different from those who violate principles and abuse their power to seek improper benefits for others in return for having solicited or taken bribes from them

In this excerpt, the defense lawyer exhibits their attitude regarding the legality of the defendant's action. A straightforward, negative evaluation of the defendant's character or behavior, "党纪国法所不允许的" (not allowed by the disciplines of the Party and the national law), is presented in terms of Culpability in the legal sense. However, this evaluative attitude is mitigated by contextualizing what the defendant received from others in a situation where he offered help to others and earned gratitude from them in return. What was received is phrased vaguely in ordinary language as "财物" (properties), in relation to what he provided, "不论为领导还是为个人在工作上给予一些支持帮助" (regardless of whether it is for personal or leadership support). By encoding the properties involved into the context where the defendant helped others and received returns from others, the lawyer avoids the alleged connection between the properties taken and the defendant's position, thus subduing the prosecution's (potential) evaluation of the defendant as a bribe taker.

Following the conjunction of conversion "但是" (however) and the metaphorical expression of high-value certainty, "上述事实表明" (shown in the facts), the defense lawyer makes further graded Judgments of the defendant's behavior by placing it in contrast to typical behaviors of bribe takers that are speculatively described in the law. Of course, this attitude may be used to highlight the leniency of the bribe-taking to a certain extent. The graded Judgement of the defendant is unequivocally shown in the relational processes: "他毕竟不同于……, 更不同于……" (different from those who …, and even more different from those …). Meanwhile, the adjunct of mood "毕竟" (fundamentally) and the adverb of degree "更" (more) intensify the comparative meanings in the Judgement. As a result, the negative Judgment of the defendant's character in Social Punishment is softened in comparison to the legally condemned behaviors of the two kinds of persons who take bribes blatantly and purposefully.

Similar to criminal trials, civil trials also have Judgments of characters or behaviors in legal terms.

Excerpt (13) No M-D-010

原代: 被告目前的态度和做法, 不仅极大伤害了原告和其他家属的感情和身心健康, 而且是对社会广大消费者基本权益的极端蔑视, 并在死者的外国友人中给中国造成了非常 恶劣的影响	PL: The defendant's attitude and behaviors not only inflicted great harm to the feelings and the physical and mental health of the plaintiff and her family members, but also showed **extreme contempt** for the basic rights of the consumers, of which the plaintiff is a member. In addition, they have had a **terribly negative impact** on the national image among foreign friends of the deceased [plaintiff]

In this excerpt, the plaintiff's lawyer expresses a strong negative Judgement of the defendant's behaviors and related consequences in terms of Respectfulness, as is demonstrated in the predicate verbs with derogatory meanings in three material processes, "伤害了" (inflicted great harm to), "蔑视" (showed contempt for) and "造成了……影响" (have had a negative impact), which are intensified by modifiers specific to each phrase, "极大" (great) [harm], "极端" (extreme) [contempt], and "非常恶劣的" (terribly) [negative]. Meanwhile, the force of the evaluation is augmented by the semantic cohesion formed between these predicated verbal phrases and the large number of people affected by the said behaviors, which includes the directly affected, the plaintiff and their family, and those who are less directly affected, the general public and the international community. In the socialist country, one of the functions of law is to safeguard and maintain social and political stability, and any potential damage to the unity in the social and political senses would be thus deemed unacceptable and inappropriate. By evaluating the negative influence of the disputed action on so large a population, the lawyer attempts to boost the severity of the action under discussion.

As has been shown in data analysis, Judgments of the characters of a specific party or participant in terms of Social Punishment, which are an essential part when determining the facts of a case, may vary in the degree of force and the ways of linguistic expression, which provides a large room for lawyers to explore meaning.

In summary, lawyers' Judgments are analyzed in the three variables: Social Esteem, Social Sanction, and Social Punishment. Social Esteem leads lawyers to judge the personal qualities of the party involved in a case, such as their normality, capacity, and tenacity. Social Sanction enables lawyers to judge characters in a moral aspect, such as veracity and propriety. The variable of Social Punishment is of particular significance in lawyer evaluation as it enables lawyers to explore meanings related to the legal aspect of the characters or behaviors of the person concerned in a case. Judgment may be realized both congruently in lexis and incongruently in grammar. Although both expressions are deployed and integrated, the incongruent one is exceptionally prominent since the use of it may fit in with the normative requirement of objectivity, which is given priority in the trial talk.

4.4 Lawyer Evaluation as Appreciation

Appreciation refers to evaluations of properties or values of evidence or related entities, objects, or other things in a trial. As a constituent that permeates lawyer talk in court, it is to be analyzed thoroughly in three sub-variables: Reaction, Composition, and Valuation, in accordance with Martin and Rose (2003: 62–63). Reaction pertains to how objects or entities are perceived in terms of their impact or quality. Composition is concerned with how the inner structure of the entities or objects is perceived. Valuation explores the meanings of how the objects or entities are valued in their worth.

As an indication of legal standpoints in a trial, lawyers' Appreciation may be realized either in congruent expressions (through lexis) or in incongruent ones (in grammar), and more often than not, it is conveyed through a combination of the two. In the incongruent expressions, some structures are especially distinctive, such as relational processes in ideational meanings and the semantic link created by a network of lexis which share similar meanings (Wang 2001, 2006; Zhang 2005).

4.4.1 Reaction

The sub-variable of Reaction can be described as a speaker's perception of the impact or quality of objects or entities. It may be explored with the inquisitory question: *How is something received by people?* (see Martin and Rose 2003: 64).

Appreciation in terms of Reaction appears when lawyers evaluate the opposing viewpoints. See Excerpts (14) and (15) below. In (14), the lawyer explicitly expresses their disagreement with the judicial stance from the first-instance court by the predicated clause, "持保留态度" (hold[ing] a reserved attitude).

Excerpt (14) No X-D-027

上诉人代理: ...... (但)一审判决书对我们的大部份意见没有采纳, 并指出这些意见 "与事实不符" 。对此, 我们持保留态度	Appellant L: ... (however) the Judgement made by the first-instance court did not adopt most of our opinions and pointed out that these opinions "are not consistent with the facts". We hold a reserved attitude to the Judgment

Excerpt (15) No X-D-001

被代: 被告人Z某非法剥夺他人生命的事实是清楚的, 其行为已经构成了故意杀人罪, 所以, 我们对公诉人所指控的罪名不持异议	DL: It is a **clear fact** that defendant Z took away another person's life unlawfully, and his action has constituted the crime of intentional homicide. Therefore, we hold no objection to the charge against the defendant

In Excerpt (15), the defense lawyer presents Appreciations of three different issues: the alleged event, the defendant's act, and the charge. See Table 4.3 for a summary of these evaluations.

As shown in the above analysis, lawyers frequently use particular linguistic expressions, for instance, understatements or mitigated negations when Appreciating opposing opinions. Rather than using direct affirmative agreement, such as "I agree with you", they choose to use wording like "I have no objection", which is a mitigated or understated expression. This choice of language may reflect the confrontational and competitive relationship between disputing lawyers in their roles.

The choice to understate agreement with respect to opposing arguments is conditioned and generated by the adversarial nature of the trial. In an adversary trial, the disputing parties are supposed to contest each other's viewpoints, and therefore, the choice of "disagreement" becomes the "preferred sequence" or default response in the terminology of conversational analysis (see Atkinson and Drew 1990; Schegloff 1988: 453). In addition, pragmatically, an agreement expressed directly face-to-face or in otherwise way regarding opponents' opinions may sound offensive to the party whom the speaking lawyers represent. The understated indication of agreement is thus a strategic use of language in the court debate. After all, the expression of lawyer evaluation is sensitive to the institutional context and the institutional role of the speaker (Martin and Rose 2003: 63).

Table 4.3 Appreciations expressed in Excerpt (15)

Evaluator	Evaluated	Evaluating item	Realization
The lawyer	被告人Z某非法剥夺他人生命的事实 (defendant Z took away another person's life unlawfully)	事实是清楚的 (a clear fact)	Direct, congruent
	其行为 (the action)	故意杀人罪 (intentional homicide)	Direct, congruent
	所指控的罪名 (the charge)	不持异议 (hold no objection)	Indirect, incongruent

Lawyers employ Appreciation when they discuss the facts of a case, the motive of an action, or the attitude of an offender, in particular. In Excerpt (16), the defense lawyer positively reviews the defendant's reaction to the alleged offense and considers the "认罪, 悔罪态度" (attitude of confession and repentance) as "比较好的" (relatively good), which makes a direct Appreciation in terms of Reaction.

Excerpt (16) No. X-D-026

被代: 无论是在案发前, 还是案发后, 被告人H某的认罪, 悔罪态度都是比较好的	DL: Whether it was before or after the bribery accusation, defendant H's attitude of confession and repentance was relatively good

Excerpt (17) No. M-D-019

被代: 而原告A女士却将一个整体的《H公主》剧割裂开来, 在庭审中称只诉第一部, 但在诉状中却又用第二部的录音时间, 地点来作为事实依据, 这种**偷换概念**, **肆意诉讼**的行为, <u>使我们无所适从</u>	DL: Fragmenting the TV plays that were a drama series, the plaintiff, Ms. A, stated during the trial that she only sued the defendant on the first play, but she took the recording time and place of the second play as a factual basis in her complaint. This kind of **conceptual substitution** and **reckless litigation** <u>puts us at a loss</u>

Excerpt (17) demonstrates the defense lawyer's Appreciation of the plaintiff's litigation in the trial. First of all, the inconsistency in the plaintiff's arguments is appreciated negatively through the nominal phrases "偷换概念" (conceptual substitution) and "肆意诉讼" (reckless litigation). By nominalizing and thematicalizing, "这种偷换概念，肆意诉讼的行为" (this kind of conceptual substitution and reckless litigation), the lawyer foregrounds and intensifies the evaluation (see Hewings 2004). In addition, the negative attitude [Appreciation: Reaction] of the result related to the inconsistency is presented in the idiomatic phrase "使我们无所适从" (to put us at a loss).

Data Analysis reveals that lawyers make evident their evaluative Appreciations in terms of Reaction through lexis that contains connotative meanings. Meanwhile, they are also inclined to support their congruent expressions with incongruent ones. Only in this way can lawyer evaluation stand firm.

4.4.2 Composition

Concerned with meanings regarding how the inner structure of an entity, object, or evidence is appreciated, Composition covers two aspects: complexity and balance of the entity. Typical inquisitory questions may include: *Does it hang together? Is it hard to follow?* (Martin and Rose 2003: 63).

Lawyers' Appreciation in terms of Composition is manifested when they evaluate the legal basis of an argument.

Excerpt (18) No. X-D-026

被代: 起诉书第三十三项指控, ……, 根据案件事实, 我们认为该定性所依据的证据<u>不够确实</u>, <u>充分</u>	DL: Count 33 in the bill of indictment is … Based on the case facts presented so far, we think that the evidence used to support the charge <u>is not sufficiently accurate and reliable</u>

In Excerpt (18), the defense lawyer depreciates the evidence related to one specific accusation in the indictment through the relational process, "所依据的证据不够确实, 充分" (the evidence used to support the charge is not sufficiently accurate and reliable). At the same time, an interpersonal metaphor, "我们认为" (we think), is used to soften the negative evaluation. Of course, the interpersonal metaphor *we think/believe* may also be taken as a formulaic expression to indicate the source of opinions in a trial.

Excerpt (19) No. X-D-024

被代: 关于起诉书指控的 "被告人徇私渎职"<u>存在</u> <u>部分事实不清</u>, <u>证据不足问题</u>	DL: The accusation of "the defendant's favoritism and malfeasance in office" in the bill of indictment has some unclear facts and insufficient evidence

Just as in Excerpt (18), the defense lawyer in this excerpt makes a negative Appreciation of the accusation in its accuracy and sufficiency. With a relational process of existence, "存在" (has), the lawyer unequivocally shows their negative evaluative attitude concerning the "事实不清, 证据不足问题" (unclear facts and insufficient evidence) and mitigates the attitude in force by the modifier "部分" (some), noticeably. However, the mitigated Appreciation appears as detrimental as or even more convincing than an unmitigated one. The fatal aspect of defense in a criminal case is reasonable doubt. If the facts or evidence are proven to have contained pitfalls, the whole charge should be dismissed as invalid.

Excerpt (20) No. M-D-022

上诉人代理: 原审判决认为, 1997年11月, NY公司使用 "老干爹"商品名称生产和销售豆豉辣酱时, NM公司生产的 "老干爹"豆豉辣酱已在一定范围内享有较高的知名度, 这是一个 没有任何证据 的 主观臆断	Appellant L: The first-instance court held in the Judgement that, by Nov of 1997, the time when the NY Corporation started to manufacture and sell its fermented bean pepper sauce, using the brand name of LAO GAN DIE, the products of the same kind, the fermented bean pepper sauce of the LAO GAN DIE brand produced by the NM Corporation, had already enjoyed a relatively high reputation in the market of a particular area. That point is a **speculative statement** with **no evidence of any kind**

In Excerpt (20), the appellant lawyer presents their Appreciation of the stance of the local court in the first-instance Judgment. Allegedly, the first-instance court used the adverbial phrase of time, "已经" (already), to indicate the temporal sequence in which the disputed trademarks started to be used by the two companies. According to the statement in the Judgment, the plaintiff in the local trial, the NM Corporation, had used the trademark in question for a longer time than did the defendant (the appellant), the NY Corporation.

The appellant lawyer for the NY Corporation shows their negative Appreciation regarding the validity of the local court's opinion through a phrase containing derogatory meaning, "主观臆断" (a speculative statement), and aggravates it with a negation, "没有任何证据" (no evidence of any kind). What is presented, therefore, is a sharp disapproval.

The data analysis of Appreciation in terms of Composition makes it evident that the integration of relational processes, particularly the structure of "there be …", and the lexical expressions of attitude, is a typical way to convey Appreciations toward the arguments from the other parties in court.

4.4.3 Valuation

Valuation is the sub-variable with which to explore evaluative meanings on the worth of arguments, evidence, entities, or objects in a case. Appreciations in terms of Valuation are observed when lawyers evaluate the nature of a sued act, the validity of a legal argument, the credibility of the facts of a case, and other issues.

An Appreciation of disputed acts in terms of Validity is common in a trial, as is shown in Excerpt (21).

Excerpt (21) No. X-D-024

被代: 从被告人行为时的主观方面看, 没有证据证明被告人存在滥用职权的犯罪故意。如存在工作上的判断失误, 亦应以过失相论	DL: In terms of subjective factors in the defendant's action, there is no evidence to prove that the defendant had a deliberate intent of abusing power. If there were errors in the defendant's decisions in work, his action shall be determined as negligence

Since the subjective aspect of a disputed act is a crucial factor in determining the legal nature of the act, the defense lawyer in this excerpt manifests their evaluation of the defendant's action by making two speech acts. Firstly, a negation toward the "犯罪故意" (deliberate intent) in the alleged "滥用职权" (abusing power) is presented in the relational process, "没有证据证明" (there is no evidence to prove). Secondly, with a counterfactual clause, "如存在工作上的判断失误" (if there were errors in the defendant's Judgment in work), "过失" (negligence) is proposed instead of the prosecution's stance, abusing power.

Lawyers' Valuation is observed when the categorical boundary in a claim/charge is discussed in court.

Excerpt (22) No. X-D-024

被代: 徇私并非一定舞弊。所谓舞弊是指: 在从事公务活动中, 故意违背法律和事实, 弄虚作假, 该为不为, 不该为而为或者作出违法的处理决定。在起诉书指控的三件事上, 被告人当时并没有 "故意违背法律和事实, 弄虚作假, 该为不为, 不该为而为"的舞弊行为, 期间被告人虽念及亲情地徇私, 但被告人在三件事的大部分行为上并没有在舞弊, 在滥用职权	DL: Favoritism in the office is not necessarily malfeasance. The term "malfeasance" refers to situations where, when handling public affairs, a government employee distorts the law and facts deliberately, makes fake reports, does not do what shall be done or does what shall not be done, or makes decisions that violate the law. In the three facts alleged in the bill of indictment, the defendant [a male] did not engage in such malfeasant behaviors as distorting the law and facts deliberately, making false reports, undoing what shall be done, or doing what shall not be done. Although the defendant did show favoritism in his behaviors at that time due to family ties, he did not have malfeasant behaviors or abuse his power in most cases

In this excerpt, to present their reconstructed interpretation of the defendant's behaviors in the legal sense, the defense lawyer starts by making an evaluative distinction between the two terms, "徇私" (favoritism in office) and "舞弊" (malfeasance). Counter to the common perception that the two are usually intertwined, the lawyer discusses the link between the two through a negation: "徇私并非一定舞弊" (favoritism in the office does not necessarily mean malfeasance). Then, in their Valuation of the term "malfeasance" by way of definition, terms with negative prosody are used, "故意违背法律和事实, 弄虚作假, 该为不为" (to distort the law and facts deliberately, make fake reports, not do what shall be done or do what shall not). In addition to the behaviors described in the definition, the speech act of defining may be read as conveying a negative attitude in the metalinguistic sense. According to Halliday's (1994) functional view, language choice is a meaning-making process. On the one hand, when "舞弊" (malfeasance) is chosen over "徇私" (favoritism) for illustration, a meaningful point is being made in this language use. On the other hand, some of the typical behaviors listed under the term "malfeasance" are repetitively and redundantly used in the utterances after the definition, which increases the force of negation in the evaluation. Semantically, "舞弊" (malfeasance) is valued as more severe than "徇私" (favoritism) in the legal sense.

Based on the evaluative attitude on the two terms conveyed in the definition, the defense lawyer demonstrates their evaluations of the defendant's behaviors against the allegation indicated in the indictment. As is shown in the clause of concession, "虽念及亲情地徇私" (although the defendant did show favoritism …), the disputed action of the defendant is evaluated as a less serious offense, as in "并没有在舞弊" (not have malfeasant behaviors), with a mitigated expression realized by the adverbial phrase of degree, "大部分行为上" (in most cases).

Along with valuations of the categorial boundary in a charge or claim, valuations are also found in the semantic loading of a specific object/entity in a trial. See Excerpt (23) below.

Excerpt (23) No M-D-021

被代: 尽管双方均在商品名称上使用了 "老干爹", 但是 "老干爹" 是一个普通称谓, 就好像 "老表" "老同志" 和 "老先生"一样, 它不为任何一方所特有	DL: Though both parties used LAO GAN DIE as trade names for their products, the phrase "LAO GAN DIE" is an **ordinary term of address**, just as **"Lao Biao" (Old Cousin)**, **"Lao Tong Zhi" (Old Comrade)**, and **Lao Xian Sheng (Old Man)**. It is not owned exclusively by either party

In this excerpt, the defense lawyer presents their evaluation of the particularity of the brand name "LAO GAN DIE". As a general rule in marketing, a brand, which is the symbolic embodiment of all the information connected with specific products or services, typically includes a name, logo, and other visual elements such as images or symbols. It also encompasses a set of expectations associated with the products or services that typically arise in the minds of consumers. In other words, the brand name contains plenty of information in its semantic load. In this excerpt, the defense lawyer expresses their evaluation of the term "老干爹" (LAO GAN DIE) through a reductive reading of its semantic meanings.

In the first place, the noun "老干爹" (LAO GAN DIE) is appreciated as an "ordinary term of address" in an attributive relational process. This evaluation strips off the semantic attribute that is supposed to be embodied in the noun as a brand name. Meanwhile, classifying it into the category of ordinary addresses, as in "就好像 '老表' '老同志' 和 '老先生'一样" (just as 'Lao Biao', 'Lao Tong Zhi' and 'Lao

Xian Sheng'), further reduces the semantic force in the term and intensifies its ordinariness. Finally, the lawyer's evaluative attitude toward the name is conclusively demonstrated in the negated statement that the term is "不为任何一方所特有" (not owned exclusively by either party).

In summary, Appreciation in terms of Reaction, Composition, and Valuation enables lawyers to express viewpoints with respect to the various topics involved in a trial talk. Within Appreciation, Valuation occupies a crucial part and serves as an effective linguistic means through which lawyers advance their legal standpoints.

4.5 Summary

This chapter has analyzed the three constituents of lawyer evaluation in text. Among them, Judgement and Appreciation have both been investigated in terms of three subvariables. Judgment is further analyzed in terms of Social Esteem, Social Sanction, and Social Punishment. Appreciation is explored in terms of Reaction, Composition, and Valuation.

A distinctive feature occurs in the realization of the three constituents. While either congruent (in lexis, such as adjectives, nouns, verbs, or other derivative forms) or incongruent expressions (in grammar) may be used, the coordination of the two is very pervasive in most situations. The integration of the two expressions is generated from and conditioned by the institutional context of the courtroom, the tasks of lawyer talk, and the normative requirements in a trial. In accordance with the principle of objectivity in trial proceedings, opinions have to be made explicit and unbiased at the same time.

As lawyer evaluation has been identified textually in data, the constraints of the trial context on it are to be explored in Chap. 5.

References

Atkinson, R.C., and P. Drew. 1990. *Order in court*. Hampshire and London: Macmillan Academic and Professional Ltd.

Halliday, M.A.K. 1994. *Introduction to functional grammar*. London: Edward Arnold.

Hewings, A. 2004. Developing discipline-specific writing: An analysis of undergraduate geography essays. In *Analyzing academic writing*, ed. L. Ravelli and R. Ellis, 131–152. London & New York: Continuum.

Martin, J., and D. Rose. 2003. *Working with discourse*. London, New York: Continuum.

Rogers, L., and E. Erez. 1999. Contextualization of objectivity in sentencing among legal professionals in South Australia. *International Journal of the Sociology of Law* 27: 267–286. https://doi.org/10.1006/ijsl.1999.0092.

Schegloff, E. 1988. On an actual virtual servo-mechanism for guessing bad news: A single case conjecture. *Social Problems* 32: 442–457. https://doi.org/10.2307/800596.

Wang, Zhen-hua. 2001. 评价系统及其运作 [Appraisal system and its operation]. 外国语 [*Journal of Foreign Languages*] (6): 13–20.

Wang, Zhen-hua. 2006. 自首的系统功能语言学视角 [Confession: A systemic functional perspective]. 现代外语 [*Modern Foreign Languages*] (1): 1–9.

Zhang, Li-ping. 2005. 庭审叙事的对立与诉讼对抗: 话语分析对法官的启示 [Confrontation and contest in the courtroom narrative: Implications of discourse analysis for trial judges]. 山东外语教学 [*Journal of Foreign Language Research in Shandong*] (5): 12–15. https://doi.org/10.16482/j.sdwy37-1026.2005.05.006.

Chapter 5
Lawyer Evaluation Under Contextual Constraints

Abstract Based on data from three civil cases and three criminal cases, this chapter investigates how contextual constraints of the courtroom are observed and reflected in lawyer evaluation in the text. The constraints of context in the two levels are to be functionally analyzed in ideational, interpersonal, and textual meanings.

5.1 Introduction

This chapter aims to investigate the contextual constraints of the courtroom on lawyer evaluation in text. In line with the Hallidayan definition of context (Halliday 1978, 1985, 1994), the contextual constraints may be described in two respects: the situational context of the courtroom and the context of legal culture.

In the theoretical construction in Chap. 3, an overall analysis of the contextual features of the courtroom in terms of Field, Tenor, and Mode has made clear that confrontation between opposing lawyers in roles is an essential feature that shapes the discourse of lawyer evaluation in adversarial trials. With the mediating role of the higher-level context, the context of legal culture in the Chinese courtroom, which refers to the Habermasian interpretations of advocacy in legal communication in court, indicates that rationality or effective communication in law enables lawyers to orient their speech to confrontation in roles on the dimension of solidarity. Hence, the rational discourse of lawyer evaluation is pervasive in the Chinese court.

L. Zhang, *Lawyer Evaluation in Chinese Courtroom*,
https://doi.org/10.1007/978-981-97-1211-3_5

This chapter investigates how these contextual constraints are observed and reflected in lawyer evaluation in text. As the functions of language are realized in meanings in texts (Halliday 1994), the constraints of context in the two levels on lawyer evaluation are to be functionally analyzed in ideational, interpersonal, and textual meanings.

Data analysis will be mainly based on trial transcripts related to three civil cases, including two tort cases and one infringement case, and photocopied materials of three criminal cases. To save space and avoid repetitive representation, texts of the excerpts in trial transcripts would be referred to by designated turn numbers rather than being reproduced as the original ones. The selected portions of the trial transcripts that are involved in this chapter are attached in Appendix B.

5.2 Lawyer Evaluation in the Situational Context

As a linguistic act situated in the context of the courtroom, lawyer evaluation is conditioned and constrained by the situational context of the courtroom in China, or the context of situation in Halliday's term (1994). This section takes a closer look at this.

5.2.1 The Situational Context and Its Constraints on Lawyer Evaluation

The contextual features of the courtroom are outlined below in terms of the three variables: Field, Tenor, and Mode. In the highly institutional context of the courtroom, the task of the talk is to discuss the legality of a disputed social act. The trial talk consists of two orders of verbal activities: the construction of the subject matter or the facts of a case and the discussion of the case. In terms of the roles, the judge is an arbitrator above everyone engaged in the trial talk, and the opposing parties are competitive arguers who are supposed to advance their legal positions, justify their legal standpoints, and prove to the court which side of positions is more convincing. Being serious and formal, the trial talk is conducted in a predetermined sequence by following certain routines regarding turn-taking, cross-examination of evidence, and other aspects of trial communication.

In brief, the courtroom is a forum whose essential and unavoidable role is to decide or to make a decision on any issue brought before it concerning the legality of a social behavior, either criminal or civil (Maley 1994: 33). The plaintiff/prosecution is supposed to prove the claim/charge against the defendant, while the defense is required to deconstruct the claim/charge against their party. The two opposing parties are destined to contest with each other when discussing the various issues in the trial. Above all, the general outline of the contextual features highlights the contestant, competitive relationship between disputing lawyers in the trial (Maley 1994).

5.2.2 Lawyer Evaluation in Confrontation

5.2.2.1 Conflicting Conceptions of Rights and Duties

In terms of Field, the opposing lawyers are engaged in a talk on certain disputed acts in which their rights and duties conflict. Functionally, their competing conceptions of rights and duties are projected ideationally in lawyer evaluation when the facts of a case are presented and discussed in the legal framework (Zhang 2005; see also Wang 2004).

For illustrations, verbal interactions in the trademark infringement case (M-S-Z-09) are analyzed. As is shown in the presented evidence, the plaintiff, YANG FEI Toast Chicken Fastfood. Corporation Ltd., registered the brand name YANG FEI as the trademark for its products, pancakes, in 1997, and started to use the name ever since, while the defendant, HW Food Corporation Ltd., registered the name of BIN GE as its trademark in 2003. During the period from January to July in 2003, the defendant produced and sold in many supermarkets its pancakes which were labeled "XIN YANG FEI Pancakes in BIN GE". The package of the defendant's products contained information of three kinds: the characters of 新杨妃 and their corresponding pinyin at the top, the trademark BIN GE, and the Chinese characters 新杨妃烧饼 (literally, XIN YANG FEI PENCAKE) in the middle, and the full name and location of the defendant at the bottom. Upon discovering the sold pancakes produced by the defendant, the plaintiff considered that their ownership of the trademark was infringed and then filed a lawsuit against the defendant. However, the defendant did not think their pancakes with the marks mentioned above violated the trademark law. The two parties disagreed with each other on whether the case fits in with legal regulations on trademark infringement.

Discursively, the discord between the two parties is observed in ideational meanings, particularly in the relational process. Excerpt (1) (Turns 3–4 in M-S-Z-09) demonstrates the contestation between the two opposing lawyers when they evaluate the facts of the case. Starting with a material process "被告他……使用新杨妃文字以及拼音" (the defendant used the Chinese characters 新杨妃 and their pinyin …), the plaintiff's lawyer encodes their evaluation of the defendant's behavior as an assumed "事实" (fact), which is indicated in the nominalization "这个事实" (this fact). Meanwhile, the lawyer expands their evaluation of the event as a "事实"

(fact) in a relational process "是……得到确认的" (been …ascertained) and consolidates the evaluation in the perfective form "已经" (been already). Then, based on this evaluation, the lawyer explicitly presents their Appreciation of the case fact in a relational process, "对方的侵权事实也是已经成立的" (the opposing party's infringement has already been established). The present perfective conveyed by the adverb "已经" (already) is indicative of their attitude.

The defense has quite a different Appreciation of the case facts. Their negative evaluation of the factual link between the two trademarks is unequivocally shown in a relational process, "我单位的商标与原告的商标没有任何的相同或相似之处" (has no resemblance or similarity of any kind ...). The evaluative attitude is intensified by the intensifier "任何" (of any kind). Following the negation, the negative attitude from the defense toward the case facts is presented in the simple present tense in the material process "我单位商标不构成对原告的商标侵权" (the trademark we use for our products does not constitute an infringement on the plaintiff's).

As shown in the above analysis, competing views regarding the facts of the case are manifested through lawyer evaluation in relational processes. Arranged in the one-to-one correspondence in sequence, evaluations from opposing parties are focused on the same topics but with stark differences in polarity.

Conflicting conceptions of rights and duties are found in lawyer evaluation in other infringement cases. In Excerpt (2), disputants are against each other on one aspect of the fact, which is whether prior approval from the plaintiff has been obtained. They differ from each other in their choice of circumstantial elements of manner when they represent the fact.

Excerpt (2) No. M-D-018

原代: 制片人在未征得原告同意,未为原告署名的情况下将原告演唱的上述歌曲作为电视剧的插曲 被代: 原告人是在明知的情况下, 自愿为电视剧中的人物配唱歌曲的	PL: Without obtaining the plaintiff's consent or giving credit to the plaintiff [a female] as the singer, the producer used the songs sung by the plaintiff as the insert songs of the TV series DL: It is with her complete knowledge of the circumstances that the plaintiff **volunteered to** provide vocals to the songs of the characters in the TV plays

With the defendant "制片人" (the producer) encoded as the agency of the action in the material process, "将原告演唱的上述歌曲作为电视剧的插曲" (used the songs sung by the plaintiff as the insert songs of the TV series), the plaintiff's lawyer topicalizes the manner of the action, "在未征得原告同意, 未为原告署名的情况下" (without obtaining the consent of the plaintiff or giving credit to the plaintiff as the singer), by putting it emphatically before the predicate of the materialized action. Their linguistic operation highlights the manner as a primary condition of the alleged act. In this way, the plaintiff side attitudinally encodes the defendant as a party to bear civil responsibility.

The defense makes an adverse representation of the fact. First of all, by taking the plaintiff as the subject and an active agency of the material process of singing, "原

告人……自愿为电视剧……配唱歌曲的" (the plaintiff …volunteered to provide vocals…), the defense emphasizes the condition of the action as being "自愿" (voluntarily) and evaluates the plaintiff as the one responsible for the sued behavior. Meanwhile, their strong evaluative meanings regarding the sued behavior are expressed by the encoded manner of action, "明知的情况下" (her complete knowledge of circumstances), in the emphatic sentence structure, "是在……情况下" (it is …that…).

As demonstrated above, the two lawyers make contradictory evaluations of the case and exhibit their differences in distinct linguistic representations of the social actor and the situation (Francis and Kramer-Dahl 1992). Constructing the facts of a case is thus one site of contestation in lawyer evaluation, which, in turn, is indexical of the conflicting conceptions between opposing parties regarding their rights and duties in the litigation.

Similarly, Excerpt (3) (Turns 1–3, in M-S-Z-10) provides an account of how litigants compete with each other when assessing the clinical effects of a cosmetic surgery in relation to the defendant's rights in a tort case. In the trial of the tort case, after the cosmetic surgery performed by the defendant, KUN Hospital, the female plaintiff found red spots on her nose, for which she had to seek extra medical treatments. When the plaintiff filed a lawsuit against the defendant and claimed compensation related to the injury in her nose, the defendant denied such a claim, arguing that the surgery caused no injury. In Excerpt (3), competing conceptions of rights and duties through Appreciations of the clinical effect are observed in three steps.

Among the three topics under discussion, the first is the legality of the said surgery. In the first move, the plaintiff's lawyer expresses an affirmative Appreciation of the surgery through the choice of the past tense, "被告的行为构成了美容损害" (the defendant's act constituted medical malpractice in the cosmetic surgery), and proposes a solution with a modalized expression "应当承担损害赔偿责任" (shall be held liable for the injury compensation). In their interactive turn, the defense lawyer holds quite different positions. Demonstrating their Appreciation of the medical operation to be "成功的" (successful), the lawyer shows their denial in a relational process "既不存在伤害问题, 也不存在手术不成功的问题" (there was neither any injury nor any failure in the operation) and concludes with a polarized negation, denying the alleged legal liability. In addition to the first topic, contestation between the two parties occurs in two other topics, namely, the clinical effect and the validity of the presented evidence (medical treatment record). Affect and Appreciation are both employed in these contestations.

Conflicting conceptions of rights and duties are realized and manifested in lawyer evaluation in ideational meanings. They may be located in different processes of the transitivity system, where various elements of an event or narrative, such as participants (who), actions (what), circumstances (how), and purposes (why), are encoded differently in structure, modulation, and tense. Overall, competing views can be analyzed through the language used in lawyer evaluation.

5.2.2.2 Contesting Interests

As indicated in the triangle in Fig. 2.1 (Chap. 2), lawyers from opposing parties represent conflicting interests and, therefore, are situated in competition in the court. The plaintiff/prosecution has to prove that the defendant's action is against the law and request corresponding compensation or penalty related to such an action. In contrast, the defendant has to defend themselves against the charge/complaint and clarify their behaviors in the disputed act. Each side is destined to win the court's support in favor of its interest (Maley 1994). Discursively, the contesting interests between the two parties give rise to a competitive role relationship constructed in the trial talk, which, interpersonally, is observed both in the speech roles and the ongoing discourse relations.

Excerpt (4) (Turns 1–2 in M-S-Z-09) provides an excellent example to demonstrate lawyers' contest in speech roles and discourse roles. Firstly, the adversary relationship in speech roles is reflected sequentially in the accusation-reply adjacency pair of the conversation, especially in the cross-examination stage of the trial. In the first move, the plaintiff's lawyer takes the initiative to launch their "诉讼请求" (claims). In the second move, the defense lawyer interacts by providing a "答辩" (reply) to the claims. The claim-response sequence recursively comprises the whole trial talk. Secondly, evaluative viewpoints in contradictory positions are expressed through the adjacency pairs. The plaintiff's lawyer evaluatively considers the defendant the one to blame, which is conveyed in the use of the modulation "判令被告" (the defendant should be ordered to…). However, the defense lawyer Appreciates the responsibility differently by means of two polarized negations in clauses, "不构成" (does not constitute) and "没有客观依据" (has no factual basis). In this way, the two parties assume the discourse roles of arguers and counter-arguers, respectively. Conflict in the role relationship between the two sides is pervasive in all cases, such as in Excerpt (5) (Turns 1–2 in M-S-Z-10), which involves the tort case.

In addition to contest in speech roles, confrontation is also manifested when lawyers construct interpersonal relationships as discourse unfolds. A typical indication is the antagonistic use of the personal pronoun "你 (们)" (you). According to Kuo (2002), the use of the Chinese pronoun "你" (you) as a second-person singular in political discourse conveys a hostile relationship between interactants. A similar usage is observed in the courtroom discourse as in Excerpt (6) (Turns 1–2 in M-S-Z-08), which is related to a tort case.

In this case, the plaintiffs, three computer resellers, sued the defendant, the X Consumers Association, on the grounds of tort affecting reputation. In 2012, the defendant organized an experiment to check the radioactivity status of computers, and the computers produced by the three plaintiffs were chosen as part of the samples. In the experiment report issued later, the said computers of the plaintiffs were rated high in radioactivity, which means a high possibility of emitting harmful waves into the environment. The plaintiffs claimed in litigation that the defendant's behavior caused harm to the reputation associated with their products.

In this case, the social status between the two sides is strikingly asymmetrical. As business owners, the plaintiffs encountered a powerful defendant, who is a social organization standing for the large population of consumers in a local region of China. When the interests of business managers ran counter to those of the consumers' organization, the role relationship between the two was in great tension, which is reflected in two respects in text.

On the one hand, discord is noticed in lawyers' mutual perceptions of their contestants' roles. Remarkably, both parties address each other and are addressed in a hostile manner. An evident demonstration of the hostility is the antagonistic use of the second-person singular pronoun "你" (you) (Kuo 2002).

The plaintiffs' lawyer expresses explicit negative Judgements of the defendant in "你不能既当运动员, 又当裁判员" (you can not work as both athletes and referees) and critical attitudes toward the defendant in the clause "你既然起草了, 又为什么要去执法?……最起码的观点, 你怎么能执行这个法律?" (now that you are the drafter of the law, how could you be the executor of the law? … The simplest question is, how can you be the implementer of the law?) Meanwhile, the lawyer uses the first person singular pronoun "我" (I) in the clause "我…看不出"… (I cannot see…) to sharpen the fight between "我" (I) and "你" (you) (Arroyo 2000). In the subsequent discourse, the lawyer gives off a stronger sense of hostility in the use of the second person pronoun plural "你们" (you) when discussing topics regarding the function of the defendant. The speaker depreciates the function of the defendant in terms of Valuation with a low-value verb phrase "协调" (assist), and adds a meta-comment of contempt, "就这么回事" (that is all you can do). Intriguingly, the use of "你们" (*you* in plural form) in succession, "把你们的职责……你们的职能就是……这就是职能。……有了投诉, 你们协调一下" (your duties …Your function is to …Upon receiving complaints, you may mediate the negotiation process), accelerates the antagonism.

A similar use of the pronoun as an indication of antagonism is found in the defense's turn. The antipathy between the two parties is perceived in the contrast between "我" (I) and "你" (you), and in the repetition of the rhetorical question "我不知道你注意到了没有" (I do not know whether you have noticed). Meanwhile, negative Judgements of the plaintiffs are given blatantly in the clause "这个不是说, 就只有你一家" (this is not to say that you are the only one whose…) and subsequent utterances.

On the other hand, the contest between disputing lawyers is traced in the hostile Judgements of the personality of each party, as is shown in Excerpt (7) (Turns 3–6 in M-S-Z-08). To begin with, in Excerpt (7), the plaintiffs' lawyer negatively judges the defendant's character in terms of Social Sanction and Social Punishment. As indicated through lexical choices, the defendant is judged as malicious in sampling commodities. The verb *incite* in *the defendant* "指使" *(incited) its workers to buy the commodity* contains a strong derogatory meaning. It evokes the Judgement that the defendant was ill-purposed in its behaviors. The defendant's behaviors are also judged negatively in terms of Social Punishment in "违背其工作 (原则)" (in breach of its duties). What is conveyed is that the defendant is a law-breaking, untrustworthy organization.

Meanwhile, unfavorable evaluations of the defendant are accumulatively expressed. The alleged practice of buying commodities as ordinary customers do is appreciated as "陷阱取证" (trapping evidence), which, if proven, is strictly condemned as illegal in accordance with the law. Since it is unpleasant and improper for the defendant, as a public organization, to be associated with illegal activities, these negative Judgements of the defendant's behaviors, taken together, would be signs of degradation of the defendant's professional identity. In addition, the degradation is also shown in the derogatory idiomatic phrase "心知肚明" (been aware), concerning the motive of the testing. To counter these arguments from the plaintiffs, the defense positively evaluates their own behaviors through the intensified statement "完全是公益的" (utterly non-profitable).

Text analysis has shown that with conflicting interests in the trial, disputing lawyers tend to construct a confrontational role relationship between them. The manifestation of confrontation is pervasive in various aspects of the interpersonal meanings in text, including speech roles, terms of address, modality, polarity, lexis with connotative meanings, and other structures.

5.2.2.3 Competing Information Presentation

In the trial talk, where the legality of a social act is discussed, there are routine regulations to govern which evidence is admissible and which kinds of opinions are allowed (Yong et al. 2002). To win the case, disputing parties compete to present information favorable to their side.

Textually, competition in information presentation is reflected in the thematic structures and the thematic progression in the text co-created by both parties. In a sense, the textual meaning is more important for the realization of confrontation since it possesses the attribute of "enabling" other functions to come into play (Halliday 1978: 130). In line with the functional analysis of the textual meanings in text (Halliday 1994), the organization of textual structure can be investigated in the thematic structure of the text. Data analysis shows that confrontation between disputing lawyers in textual structure is mainly demonstrated in the thematic progression, such as the organization of Theme and Rheme, cohesion in lexical repetitions, and substitutions in discourse (see also Liao 2003). For an illustration, Excerpt (8), which relates to the physical injury case, is analyzed below.

Excerpt (8) (Turns 5–10 in M-S-Z-10) contains three rounds of contestation carried through the thematic progression in text. Whatever the plaintiff initiates, either topics in the place of the Theme or elaborations developed in the place of Rheme, is continued by the defense and arranged as the Theme of their responding speech and argued against in the place of Rheme in the textual structure of their speech. In the one-to-one correspondence, sharp distinctions in viewpoints are presented.

To begin with, divergences in information organization related to the topic, Exhibit No. 1, are presented. In the turn of the plaintiff's lawyer, "证据一, 广告信息一份" (Exhibit No. 1, one copy of the advertisement) is encoded as the Theme, the starting point of the information in the text. The development of the topic is put in the Rheme. See Table 5.1.

Table 5.1 Thematic structure in the plaintiff's discourse (Turn 5)

证据一, 广告信息一份 (No. 1, one copy of the advertisement)	所要证明的事项是…… (Proves two things…)
Theme	Rheme

In the defense's turn, the starting point of the information is also "证据一" (Exhibit No. 1), but the difference appears in Rheme (see Table 5.2). In this instance, what is developed in Rheme is a negative statement, contrary to that in the plaintiff's textual information in Table 5.1.

A comparison of the thematic structures in Tables 5.1 and 5.2 shows that in the first round of the contest on Exhibit No. 1, the theme in the defense's discourse is derived from that in the plaintiff's discourse. Accordingly, the thematic progression formed by the utterances of the two parties simply follows the pattern of "TP with a constant (continuous) Theme" in Danes' (1974) term.

In the second round of the contest, which is about Exhibit No. 2, the thematic organization is different from that of Exhibit No. 1. In the plaintiff's turn, what is placed in Theme is "证据二" (Exhibit No. 2), and the topic of the evidence is developed with two coordinating Rhemes, Rheme (1) and Rheme (2), each of which is divided further into micro-Themes and micro-Rhemes, marked as Theme_x and Rheme_x in Table 5.3.

Table 5.2 Thematic structure in the defense's discourse (Turn 6)

证据一 (Exhibit No. 1)	按复印件来看, 没有我KUN医院的名字…… (As observed in the photocopy of it, has no information of the defendant's name in it)
Theme	Rheme

Table 5.3 Thematic structure in the plaintiff's discourse (Turn 7)

<table>
<tr><td rowspan="2">证据二, …治疗单和…收费专业收据各一份
(Exhibit No. 2, one medical treatment record and one official medical examination receipt)</td><td colspan="4">证明事项 …… (proves two points)</td></tr>
<tr><td>一, 证明原, 被告双方之间
(Firstly, there …between the plaintiff and the defendant)</td><td>存在美容服务法律关系的事实
(Is a legal relationship as per the beauty contract)</td><td>第二, 证明原告
(Secondly, the plaintiff</td><td>向被告缴纳的手术费650元, 与被告广告宣传的收费标准不符
(Paid the defendant 650 yuan for the surgery fee, which is not consistent with the charge specified in the advertisement)</td></tr>
<tr><td rowspan="2">Theme</td><td>Theme₁</td><td>Rheme₁</td><td>Theme₂</td><td>Rheme₂</td></tr>
<tr><td colspan="2">Rheme (1)</td><td colspan="2">Rheme (2)</td></tr>
</table>

In the defense's turn, the lawyer maintains the information that the plaintiff has developed in Theme$_2$ and Rheme$_2$ and develops them further in their own textual structures, as shown in Tables 5.4 and 5.5.

In the defense's discourse, the topic "隆鼻术" (the nose augmentation operation) is developed in the predicated clause "确实收了650元, 这个没有争议" (did charge…indisputable). However, the information is expanded further. As shown in Table 5.5, the information concerning the topic "600元与650元, 这个" (between 600 and 650 yuan) is developed with a negation in "没有根本的很大的冲突" (no substantial difference).

Noticeably, in the defense's coding in Table 5.5, the inserted conditional clause, "如果这个广告是乾坤医院的" (if the advertisement is indeed from the KUN Hospital), is coded as the topical Theme of the utterance. The defense acknowledges the plaintiff's point in Rheme$_2$ of Turn 7 as a worthy topic and retains it as the topic of their utterance. However, they put it in question in the first place.

As is indicated in Tables 5.3, 5.4, and 5.5, the thematic organization in the second round of the contest is patterned in what Danes (1974) called "simple linear progression", where each Rheme in the preceding utterance becomes the Theme in the current utterance.

The third round of the contest, which relates to "证据三" (Exhibit No. 3), has the same thematic organization as does the first round. In general, when presenting evidence, opposing lawyers display their conflict in the thematic progression and the placement of Theme and Rheme in their utterances. What is packaged in the Theme or developed in the Rheme by the plaintiff is responded to and packaged by the defense as in the place of Theme in their speech. Then, in the defense' turn, those packaged as the Theme are argued against again. In successive transmissions of information from Theme to Rheme, conflicting viewpoints are exchanged.

Along with thematic progressions, other devices, such as antonyms and cohesive links, also coordinate to convey competition in information and contestation between the two parties. Readers may refer to Excerpt (8) (Turns 5–10 in M-S-Z-10) for more examples.

Table 5.4 Thematic structure in the defense's discourse (Turn 8: Move 1)

隆鼻术 (The nose augmentation operation)	确实收了650元, 这个, 没有争议 (Did charge the defendant 650 yuan, which is indisputable)
Theme	Rheme

Table 5.5 Thematic structure in the defense's discourse (Turn 8: Move 2)

如果这个广告是KUN医院的 (If the advertisement is indeed from the KUN Hospital)	600元与650元 (600 or 650 yuan)	这个没有根本的很大的冲突 (There is no substantial difference between them)
Theme	Theme$_1$	Rheme$_1$
	Rheme	

In summary, data analysis proves that with the impact of the context of situation in the courtroom, lawyers display conflicting conceptions of rights and duties, contesting interests, and competing information presentation when they present their evaluative attitudes regarding various issues in the trial. The confrontation is reflected in the three functions of language in text, the ideational, the interpersonal, and the textual meanings.

5.3 Lawyer Evaluation in the Legal Culture

In the preceding section, investigations into the situational context in the courtroom have made evident that, generally, the presentation of lawyer evaluation is centered on confrontation. However, if we transcend "the immediate context" of the courtroom and draw upon descriptions of the broader context of legal culture (Halliday 1985: 46–47), we may interpret more specifically how lawyers present their evaluative attitudes in the confrontational environment of the Chinese court.

The context of culture, in Halliday's term, is an all-embracing term that covers many issues such as social structure, ideology, and material culture (Halliday 1978: 68). What is meant by culture in this research is the legal ideology concerning how an effective courtroom discussion should be conducted. As has been reviewed in Chap. 2 and elaborated in Chap. 3, the predominant legal ideology in the current legal context of China is the intersubjective view of law and legal communication in the theory of Habermas. The communication theory of law plays a vital role in understanding lawyer evaluation in the Chinese courtroom.

5.3.1 Habermasian Law and Rational Confrontation Between Lawyers

The essence of the Habermasian legal theory is a procedural view of law or, more precisely, an intersubjective view of the law. For any law to be called legitimate, it has to be rationally agreed on its acceptance. The only way to determine whether norms and values can gain the rational agreement of all those impacted is by looking at it from a broader perspective that includes the viewpoints of all individuals involved. The broader perspective may integrate "the perspectives of other participants' world-view and self-understanding in a manner that is neither coercive nor distorting" (Habermas 1996: 228). Any decision on a disputable issue has to go through the dialogical process of argumentation before it is accepted as a norm. Accordingly, Habermas proposes a set of criteria that he believes must be met in order for judicial arguments to be considered rationally accepted, and he outlines the structure of the argumentative process that must take place in order to arrive at this rational acceptance (Habermas 1996: 226).

If the argumentation process is to be conducted rationally, there are some "idealizing" presuppositions regarding the communicators in legal settings (Habermas 1996). Accordingly, all participants share the common aim of reaching agreement with regard to the validity of any disputed claim; meanwhile, they may engage in the discussion equally and intensively, with no force except that of the better argument exerted, no competent parties been excluded from the discussion, and no relevant argument been suppressed knowingly; lastly, they have to present arguments or counter-arguments based on reasons and justifications and organize their speech in regulated contest (Cooke 1998: 4–5; Habermas 1996: 230). Needless to say, in the process of communication, the choice of the same language is vital for participants because it guarantees mutual understanding in discussion. Considering that lawyers are all legal professionals, who speak in the same way, the requirement of the same linguistic expression in a general sense is not relevant in this study. These three conditions are called idealizing in the sense that "they are typically counterfactual and will not, as a rule, be satisfied more than approximately" (Cooke 1998: 4). At the same time, these conditions are unavoidable because they belong to the very meaning of what it is to take part in argumentation (Cooke 1998: 5). To put it straight, though largely counterfactual, they are necessary preconditions for the success of communicative action and also for the success of rational communication between lawyers in the court debate (Habermas 1996: 229).

These idealizing presuppositions are inspiring for understanding the courtroom communication between lawyers. Under these presuppositions, "the communicative actor undertakes the obligation to provide reasons for the validity of the claims they raise with their utterances, while the counterpart in action may either accept the preferred reasons or challenge them on the basis of better reasons" (Cooke 1998: 4). Viewed in this way, the interpersonal relationship between lawyers in the court tends to be one of solidarity and cooperation (Beaugrande 1997).

In the Habermasian view of the structure of legal argumentation, the presentation of lawyer evaluation in a court follows requirements in the following aspects: first of all, lawyers from disputing parties share the same purpose of reaching an agreement on the resolution of a legal dispute by referring to their shared "lifeworld"—the "judicial knowledge" (Phillips 2003: 140); secondly, mutual respect and equal concern is given to the perspective of all concerned in a case; thirdly, during the argumentation conducted in a regulated contest, as a communicative actor, lawyers undertake the obligation to provide reasons for the validity of the claims they raise, while their opposing counterparts may either accept the reasons or challenge them on the basis of better reasons. These three aspects guide lawyers to present their evaluations properly in the conflictual context of the trial talk. Since rationality is the core of the legal theory of Habermas, lawyer evaluation shaped under these constraints is designated as the rational discourse of lawyer evaluation in this study. The impact of these three aspects of rationality on lawyer evaluation can be described in the detailed data analysis below.

5.3.2 Lawyer Evaluation in Rational Confrontation

5.3.2.1 Graded Interpretations of Legal Cases

In the legal communicative process, any cooperative search for the resolution of a dispute is to be made against the common background of lawyer talk (Habermas 1996: 229). In order to discuss the implications and meanings of the rights and duties of each party in a legal dispute, one particular perspective should not be considered to be the "single right" decision unconditionally. Instead, participants have to consider the perspectives of others, including the opposing party's view and the universal perspective of the general public. When the perspectives of the opponents and the general public are drawn together, there will not be "single right" viewpoints but a gradable perception of the issue concerned in the legal dispute. In this way, although conflict remains in the case, various opinions may rationally stand to each other.

Ideationally, the rational confrontation between disputing lawyers means graded evaluations may occur regarding the various issues in a trial (Zhang 2011). Firstly, every claim or evaluative attitude presented in court must be supported by reasons based on the factual basis or the law. Secondly, the issues may be evaluated to varying degrees based on the strength and relevance of the reasons supporting them.

Excerpt (9) No. X-D-030

公诉人: ……被告人C某的行为已构成杀人罪 被代: 虽然C某作为一个正常的成年公民其行为已触犯了法律, 但在共同犯罪中只起到了次要作用, 是从犯	Prosecutor: The act of defendant C has constituted the crime of **murder** DL: As a normal adult citizen, defendant C has **violated the law with his actions.** But he only played a subordinate role as an **accomplice in the joint crime**

In this excerpt, the prosecution charged the defendant with murder. In rebuttal, the defense presents a slightly different evaluation of the alleged action of the defendant. At the very beginning, without attending to the ideational meaning of "murder", the defense lawyer just acknowledges the defendant's action is illegal, "触犯了法律" (violat[ing] the law). In contrast to the specific term of the crime "杀人罪" (murder), violating the law sounds more like a general, vague determination or a rough super-ordinate. Using the super-ordinate allows the defense to make a graded evaluation of the alleged act, which is anchored on the role the defendant plays in the crime. In the semantic field of the term "crime", the lawyer chooses the sub-category of "共同犯罪" (joint crime) and takes one hyponym/subordinate "从犯" (accomplice) to convey their evaluation of the defendant in terms of Social Punishment. Moreover, the lawyer supports their evaluative attitude with a justification in the clause "只起到了次要作用" (only played a subordinate role). As it is, the defense lawyer not only grades their evaluation about the viewpoints of the opposing party but also provides justifications to support their graded evaluation. In this way, a rational argument is delivered.

Excerpt (10) No. X-D-026

公诉人: 被告人在工作中有多次受贿行为……	Prosecutor: The defendant took bribes many times in his work …
被代: ……被告人在工作期间, 虽然有错误和失误, 但对当地的经济发展, 市政建设还是做了一些有益的工作	DL: …When the defendant was in office, he still made some contributions to the economic development and infrastructure construction, though he had **mistakes and malpractices**

What is directly evaluated in Excerpt (10) is the defendant's work during his term in office. The prosecutor Appreciates the defendant's act negatively in "多次受贿行为" (taking bribes many times). Different from the prosecution, the defense lawyer appreciates the defendant's work positively in "有益的工作" (some contributions).

What is impressive in this conflict is the defense lawyer's skillful coding of their evaluative attitude. First of all, the defendant's contribution is placed in the main clause and thus highlighted as new information. Meanwhile, the alleged action of the defendant is skillfully packaged in the diction of "错误和失误" (mistakes and malpractices), which, as general words, contains less semantic force ideationally. The graded meaning addresses the prosecution's viewpoint and rebuts it at the same time. At last, the negative evaluation toward the defendant is placed in the concessive clause "虽然……" (though…), in contrast to his "有益的工作" (some contributions) in the main clause. This grammatical coding reduces the negative effect of the defendant's behaviors and reinforces the positive part instead.

A more dynamic and complex example of rational confrontation is observed in the negotiation of contested criteria for determining what it means for two trademarks to be "identical" in Excerpt (11) (Turns 5–11 in M-S-Z-09). In the absence of regulations specifying what kind of resemblance between the trademarks can be called "similar", the determination relies on common-sense perception and interpretation. As a result, the process of discussing the level of resemblance between two trademarks becomes a central point of contention and negotiation in the legal dispute.

The contestation regarding criteria for "being identical" is initiated when the plaintiff Appreciates the disputed act. To begin with, the plaintiff asserts that the infringement is self-evident, and the criterion for infringement is common knowledge. This assertion is conveyed in their expressions that the case facts are "清楚" (clear) and the alleged act is "明知的" (deliberate). In both evaluative expressions, the plaintiff's lawyer takes "他的侵权" (the infringement by the opposing party) as a presumption which needs no testing of reason.

In the defense's turn, the lawyer barks at the assumed evaluation, the infringement. To back up their position that the alleged act "不构成商标的侵权" (does not constitute an infringement), the defense refers to legal regulations concerning the concept of the trademark in law, as in "对于商标的这个概念和定义, 法律都有明确规定" (there are specific regulations regarding the concept and definition of the term *trademark*). Intriguingly, the accurate location or source of the regulation is not provided in their speech. In terms of this vaguely designated "明确规定" (specific regulation), the lawyer loosely phrases the concept of the trademark as "图形和文字的组合" (combination of graphics and words). The vague definition enables the defense to explore the ideational meanings in the "相同与相似" (identical or similar) between the two trademarks. In line with the vague and broad concept, the defense argues in an intensified manner that "它不可能是相同的, 相同不存在" (it is impossible for the two to be identical. There is nothing identical between the two), based on "从图形和文字的组合, 从双方的商标对比来看" (a comparison of the two trademarks in terms of the combination of graphics and words). As is shown, the definition of the trademark enables the defense to negotiate the criteria for the "infringement" in terms of "identical between the two". It is justifiable for the defense to do so since, conceptually, the meaning of the "相同" (identical) is a matter of degree.

The plaintiff insists, in their turn of speech, that the alleged act does constitute an infringement, which has already been established in the stage of court investigation. In this situation, the plaintiff emphasizes the fact "被告……使用新杨妃文字以及拼音" (the defendant used the Chinese characters XIN YANG FEI and the pinyin…) and deems it the default criterion for infringement. This criterion is indicated in the coding of the logical meaning in the clauses, "这个事实……是已经得到确认的。所以我们认为呢, 对方的侵权事实呢, 也是已经成立的" (this fact has already been ascertained …. Therefore, we think that ... infringement has already been established). In their subsequent turn, the defense firmly clings to the position of "being identical" and reinforces the evaluation from their side. The lawyer contends once again that there is no infringement because "我单位的商标与原告的商标没有任何的相同和相似之处" (our trademark has nothing identical or similar to the plaintiff's). Encountered with the defense's reinforced evaluation of the criterion for "being identical", the plaintiff's lawyer forwards a more specific criterion, the regulation of Article 50(1) in the Rules for the Implementation of the Trademark Law. By means of this, the lawyer is able to extend the criterion from "being identical" to "being identical or similar", which covers a more flexible space of "being alike" between two trademarks.

As such, the defense's contested categorization of the criterion is frustrated. According to the available data, it appears that the defense has abandoned the argument regarding the definition of "相同" (identical) and shifted their focus to advancing their case in a different manner. As seen from the use of the modal expression "我觉得, 应该以" (what I mean is, we should), the defense is compelled to argue on which rule should be referred to when determining infringement. Consequently, the plaintiff replies in an affirmative tone that "本案呢…是符合这一规定的" (this case does fit in with those regulations) and justifies the point by the logical meanings arranged between the several events.

The above analysis outlines how rational argumentation exerts its effect on lawyer evaluation in ideational meanings. In short, lawyer evaluation in rational confrontation is realized in graded evaluations regarding the significant issues in a trial talk.

5.3.2.2 Equal Participation in the Trial Talk

In accordance with the Habermasian statements of the speakers' role relationships in legal communication, equal concern shall be given to all who are affected, and all parties concerned shall equally participate in the trial talk. Interpersonally, the construction of an equal interpersonal relationship between lawyers and a multi-voice discourse environment in legal communication is indicative of lawyers' awareness of integrating different perspectives into an enlarged one.

In Excerpt (11) (Turns 5–11 in M-S-Z-09), three points are worth attention. Firstly, the pronominal choice, *we*, *you*, and *they*, indicates the speaker's perceived role relationship of mutual respect and recognition. Secondly, multiple voices are engaged in the dynamic interaction of the court debate. Thirdly, alignment and alienation are conducted through lawyer evaluation.

First of all, the pronominal choice manifests the speakers' effort in constructing an equal relationship with the other participants in the court. These personal pronouns are to be explained functionally in two aspects. On the one hand, the co-occurrence of the three plural pronouns symbolizes a less intense confrontation between them than when the singular pronouns of *I* versus *you* are used (Arroyo 2000; Kuo 2002). The pronoun, "我们" (we), is the self-referential address used by the speaking lawyer to designate their side as a collective unit. As referential addresses, the pronouns in plural form, "你们" (you) and "他们" (they) are both employed. The term "你们" (you) is used to designate the addressee when the speaking lawyer directly converses with the opposing lawyer, and "他们" (they) is employed to refer to the opposing lawyers when the speaking lawyer talks to the judge. Both the plaintiff and the defense use these plural personal pronouns in the same way. Comparatively, such a designation reduces the tension between the lawyers from opposing parties in person (Arroyo 2000; Hyland 2002; Kuo 2002). The pronominal choice suggests, therefore, that the two disputing sides have equal interactional roles at the trial.

On the other hand, the inclusive first-person plural pronoun "我们" is deployed to construct a community of legal professionals in the debate, or "colleagiacy" in Gaines' (2002) term. When quoting the specific rule of the trademark law, the plaintiff points out that "我们呢这属于是同一种商品上" (it is in the same goods in our case). In this context, "我们" (we) refers to a collective unit including the plaintiff as the speaker, the defense, and the judge as the addressees. The same usage of the pronoun "我们" (we) occurs in the defense's speech, for instance, when the defense lawyer proposes that "应该以商标法, 以及最高人民法院所颁布的有关司法解释作为我们审判的依据" (we should take the rules in the Trademark Law and the relevant interpretations issued by the Supreme Court as the guidelines for determining this case). Evidently, in this context, the pronoun "我们" (we) is used in a more inclusive sense, including both the defense, the judge, and the plaintiff. The inclusive plural personal pronoun "我们" (we) thus helps to construct a different "ongoing discourse role-relationship" between the three major participants in court (Wang 2001) or the perceived interactional role relationship between them. With the pronoun "我们" (we), the three major participants are encoded to belong to a community of legal professionals sharing more similarities than differences. Accordingly, diverse perspectives are transformed into the perspective of the first person plural (Habermas 1996: 229). Noticeably, an equal relationship may have been constructed between them in text.

Secondly, multiple voices can be projected in the interaction. First of all, the opposing parties are dialogically engaged in the trial. For instance, in the first turn, when presenting their evaluative attitude, the plaintiff draws their speech in close connection with the voice of the defense. In "而且被告代理人也已经承认了, 他们当时在采用这个新杨妃的这个称呼的时候, 也是考虑到有一个杨妃在先" (the defense lawyer has admitted that when they decided to use the name XIN YANG FEI, they were aware that there had been a brand-name YANG FEI), the voice of the defense is projected through the projecting verb "承认" (admitted). In other words, the voice of the defendant is introduced into the discourse and given the place to develop. Thus, it is evident that the plaintiff has a dialogical engagement with the defense.

Meanwhile, a similar dialogical engagement with the opponents is found in the defense's utterance. In the defense's turn, the lawyer begins by mentioning the position of the plaintiff, as in "对于原告所谓使用商标条例里的这一规定" (regarding the rule that the plaintiff proposes). The thematic structure of the defense' utterance is striking because the multiple and marked Theme functions not only maintain topic coherence but also indicate evaluative or interpersonal standpoints and logical frameworks, which can help identify which argument and evidence is valued.

In addition, the external voice of the law is also engaged in the dialogue. Both lawyers refer to regulations in law when they develop their own positions. For instance, the voice of the law is found in the plaintiff's quotation of Article 50(1) of the Trademark Law.

Along with the dialogical engagement of the voices mentioned above, the voice of the court is also present. For example, the plaintiff draws the voice of the judge into the speech of their side by means of the adjunct "已经" (already) in the clause, "经过刚才的法庭调查呢是已经得到确认的" (has been already ascertained in the court investigation). Co-textually, with the adjunct, the stance that the judge may have expressed in the court investigation is called to attention. All in all, a discourse environment where multi-voices are available in the speech is constructed gradually. This construction textually reflects what Habermas says: equal concerns are given to different viewpoints.

Thirdly, evident traces of alignment and alienation in the multi-voiced discourse environment are observed as the trial interaction moves on. The defense lawyer alienates their contestants by countering their arguments. For example, the defense Appreciates negatively the relation between the two brands, as in "没有任何的相同和相似之处" (nothing identical or similar) to each other. With this negative Appreciation, the defense implicitly denies the plaintiff's claim. In this way, the plaintiff is textually distanced and alienated from the community of legal professionals. At the same time, efforts to align with the judge are noticed. By the use of the pronominal choice, such as "we" in the clause "作为我们审判的依据" (we should …as the guidelines for determining this case), the defense lawyer attempts to establish solidarity with the judge, which is evidenced by the accompany of the lawyer's body movement (turning to face the judge).

Data analysis of Excerpt (12) (Turns 12–14 in M-S-Z-09) in terms of the pronominal choice and the voices recognizable in the text provides another example to illustrate how rational confrontation between lawyers can be observed. What is eye-catching in this excerpt is the combined use of alignment and alienation when lawyers discuss contested criteria related to the infringement quantity.

In the infringement case, estimating the financial loss is a very crucial factor for compensation. Accordingly, it becomes a crucial site of contestation between the two sides. As both parties try to draw the empathy of the judge to their side, similar strategies to achieve such purposes are observed. Both parties have attempted to align the judge and the audiences and alienate the opponents, but divergence occurs in the discursive means they employ.

The plaintiff's claim, a compensation of 300,000 yuan, which is based on a series of "rough" figures like "大概" (about) 2000 bags per day, runs into challenge from the defense, who states that "我方表示疑义" (we have doubts). To negotiate an alternative determination of the figure, the defense employs Appreciations as follows. First of all, the lawyer makes a negation of the claim in terms of Composition, "构成依据不存在" (there is no supportive evidence). Meanwhile, the lawyer Appreciates negatively the supportive figures in terms of Reaction by asserting that "这个推算数字也不符合情理" (the estimation does not fit in with the common-sense perception). Their appeal to Appreciation in terms of Reaction is made more evident in the concessive clause, "即使是一天有……, 也不可能是……" (even though there were ... single day, it is impossible that ...). Moreover, through a conditional clause, "如果有六万袋的话" (if it is claimed to be 60,000 bags), the lawyer exposes the "logical fallacy" (Qin 1998) buried in the plaintiff's legal argument. Then, the defense presents their position to the court by arguing that "必须有依据" (there must be evidence to support it). Above all, the defense lawyer's appeal to Appreciation is made forceful and predominant. It works both to alienate the contestants and align the judges at the same time. The defense distances and alienates the opposing party as a community with alien viewpoints by exposing the pitfalls in the plaintiff's viewpoints, and attempts to influence the position of the judge by proving that their own position is worthy of attention. What is presented before the audiences is a dyadic of changes in role relationships. Initially, the judge is merely a third party, aloof to both parties. Now, with the lawyer's Appreciation in argumentation, the judge may be drawn to be the persuadee and co-interactant.

Similarly, the plaintiff's lawyer tries to construct an ally with the judge through Judgment and Appreciation regarding the criteria for compensation. However, Appreciation is expressed in terms of Valuation rather than Reaction. Firstly, the lawyer presents a negative Judgement of the defendant's character in terms of Social Punishment, as in the phrases "拒不提供" (refus[ing] to present) and "明显虚假" (apparently false). With this negative Judgement, the defense may be distanced and pulled away from the judge. By quoting the legal regulation of Article 56 in the trademark law, the plaintiff's lawyer draws the judge close to the Valuation of their claim within the framework of law and concludes, therefore, that their claim of compensation "应该" (shall) be "应当的" (legitimate) and "有理有据的" (reasonable and well-supported).

In summary, under the constraints of the Habemasian views of legal communication, different perspectives shall be integrated into an enlarged perspective of the first-person plural. Discursively, full and equal participation of all those affected is realized in the trial talk. As illustrated in the data, the rational confrontation between lawyers in interpersonal meanings is demonstrated in the use of pronominal choice, the co-existence of different voices in discourse, and the construction of aligning in the trial talk.

5.3.2.3 Presentations of Information in the Regulated Contest

The essential intuition in the practice of dialogical argumentation in law is characterized by participants' expectation of winning the assent of a universal audience to a proposition in a rational but regulated contest, and the way for such a result depends on presenting arguments supported with reasons (Habermas 1996: 228). In the trial talk, disputing parties have to present their information in a regulated way, though they have diverse and adverse information to present. Alongside the sequential organization of the trial talk (Atkinson and Drew 1990), there are rules on who speaks first and who speaks next. Discursively, through the orderly organization of the interaction in text, the rational confrontation between lawyers regarding presenting evidence and arguments is realized and manifested. The information proposed by one party is maintained by the other party and responded to in the following utterance. The pattern of information organization is typically captured in the thematic progression in the functional sense.

For an illustration, the thematic progression in Excerpt (13) (Turns 12–14 in M-S-Z-09) will be sketched. In the first move, the plaintiff's lawyer textures "这个侵权数量" (this infringement quantity) as the Hyper-Theme and expands the topic in the predicated clause (Rheme), "应该可以作为本案的这种赔偿的定案依据的" (should be taken as the evidence for the determination of compensation in this case). In their turn of response, the defense packages their information textually in the following way. The lawyer encodes their doubts toward the plaintiff's argument, "对于刚才原告方关于三十万损失的证据, 我方表示疑义" (as for the plaintiff's evidence in support of their claim for 300,000 yuan in compensation, we have some doubts) in the hyper-Theme and their justification or elaboration of their attitude in the Rheme. In their subsequent turn, the plaintiff's party organizes their information in the form of a request, where the court is encoded as the addressee. The lawyer puts the request "在被告……的情况下, 法院应该采纳我们这方提供的证据" (under the circumstances that the defendant…, the court should take the information we present as evidence) in the Hyper-Theme of their text and justifies the request in the Rheme.

The thematic progression in Excerpt (13) may be diagrammatically shown in Fig. 5.1.

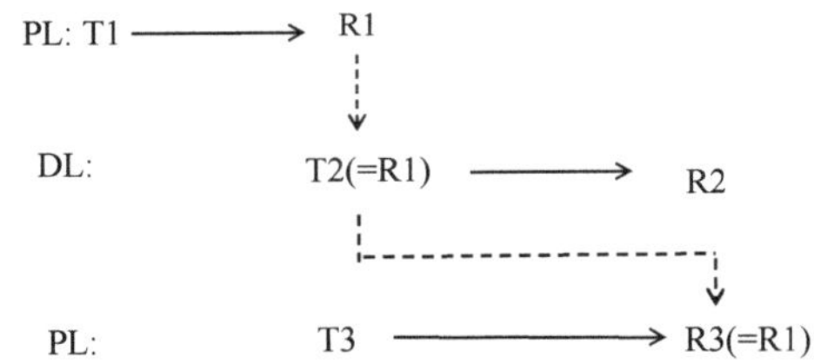

Fig. 5.1 Thematic progression in Excerpt (13)

As indicated, with the thematic progression, the divergent information between the disputing parties is displayed in an orderly and regulated way, and the competition between the two sides progresses as texts unfold.

5.4 Summary

This chapter has analyzed how the contextual features of the courtroom in China exert their impact on lawyer evaluation in text. Constrained by the context of situation in court, confrontation becomes a striking feature of the interpersonal relationship between disputing lawyers in the trial talk. This feature finds reflections in the three functions of language in text, ideational, interpersonal, and textual meanings. With the mediating role of the context of legal culture, specifically, the Habermasian statements on legal argumentation via communicative action, disputing lawyers tend to contest with each other in a rational manner. Rational confrontation permeates the three functions of language in text.

The discussion of rational confrontation in this chapter is no more than a brief sketch on the whole. A more detailed and thorough analysis of how lawyer evaluation is discursively organized in the rational discourse is to be followed in Chaps. 6 and 7.

References

Arroyo, J.L.B. 2000. Mire usetd Sr. Gonzales... personal deixis in Spanish political-electoral debate. *Journal of Pragmatics* 32: 1–27. https://doi.org/10.1093/applin/23.2.215.

Atkinson, R.C., and P. Drew. 1990. *Order in court*. Hampshire and London: Macmillan Academic and Professional Ltd.

Cooke, M. 1998. Introduction. In *On the pragmatics of communication*, ed. M. Cooke, 1–20. Cambridge: MIT Press.

Danes, F. 1974. Functional sentence perspective and the organization of the text. In *Papers on functional sentence perspective*, ed. F. Danes, 106–128. The Hague: Mouton.

de Beaugrande, R. 1997. *New foundations for a science of text and discourse: Cognition, communication and the freedom of access to knowledge and society*. Norwood: ABLEX.

Francis, G., and A. Kramer-Danhl. 1992. Grammaticalizing the medical case history. In *Language, text and context*, ed. M. Toolan, 56–90. London & New York: Routledge.

Gaines, P. 2002. Negotiating power at the bench. *Forensic Linguistics: The International Journal of Speech, Language and Law* 9 (2): 213–234. https://doi.org/10.1558/sll.2002.9.2.213.
Habermas, J. 1996. *Between facts and norms*, trans. William Rehg. Cambridge: MIT.
Halliday, M.A.K. 1978. *Language as social semiotic*. London: Edward Arnold.
Halliday, M.A.K. 1985. Text, context, and learning. In *Language, context and text*, ed. M.A.K. Halliday and R. Hasan, 44–51. Oxford: Oxford University Press.
Halliday, M.A.K. 1994. *Introduction to functional grammar*. London: Edward Arnold.
Hyland, K. 2002. Directives: Argument and engagement in academic writing. *Applied Linguistics* 23 (2): 215–239. https://doi.org/10.1093/applin/23.2.215.
Kuo, Sai-hua. 2002. From solidarity to antagonism: The uses of the second-person singular pronoun in Chinese political discourse. *Text* 22 (1): 29–55. https://doi.org/10.1515/text.2002.004.
Liao, Mei-zhen. 2003. 法庭审判问答推理分析 [Argumentation in questions and answers of the courtroom]. In *New perspectives on language and the law* [语言与法律研究的新视野], ed. Qinsheng Zhou, Jie Wang, and Jinzhi Su, 202–212. Beijing: Law Press.
Maley, Y. 1994. The language of the law. In *Language and the law*, ed. J. Gibbons, 11–50. London: Longman.
Phillips, A. 2003. *Lawyer's language: How and why legal language is different*. London and New York: Routledge.
Qin, Pu. 1998. 律师实用口才 [*Professional speech for lawyers*]. Beijing: Law Press.
Wang, Jian-hua. 2001. 话语礼貌与语用距离 [Discursive politeness and pragmatic distance]. 外国语 [*Journal of Foreign Languages*] (5): 25–31.
Wang, Jie. 2004. 控辩式法庭审判互动语言探索 [Exploring the interactive language in an adversarial trial]. 语言文字应用 [*Applied Linguistics*] (3): 75–82. https://doi.org/10.16499/j.cnki.1003-5397.2004.03.016
Yong, Q., Cheng-guang Jin, and Rong-mao Yao. (2002). 法律适用中的逻辑 [*Logic in law application*]. Beijing: China University of Political Science and Law.
Zhang, Li-ping. 2005. 庭审叙事的对立与诉讼对抗: 话语分析对法官的启示 [Confrontation and contest in the courtroom narrative: Implications of discourse analysis for trial judges]. 山东外语教学 [*Journal of Foreign Language Research in Shandong*] (5): 12–15. https://doi.org/10.16482/j.sdwy37-1026.2005.05.006
Zhang, Li-ping. 2011. Arguing with otherness: Intertextual construction of the attorney stance in the Chinese courtroom. *Text and Talk* (6): 753–769. https://doi.org/10.1515/TEXT.2011.036

Chapter 6
Lawyer Evaluation as Rational Discourse

Abstract This chapter discusses in detail how lawyers construct their rational stance in relation to the opposing lawyers and the judges. The rational discourse, which consists of three features, is constructed through lawyer evaluation in various ways. First of all, by evaluating the common ground or the "life-world" shared by participants in the court, lawyers build an equal role relationship with the other participants. Secondly, by projecting and acknowledging the various voices of the participants and the audiences in the court, they construct a multi-voiced environment, which is necessary for legal communication to be carried out. Thirdly, in the heteroglossic environment, lawyers polarize their attitudes with respect to their contestants' positions and various issues in the trial and eventually develop two distinct discursive communities of *us* versus *them*.

6.1 Introduction

This chapter is devoted to an investigation of how lawyers position themselves rationally in discourse by means of lawyer evaluation in China's current legal system. The central research question is: How do lawyers construct, in the adversary trial, cooperative and rational interpersonal relationships with other participants by means of lawyer evaluation? Precisely, how do lawyers position themselves in relation to opposing lawyers, judges, and other audiences?

As elaborated in the theoretical discussions of the contextual constraints of the courtroom on the language used in lawyer evaluation in Chap. 3, the rational discourse of lawyer evaluation consists of three aspects: an equal role relationship, a multi-voiced environment, and distinct discursive communities of *us* versus *them*. These three aspects may emerge sequentially, but they may work coordinately and simultaneously so as to contribute to the construction of lawyers' rational speech. The rational discourse is mainly achieved through lawyer evaluation regarding topics in the two levels: the opposing party's viewpoints (coded as FT_O) and various issues of the trial (including FD, FT_A, and FT_S).

L. Zhang, *Lawyer Evaluation in Chinese Courtroom*,
https://doi.org/10.1007/978-981-97-1211-3_6

To explore how the rational discourse is discursively constructed in text through lawyer evaluation, this chapter will conduct a detailed discourse analysis of the data.

6.2 An Equal Role Relationship

In the Tenor of the courtroom talk, the participants' social status is quite different. As was indicated in the isosceles triangle (Fig. 2.1), situated hierarchically below the judge, disputing lawyers are confrontational with each other since they represent different interests. How can lawyers create a relationship in roles that would contribute to the argumentation process? According to Habermas (1996: 230), participants share the same aim of reaching an agreement with regard to the validity of disputed claims, and no force except that of a better argument is exerted. All participants enjoy equal status in trial communication. In line with these views, lawyers can construct an equal role relationship by making positive evaluations on various topics, including those conceptions they share in common and the life-world they share as members of the community of legal professionals.

6.2.1 Underlining the Common Ground

To begin with, lawyers present positive evaluations of the common ground they have with their opposing party. By establishing shared evaluative attitudes, they construct all participants to be equal contestants in the trial talk. Typical examples are pervasive in criminal trials, as in Excerpt (1).

Excerpt (1) No. X-D-024

被代: 在目前党内外视反腐倡廉为 "生死抉择"之机, 关注及呼吁加大反腐倡廉力度, 运用法律手段有效扼 (遏) 制国家机关工作人员有法不依, 执法不严, 滥用职权, 玩忽职守问题, 是辩护人与公诉人的共识	DL: It is a **shared understanding between** the defense and the prosecution that in the current situation where anti-corruption is regarded as a life or death decision both inside and outside the Party, attention and advocacy should be paid to strengthening anti-corruption efforts, and legal means should be used to effectively curb issues such as the government officials' disregard of the law, lax enforcement of the law, abuse of power and dereliction of duties

In this episode, the defense lawyer expresses their attitude regarding the social function of the law in society. Unequivocally, the lawyer positively Appreciates the viewpoint "关注及呼吁……运用法律手段有效……" (attention and advocacy should be… and legal means should be used…) as "共识" (a shared understanding). Their affirmative attitude is highlighted in the relational process "……是……" (…is…). Underlining the common ground between the disputing parties opens up the possibility that the two parties are equal in discourse roles in trial communication.

The social function of the law in safeguarding the social order and protecting security and peace is often acknowledged and positively received in criminal trials. Meanwhile, it may be skillfully employed when lawyers discuss issues susceptible to biases or prejudices, such as the measurement of a penalty.

Excerpt (2) No. X-D-026

被代: 作为辩护人, 我们希望二审法庭对被告人的主动坦白情节应当充分肯定, 量刑时应当充分体现。少杀一个人是小事, 维护党的威信, 体现党的政策, 取信于群众, 取信于犯罪人是大事	DL: As the defense, we hope that the court of appeal should give full consideration to the defendant's voluntary confession and impose a penalty accordingly. Sparing an individual is less important than maintaining the credibility of the Party, enforcing the Party's policies, gaining the trust of the public, and addressing the concerns of criminals

In this excerpt, the lawyer requests the judge to impose a less severe penalty on the defendant on account of the latter's voluntary confession. The speaker first foregrounds their speech role as the "辩护人" (the defense) and then proposes a less severe penalty represented in a modalized statement "二审法庭对……应当充分肯定, 量刑时应当充分体现" (the court of appeal should give full consideration to …a penalty accordingly). To justify the legitimacy of their position and role, the lawyer provides two distinct evaluations of the goals of the law in the trial. What is of significance here is that the two Appreciations are placed in harmony with each other. Sparing the defendant, which concerns the interest of the defendant, is evaluated as minor in the phrase "小事" (less important). The credibility, the policy of the Party, and other things shown in the clauses "维护党的威信, 体现党的政策, 取信于群众, 取信于犯罪人" (maintaining the credibility of the Party, enforcing the Party's policies, gaining the trust of the public and addressing the concerns of criminals), which reflect the basic principle of the law in society, are evaluated as a significant issue. Such an affirmative evaluation of the social function of the law enables the defense to demonstrate a stance similar to that of the prosecution.

In addition to the general social function of the law, the basic principles of a trial are also evaluated as a consensus, which helps to construct disputing parties as arguers adopting the same stance.

Excerpt (3) No. X-D-024

被代: 公诉机关提到: 权力的滥用是……没有依法行事。因此, 在如何认定X某徇私舞弊滥用职权案问题上, 依法行事将是控辩审三方的共识 基于辩护人的法定职责是据实依法表明公诉人的指控是否成立的辩护意见, 提出有利于被告人的材料和意见, 以利法庭兼听则明。辩护人的诉讼职能、角度与公诉人虽有所区别, 但在寻求依法办事, 通过法律手段依法制裁……犯罪问题上的根本目的是一致的	DL: The prosecution has pointed out that the misuse of power…can be attributed to the failure to act in accordance with the law. Therefore, to act in accordance with the law will be a consensus among the prosecution, the defense, and the judge regarding how to determine defendant X's case of irregularity for favoritism and abuse of power The statutory duty of the defense is to present defense opinions in accordance with the law regarding the tenability of the accusation against the defendant, and to present materials and opinions in favor of the defendant for the court to consider from a broader perspective. Although the defense differs from the prosecution in the statutory duty and position, it shares with the prosecutor the fundamental purpose of acting according to the law and cracking down on crimes through legal means

In this excerpt, the defense lawyer shows a positive attitude twice regarding the principles of "依法行事" (to act in accordance with the law). First of all, by way of citing the prosecutor's comment that "权力的滥用是……没有依法行事" (the misuse of power…can be attributed to the failure to act in accordance with the law), the defense bestows their positive Appreciation of the prosecutor's position. Immediately after the Appreciation, the lawyer refers to the case under deliberation and states in the manner of requesting that the principle "将是控辩审三方的共识" (will be a consensus among the prosecution, the defense, and the judge). Following this positioning, the lawyer reiterates unilaterally that they "寻求依法办事, 通过法律手段依法制裁……犯罪问题上的根本目的是一致的" (share with the prosecutor the fundamental purpose of acting according to the law and cracking down on crimes through legal means). This reiteration works more than a mere repetition. It accumulates the prosodic attitude that the principle is the common ground for the participants in the trial. By emphasizing the common ground, the speaker may construct opposing parties and judges to be interactants with equal roles, who are all gatekeepers of social justice.

It is ubiquitous for lawyers in criminal proceedings to evaluate the common interests of all participants in court, thereby shortening the distance between them in roles. One primary reason is that in a criminal court, there is a significant distance between the three parties in terms of social status and the initial discourse role relationships. The defense represents an individual or entity, the prosecutors represent the state interests, and the judges represent an impartial arbitrator. Being both government employees, the prosecution and the tribunal are closer to each other in social status.

In civil proceedings, though the distance between the disputing parties in social status is not as striking as that in criminal cases, the confrontational role relationship remains the same. In this instance, emphasizing the shared common ground and the basic principles in law and legal communication is still frequently deployed to undermine the hostile relationship between the two parties.

In civil proceedings, the defense lawyer typically employs a formulaic expression such as "依法发表代理意见" (to present legal opinions in accordance with the law) to "justify" their speech role at the very beginning of their speech. One of the main functions of this expression is to tone down the contest between the two parties, as demonstrated in Excerpt (4).

Excerpt (4) No. M-D-021

被代: 根据我国诉讼法和《律师法》所规定的律师参与民事代理活动的原则, 现特发表如下代理意见, 请在合议时能予以切实的考虑	DL: In accordance with principles governing lawyers' participation in civil representation activities prescribed in China's civil procedural law and the Lawyers Law, the lawyer hereby presents the following legal opinions and requests that the court consider them carefully during the panel discussion

In addition to the expression "根据我国诉讼法和《律师法》所规定的律师参与民事代理活动的原则" (in accordance with principles governing lawyers' participation in representation activities prescribed by China's civil procedural law and the Lawyers Law), other formulaic expressions such as "依法" (in accordance with the law) or "依照法律的有关规定" (according to relevant legal regulations) are frequently used to justify the appropriacy of lawyers' roles and speeches. These expressions invariably indicate the speaker's awareness of the need for them to publicly acknowledge the common points shared by all participants.

To summarize, by positively evaluating either the role of the law in society or the basic principles of law in the trial, lawyers highlight the common ground held by all the participants in court. It helps to construct an equal relationship between them.

6.2.2 Emphasizing the Life-World

Another important means of constructing equal roles is to stress or make reference to the life-world, which means the judicial knowledge that legal professionals share (Phillips 2003). One aspect of the life-world is the professional argumentative speech style, and the other is the frequent reference to legal regulations in lawyer talk.

A typical feature of the argumentative speech style is the use of various types of conjunctions, such as *because, as a result of*, and *therefore*, to indicate inherent causal relationships in arguments.

Excerpt (5) No. M-D-018

被代: 原告人并非电视剧《H公主》主题歌的主唱者, 也不是原唱者。《联合早报》的有关报道, 向读者传递了一个虚假的信息, 具有明显的误导倾向和欺诈性, 实属无效证据, 不足以采信。据此, 原告人据此提出的有关诉讼请求应当依法驳回	DL: The plaintiff [a female] was neither the **chief singer** nor the **original singer** of the theme song in the TV serial Princess H. Since the report by the Lian He Morning Paper was misleading and deceptive, any evidence based on it should be dismissed as invalid. As a result, the claims that the plaintiff brings to court based on that evidence should be rejected in accordance with the law

The main point in this excerpt is the defense's negated Appreciation of the plaintiff's claim in terms of Reaction. To justify their evaluation, the defense lawyer provides two reasons to support their proposal for rejecting the claim. The first reason concerns the identity of the plaintiff in relation to the said theme song, "并非……主唱者, 也不是原唱者" (neither the chief singer nor the original singer). The second reason lies in the inaccuracy of the news report as evidence, which is "误导倾向和欺诈性" (misleading and deceptive). Finally, the defense provides their negative evaluative attitude regarding the claim in the clause "据此……诉讼请求应当依法驳回" (as a result…the claims should be rejected). In this short speech, the way in which the defense lawyer presents their legal position based on reasons is in line with the spirit of the law and the search for justification.

What is significant with this speech is that by following the normative requirements of professional skills, lawyers demonstrate that they have the same "good talking" in the court. Interactively, the addressees are positioned as professional lawyers who can be convinced by nothing but reasons. The speech style thus draws the participants close to each other as they share the colleagiacy (Gaines 2002). In this way, an equal role relationship between participants is constructed. More apparent uses of argumentative speech are found in Excerpt (6).

Excerpt (6) No. X-D-025

DL: 1996年12月Lian公司所送2万元不应认定为被告人受贿 1. 利用职务上的便利是构成受贿罪的必不可少的条件, 是受贿罪各要件的核心。因为这一条件决定了受贿罪的亵渎性质。如果没有利用职务上的便利, 则不构成受贿罪 2. 被告人为L某担保不是起诉书所指控的是以Lian公司的名义担保, 而是以被告人个人名义担保 3. (省略) 4.被告人以个人名义担保的行为未利用任何职权, 也未利用职务上的便利…… 因此, 我们认为这2万元应视为被告人以个人名义担保, 承担了担保风险后刘某给的风险费, 不应视为受贿	DL: The 20,000 yuan received from the Lian Corporation in December 1996 should not be determined as a bribe for the following reasons: 1. The use of one's position for personal gain is an essential element of the offense of bribery and forms the core of its various components because this element determines the corrupt nature of the offense. Without the exploitation of one's position, bribery cannot be established 2. The guarantee that the defendant provided for the debtor L was not in the name of the Lian Company, as alleged in the bill of indictment, but in his own personal name 3. (Omitted) 4. The guarantee that the defendant provided has no relation to his position or any privileges associated with the position… As a result, we believe that this sum of money should be determined as the profit that the defendant deserved as a return for the risks he bore and should not be determined as a bribe

In this excerpt, the defense lawyer presents a very long argument to advance their legal position that "2万元不应认定为被告人受贿" (the 20,000 yuan … should not be determined as a bribe). Three points are presented to support their evaluative position. Firstly, by a relational process, the topic "利用职务上的便利" (the use of one's power for personal gain) is encoded as the "必不可少的条件" (essential element) for bribery, which is justified by a clause introduced by the cohesive link "因为" (as) and a counterfactual clause, "如果没有利用职务上的便利, 则不构成受贿罪" (without ..., bribery cannot be established). Secondly, following the evaluation on the topic, the specific factual situation of the case is presented, which is "被告人个人名义担保" (the guarantee the defendant provided... was in his own personal name). Thirdly, the alleged relationship between the situation of the fact and the essential element of bribery provided in the law is negated, as in the clauses "担保的行为未利用任何职权, 也未利用职务上的便利" (the guarantee has no relation to his position or privileges associated with the position). Argued in the logic established by the three points, the defense puts forward their conclusion introduced by "因此" (as a result). The lawyer's reasoning is instantiated by the cohesive devices and the arrangement of the three points in succession.

Another point worth attention in this excerpt is the defense lawyer's reference to the body of the law. According to Gaines (2002), frequent references to legal regulations or legal jargon are a fundamental way to construct an intimate, equal relationship. For more illustrations, see Excerpt (7).

Excerpt (7) No. X-D-024

DL: 根据刑法第397条规定, 滥用职权罪, 是指国家工作机关工作人员超越法律、法律赋予的职权, 擅自处理其无权决定、处理的事项, 或者违反规定处理公务, 致使公共财产、国家和人民利益遭受重大损失的行为。所谓滥用职权罪主要表现为不正确行使职权或超越职权, 或者利用手中的职权随心所欲, 胡作非为, 违法地处理公务……	DL: In line with Article 397 of the Criminal Law, the crime of abuse of power refers to behaviors in which an employee of governmental departments exceeds the authority granted to them by the laws and regulations and handles matters that they are not entitled to decide on or handles public affairs in violation of relevant regulations, incurring great damage to the public property, and the interests of the state or the people. This crime is mainly characterized by the irregularities that occur when the employee improperly exercises their authority, exceeds their authority, or **willfully uses** their authority to handle public affairs unlawfully

The defense lawyer's elaboration on the crime "滥用职权罪" (the abuse of power) is made up of two parts. The first part is a direct quotation (or faithful reproduction) of the rule "刑法第397条" (Article 397 of the Criminal Law). It is followed by the defense's interpretation of the rule in the second part, in which the lawyer highlights the main characteristics of the crime, using attitudinal expressions such as "不正确" (improperly) and "随心所欲, 胡作非为" (willfully). If the quotation of the legal rule is a strict use of legal jargon, then the interpretation is encoded in plain speech. The quotation of the law and the shift between legal jargon and plain language are lawyers' practices of their professional skills. By linguistic operations of this kind, the defense shows their engagement in the dynamic interaction with the opposing lawyers and the judges.

This shift between the legal jargon and the ordinary language is considered an interaction between participants with equal discourse roles for the following reasons. In accordance with Bakhtin's view (1984), the essence of a "dialogue" lies in the reciprocal relationship between the speaker and the listener at the individual or social level. Each utterance expresses a connection between the author's speech and that of the others. Because of the reciprocal responsiveness, meanings are generated in a continuous process of verbal communication and are open to change. To put it simply, dialogue could be interpreted as the speaker's attitude or orientation toward communication. In this excerpt, by interpreting the legal rule in plain language, the speaker invites the audience to join in the interpretation against the background of the judiciary knowledge. The judiciary knowledge or the life-world is assumed to be the shared background of the ongoing discussion. In this sense, an equal role relationship between the disputing lawyers is constructed and maintained.

In summary, lawyers may construct equal role relationships with disputing lawyers in two ways: positive evaluation of the common ground they have and frequent references to the life-world shared between the legal professionals. The former is concerned with the basic functions of law in society and the fundamental principles of the trial, while the latter encompasses both the legal argumentative speech style and the invocation of legal rules and terms.

6.3 A Multi-voiced Environment

In the Habermasian views of legal communication, participants in the court shall give mutual respect and equal concern to all those affected and exclude no competent parties from the trial talk (Habermas 1996: 230). In a trial interaction, lawyers must engage with voices from different sides simultaneously so as to reach a mutual understanding over which legal position deserves the court's support. Linguistically, they may show an awareness of the opposing party's existence and their voices and then acknowledge or respond to them when advancing their own legal opinions. More precisely, lawyers are engaged in a heteroglossic environment where various viewpoints co-exist, which is reflected and constructed in lawyers' evaluation toward different voices in the court.

According to Martin and Rose (2003: 44–54), sources of voices may be introduced into the text in various ways, among which are projection, modality, concession, and negation. Speech act verbs (such as *claim, argue, request*) and the related nouns (such as *a request in litigation, some hearsay*), scare quotations (such as *those so-called facts*), as well as projecting clauses (such as *he alleges/reports*) may be used to identify the attribution of voices in text. In a face-to-face interaction, nonverbal expressions (such as gestures, facial expressions, and pitch) may be used to signal unspecified but recoverable sources (see, for example, Goodwin and Goodwin 1997). In addition, modality may indicate the implication of two voices because it serves as a means to set up a semantic space between *yes* and *no*, a cline running between positive and negative poles (Halliday 1994). At last, concession, conditional clauses, and other devices can all be interpreted as indications of different voices.

Despite the flexibility in introducing the sources of voices into text, the presentation of voices in the text is constrained by the Field (i.e., the activity a speaker is engaged in) and Tenor (i.e., the institutional position of the speaker) (Martin and Rose 2003: 63; White 2003). In judicial settings, projection, scare quotation, concession, negation, modality, and conjunctive adjuncts are all frequently used linguistic means to introduce sources of voices into text (Kšrner 2000; Miller 2002).

A thorough investigation of the data highlights three ways lawyers engage with other voices in discursive interactions: dialogical engagement with the opposing lawyers via projection, dialogical engagement with other voices via conjunctive adjuncts, and the dialogical uses of *we think/believe*.

6.3.1 Dialogical Engagement via Projection

In the trial talk, where disputing lawyers are contestants to each other, acknowledging and introducing the opposing party's positions is of significance in that as debaters, both parties are given legitimate places to develop their opinions textually. In discourse, projection is an effective means to put the textual voice in dialogical engagement with the opposing voice.

Projecting clauses or speech act verbs

Through projecting clauses such as "原告诉讼请求是: ……" (the plaintiff claims that …) and "被告答辩认为: ……" (the defendant replies that …), lawyers may present their points of views unequivocally.

Excerpt (8) No. M-D-021

原代: 原告NM公司的诉讼请求是……被告NY公司……严重侵犯了原告合法权益,故请求法院根据《反不正当竞争法》第五条之规定,对本案做出公正判决 被代: 被告NY公司答辩,依《反不正当竞争法》第五条之规定,判决被告行为是否侵犯知名商品特有名称、包装、装潢的前提是看……	PL: The plaintiff, NM Corporation, claims… The defendant, NY Corporation…has gravely violated the legitimate rights of the plaintiff. In accordance with Article 5 of the Law of Unfair Competition, the plaintiff hereby petitions the court to make a fair judgment on this case DL: The defendant, NY Corporation, replies in the following: in accordance with Article 5 of the Law of Unfair Competition, the pre-condition for determining the alleged behavior of the defendant as a violation of the copyright of a famous product in terms of its name, packaging, and decoration is…

In this excerpt, both the plaintiff's lawyer and the defense lawyer unequivocally signpost their viewpoints through a projecting clause. The plaintiff prefaces their evaluative attitude with the clause "原告……诉讼请求是" (the plaintiff claims that), and the defense presents their opinions introduced by the clause "被告……答辩" (the defendant replies).

Lawyers may employ projecting clauses to introduce an opposing viewpoint that they argue against in the current speech, as in Excerpt (9).

Excerpt (9) No. M-S-Z-09

原代: …… (在) 被告提供的证据里, 他已经提供了, 而且被告代理人也已经承认了, 他们当时在采用这个新香妃的这个称呼……	PL: …In the evidence presented, the defendant has shown that point. Besides, the defense lawyer has acknowledged that when they decided to use the name XIN YANG FEI …

When developing their own position in this excerpt, the plaintiff's lawyer projects the voice of the opposing party through the projecting clauses, "他已经提供了" (the defendant has shown that) and "已经承认了" (has acknowledged that). In this way, the lawyer leaves a legitimate place for the opposing views to expand in full scale, although the expansion of those views is always within the control of the speaking lawyer. Discursively, this projection shows that the speaker bestows an equal argumentative role to the disputing party and demonstrates a concern for the legitimate discursive role of the opposing party in the debate. Obviously, the meaning of the opposing viewpoints may be slightly altered in this projection, and a kind of evaluative attitude is always conveyed in this process.

Along with projecting clauses, speech act verbs may be taken to project the alternative voices of the opposing party and construct them as co-debaters.

Excerpt (10) No. M-D-021

被代: 从原告向法庭提交的证据清单上看, 原告没有提供与证明其商品知名度有关的任何证据。其诉讼主张, 其产品在 1998 年被评为G省名牌产品, 该评比结果并不意味着其产品在G省以外的市场也有知名度, 特别是原告并没有证据证明, 在诉讼发生地X市场上, 其产品被相关消费者所知晓	DL: The list of evidence presented by the plaintiff to the court shows that the plaintiff failed to present any evidence to prove the popularity of their products. Their claim that their products were awarded the name-brand products in G Province does not mean that their products are famous enough in the market outside the Province. In particular, the plaintiff did not have any evidence to prove that their products are familiar to customers in City X, the place where this litigation takes place

In this excerpt, the lawyer presents, in the textual voice, the opposing position by means of speech act verbs, including "看" (shows), and "意味着" (means). In this way, the speaker acknowledges and addresses the opposing viewpoint.

Projection by nominalization

Nominalization is another way of projecting the opposing positions. In Excerpt (10), the opposing party's viewpoint is nominalized in "其诉讼主张" (their claim that) and developed in the appositive clause. Another example of using nominalization is provided in Excerpt (11) below.

Excerpt (11) No. X-D-001

被代: 我们认为, 被告人Z某非法剥夺他人生命的事实是清楚的, 其行为已经构成了故意杀人罪。所以, 我们对公诉人指控的罪名不持异议。但是……	DL: We believe that the fact that defendant Z took away another person's life unlawfully is clear and that this action has constituted the crime of intentional homicide. Therefore, we hold no objection to the charge against the defendant. However …

As in the preceding excerpt, the defense lawyer in this excerpt explicitly acknowledges the prosecutor's voice with a nominalization in "公诉人指控的罪名" (the charge against the defendant), and also gives the voice a full development in the preceding clauses. The projection of an opponent's voice is a little bit different in the following excerpt.

Excerpt (12) No M-S-Z-08

原代: 被告的讲法混淆了品牌和厂家这个概念	PL: The defendant's proclamation has confused the two concepts of "brand-holder" and "manufacturer"

In this instance, by the nominalized phrase, "被告的讲法" (the defendant's proclamation), the speaking lawyer acknowledges the opposing lawyer's voice in their current speech but sets it aside, leaving no opportunity for it to develop at all.

Projection by (in)direct quotation

Different voices may be projected through (in)direct quotations. Refer to Excerpts (13) and (14) below.

Excerpt (13) No. M-D-018

被代: 在刚才的庭审调查中, 我们向法庭出示了 "晚报"宣称原告为 "主唱"和 "原唱"的三首歌曲在电视剧中的材料	DL: In the court investigation held just now, we presented to the court the materials in the TV serial relevant to the three songs that the Evening Paper claimed to have been performed by the plaintiff as the "chief singer" and "original singer"

In this episode, the double quotation marks in "主唱" (chief singer) and "原唱" (original singer) reproduce vividly the opposing party's diction and tone. As the quotation represents only a part of the plaintiff's speech, it is called a "scare quote" in Martin and Rose (2003: 47). In Excerpt (14) below, an indirect quotation is employed.

Excerpt (14) No M-S-Z-08

被代: ……什么又是裁判员啦, 又是什么这个, 我觉得这个说法是不对的	DL: …the referees or whatever. I do not think those viewpoints are right

In this excerpt, the defense lawyer paraphrases the plaintiff's voice into, "什么又是裁判员啦, 又是什么这个" (the referees or whatever). This indirect quotation serves a dual function: to introduce the voice of the original speaker, and, more importantly, to convey the current speaker's comments toward the quoted voice at the same time.

In summary, by means of projection, lawyers may acknowledge or present, in a way that suits their communicative intention, the voices or arguments of the opposing parties in their current speech. In this way, the alternative voices of the opposing parties may not be excluded or suppressed, and instead, they are constructed as contestants with equal roles. It is important to note that, ideationally, what is projected is different from the original in meaning, and alterations in meaning may be made and skillfully manipulated in the process of projection (Halliday 1994: 254–255).

6.3.2 *Dialogical Engagement via Conjunctive Adjuncts*

Apart from projection, devices such as modality, negation, and concession all serve as alternative ways to represent the voices of the opposing parties or other audiences. The linguistic devices encompass conjunctive adjuncts of various kinds. The primary feature of this kind of representation lies in that the sources of voices are not unequivocally marked.

Excerpt (15) No. M-S-Z-08

原代: 作为这个商标的所有人、使用人、许可使用人, 我们是有权利起诉的。第一是, 即使我们签订的联营协议是暗箱协议, 中国的法律没有规定, 签订协议一定要向新闻界公开。我们爱怎么签, 就怎么签, 这是我们的权利。所以说, 我们的主体资格是一点问题都没有的	PL: As the owner, user, and licensed user of the trademark, we are entitled to file this case. First of all, even if the coordination contract we signed was executed behind the scenes, since the Chinese law does not have any regulations mandating that signed contracts be released to the media, we may sign whatever we want, which is our lawful right to do. Therefore, there is definitely no problem of any kind concerning our qualification as the legal subject in this lawsuit

In this excerpt, the plaintiff's lawyer argues against the defense's challenge to their legal qualification as the subject of the litigation. Through the link verb "是" (be) in the positive statement, "我们是有权利起诉的" (we are entitled to …), the speaker is dialogically engaged in a dialogue with different voices. Retrospectively, the speaker responds to the defense's challenge, and, prospectively, interacts with the potential alternative voice from the audience, who may have some doubts concerning the topic, co-textually.

Through the concession "即使我们签订的联营协议是暗箱协议" (even if the coordination contract we signed was executed behind the scenes), the possibility of doubt that may be generated from the audience is acknowledged and then responded to with two reinforced affirmative conclusions in the clauses "是我们的权利" (is our lawful right) and "是一点问题都没有" (is definitely no problem of any kind). The affirmation is prefaced with a high-value modalized expression "爱怎么签" (whatever we want), indicating that the exercise of rights with the slightest possibility is still within the limits of the law. Thus, through the use of modality, concession, and negation, the various possibilities and interpretations concerning the legal subject on the part of the plaintiff are addressed.

Apart from modalization, concession, and negation, a presupposition conveyed by conjunctive adjuncts is another effective way to allow alternative voices to be transplanted into the discourse, as demonstrated in Excerpt (16).

Excerpt (16) No. X-D-018

被代: 被告人没有利用职务上的便利收受过W某的财物。虽然他确实收受过W某的一些财物, 但那完全是W某出于朋友之情送给他的或是暂时交换使用, 与被告人H某的职务并无关联	DL: The defendant did not accept any property from W by taking advantage of his position. Although he did receive some properties from W, it was absolutely for the sake of their friendship or a temporary exchange between them. Therefore, defendant H's behavior had nothing to do with his position

Here in this excerpt, to argue against the accusation that the defendant accepted properties by taking advantage of the duty, the defense draws several voices together in their speech. Firstly, the prosecutor's voice is presented in the clause "利用职务上的便利收受过W某的财物" (accept[ing] any property from W by taking advantage of his position). Secondly, the presumption "收受过吴某的一些财物" (receiv[ing] some properties from W) introduced by "虽然" (although) presents the potential speculation that the judges or the audience may have in their mind. Thirdly, in the textual voice, the lawyer presents their denial, which contains "完全是" (absolutely for the sake of…).

As is shown in the text, the defense lawyer engages with various voices in diversified manners. The lawyer responds to the prosecution's voice with a negation but accepts the presumption from the audience and the judges, as is indicated in the adverb "确实" (did receive). Intriguingly, with the conjunction of conversion "但" (but), the speaker manages to rebut the accusation with a denial, "与被告人H的职务并无关联" (has nothing to do with his position). Immediately after this, the lawyer manifests their interpretation of the fact, which is intensified by the adverb "完全" (absolutely) in the clause "完全是吴某出于朋友之情送给他的或是暂时交换使用" (was absolutely for the sake of their friendship or a temporary exchange between them).

6.3.3 The Dialogical Uses of We Think

In the various means for introducing voices in discourse, a formulaic expression identified by the interpersonal metaphor (or discourse marker) *we think* is an exceptional way for lawyers to mark their attitudes. Variations for this expression include *I think/reckon* and *the defense/prosecution believes*. The expression is distinctive in legal discourse because it explicitly signposts the speaking lawyer's voice in the text. It enables lawyers to highlight their opinions and negotiate with others. By putting their opinions in interaction with those of others, lawyers can engage in the constructive dialogue through which to reach an agreement finally.

Excerpt (17) No. M-S-Z-09

原代: 我们认为呢, 本案的事实清楚, ……所以我们认为这个事实, 而且被告代理人也已经承认了, 他们当时在采用这个新香妃的这个称呼的时候, 也是考虑到有一个香妃在先, 所以我们认为他是属于明知的 被代: 我们认为呢, 不构成商标的侵权。对于商标的这个概念和定义, 法律都有明确的规定……	PL: We think that the facts of the case are clear …As a result, we think the facts, and the defense lawyer has acknowledged that they were aware that the brand name YANG FEI had been in use when they decided to use the name XIN YANG FEI. As a result, we think that their infringement was deliberate DL: We think that our action does not constitute a trademark infringement. There are specific regulations concerning the concept and definition of the term *trademark*…

In this excerpt, four instances of *we think* are employed to preface evaluative opinions. The meaning of the phrase underwent changes in accordance with context (see Ostman 1981). Initially, it was analyzed at length in the local context in terms of its semantic meaning. Later, explored pragmatically in terms of the speaker's epistemic state, it was regarded as an indicator of "being vague" (Channell 1994) and "being powerless" (Lakoff 1990), leading to a presentational style with weak credibility in adversary courts (O'Barr 1982). Recently, however, it has been dynamically interpreted. Given the high frequency of the phrase in the context of the Chinese court, it should not be understood statically as an expression of uncertainty or an indicator of the powerless style (see also Simpson 1993). Owing to the fact that the discursive environment of lawyer evaluation where it occurs is different from the context of the witness statements in the Western courts that were observed in O'Barr's (1982) study, we may re-interpret the function of the phrase with a refreshed eye.

According to Stubbs (1996), the function of *I think* or *we think* may be determined in accordance with the clause that follows it. When followed by a fact (a claim about some observable, verifiable state of affairs in the experienced world), it expresses the speaker's epistemic doubt. When followed by an opinion, it may signal a low certainty but may also be used to foreground the speaker's attitude and put their opinions in focus. It can be seen as the speaker announcing, "Here I come" (Simon-Vandenbergen 2004), making their opinion an option for the listener to consider. Among similar views documented elsewhere, White (2003: 265) points out, with inspiration from Bakhtin's dialogical view of language, that the expression of *we think* signals to put forward the textual voice as an alternative for the audience to consider, to accept, or to deny. This proposal is consistent with the notion of "negotiability" of language (Verschueren 2000). In this sense, the phrase facilitates the negotiation of meanings between the speaker and the audience.

Interpreted dynamically in a large pragmatic context, the expression *the defense thinks* or *we think* in Excerpt (17) serves to foreground the speaking lawyer's claim, drawing attention from the judges while still allowing room for judicial discretion. It indicates the lawyer's efforts to interact dynamically with other voices in the court and construct equal roles between participants as arguers and debaters.

In short, by means of diversified linguistic devices, including projection, conjunctive adjuncts, and discourse markers, lawyers may be engaged with different voices in the trial talk. The discursive introduction of various voices in the text is not only a reflection of the adversarial environment in which two or more voices are in interaction and contestation. It also demonstrates the role relationships between different participants. The representation of various voices in text makes evident that the courtroom is a place of heteroglossic culture, where all participants are equally involved in the conversation. Therefore, the discursive involvement of various voices in the trial talk meets the requirement proposed by Habermas (1996) regarding the role relationships in legal communication.

Although the multi-voiced environment is an essential feature of the rational discourse of lawyer evaluation, it does not suffice for trial communication. The discursively constructed multi-voiced, democratic environment serves a more profound purpose, which is to establish oppositional discursive communities. In other words, the representation of different voices in the legal discourse reflects the existence of diversified yet opposing perspectives and positions, based on which lawyers are to establish opposing discursive communities through more convincing and significant evaluations.

6.4 Distinct Discursive Communities

It has been made evident in the preceding sections that lawyers are able to construct equal relationships in roles with their opposing party and create a multi-voiced verbal environment. However, in the competitive courtroom, lawyers are primarily responsible for presenting legal opinions regarding the legality of a disputed act in the trial discussion. To prove the validity of their opinions and gain support from the court in the multi-voiced discourse environment, lawyers have to construct their own legal positions, counter opposing viewpoints, and address any possible doubts that may arise from the audience.

In accordance with the Habermasian views of legal argumentation, all arguments have to be supported by reasons, and responses given to an argument, whether in agreement or denial, must also be based on reasons (Cooke 1998: 4–5). Accordingly, it would be meaningless for lawyers to confine their positions to blatant negations toward the opposing party's legal positions, and they have to provide responses of various kinds to the opposing viewpoints and other issues in the trial.

Discursively, lawyers position themselves differently through lawyer evaluation. When a legal argument is perceived to be valid after the process of discussion and debating based on reasons, they may present a positive evaluative attitude. By showing agreement in the multi-party talk, lawyers construct an alignment or a discursive community of *us* with the addressees (Kangasharju 1996). Conversely, when lawyers present negative evaluations of their arguments from the opposing party, they distance and alienate the latter. In this case, they attempt to construct the opposing party as an antagonist in the discursive community of *them* (Kuo 2002). In the process of arguing and counter-arguing, lawyers divide all participants in the court, including the opposing party, the judges, and the ordinary audience, into two oppositional allies or discourse communities by means of aligning and disaligning. The establishment of distinct discursive communities is achieved through the polarization of attitudes in various ways: positive evaluations, negative evaluations, or graded evaluations of various issues and topics in a trial.

6.4.1 Positive Evaluations

In rational communication, the resolution of a disputed argument depends on reasons and justifications (Habermas 1996). To any legal arguments that are justified solidly with corresponding reasons based on facts or the law, lawyers are compelled to express agreement or consent unless they have better arguments than their contestants'. Lawyers usually demonstrate their agreement, subject to two situations: firstly, the evaluated topic concerns the general principles of the trial or the social function of the law, and secondly, the legal arguments are sufficiently supported by the law and facts of a case.

As a general rule, when a positive evaluation is given to the position held by the opposing party, the lawyer's textual voice is aligned with the addressee's position. The expression of agreement allows lawyers to form an alliance with their addressees (Kangasharju 1996, 2002). Discursively, only when a positive lawyer evaluation is given unequivocally can the alignment be constructed, revealed, and maintained between the speaker and the addressee (Martin 2004a; Miller 2004).

Firstly, alignment may be achieved when lawyers provide positive evaluations regarding the character or work of their opposing party.

Excerpt (18) No. X-D-026

被代: 开庭前, 我们认真查阅了案卷, 会见了被告人, 两天来又参加了法庭调查活动, 由此使我们对本案有了比较全面、系统和客观的了解。我们首先感到, 检查机关在本案的侦察、起诉阶段做了大量**艰苦**、**细致**的工作, 他们的**辛勤劳动**对于T市乃至S省的反腐败斗争将产生**积极的影响**。在此, 我们向所有参加本案的检查人员表示**由衷的敬意**。其次, 我们认为《起诉书》指控的被告人的犯罪行为, 大部分事实基本上是**清楚的**, 证据也是确实、充分的, 在此基础上提出的定性意见也是正确的	DL: Prior to the court session, we reviewed the case files carefully and interviewed the defendant. Over the past two days, we have participated in the court investigation here. All these activities have enabled us to have a comprehensive, systematic, and objective understanding of this case. Firstly, we wish to acknowledge the prosecution's **arduous work** in the stages of investigation and prosecution of this case. Their **strenuous effort** will surely have **a positive impact** on the anti-corruption work in the City of T and S Province. Here, we would like to pay **our heartfelt tribute** to the prosecutors involved in this case. Next, we believe that most of the alleged criminal behaviors outlined in the Bill of Indictment are **basically clear** and **adequately supported** by evidence and that the legal opinions they proposed on the basis of their work regarding the determination of the case are **correct**

In this excerpt, the defense lawyer focuses explicitly on evaluating the prosecutors' work and their viewpoints. What is striking here is the accumulation of their positive evaluations. The prosecutors are judged favorably for their work, as seen in phrases like "艰苦、细致的工作" (arduous work), "辛勤劳动" (strenuous effort), and "积极的影响" (positive impact). These positive evaluations are interpreted as tokens of favorable Judgement towards the prosecutors in terms of Social Sanction. The favorable Judgements are followed by the lawyer's affective attitude in terms of Reaction, expressed as "由衷的敬意" (our heartfelt tribute).

Along with the Judgement of the prosecutors' character, affirmative Appreciations are provided regarding the prosecutors' viewpoints. The alleged criminal facts in the bill of indictment are evaluated positively in "基本上是清楚的" (basically clear), the evidence is "也是确实、充分的" (adequately supported), and the legal opinions are "正确的" (correct). The combination of favorable Judgements and affirmative Appreciations has composed a very impressive prosody of praise on the prosecutors' character. Naturally, this brings the disputing parties closer.

Meanwhile, the favorable praises bring the defense lawyer closer to the judge and the audience. In the Chinese culture, prosecutors are considered the respected defenders of social justice. When the prosecutors' work and their legal opinions are evaluated positively, the prosecutors' professionalism is affirmatively acknowledged. The demonstration of such evaluations enables the defense lawyer to align with the public value system concerning the official role of the prosecution. Thus, a similarity between the defense and the audience emerges. Subsequently, an alliance is created between the defense, the judges, and the audience in the court.

Con-textually, the defense's positive evaluation of the prosecutor's work would be deemed entirely rational. Technically, making proper evaluations is perceived as a primary and essential quality possessed by the staunch legal agents and a quality consistent with the normative principle of "calling a spade a spade" in Chinese culture. By doing the right thing in conformity with public expectation, the defense lawyer constructs themselves as cool-headed legal professionals. The demonstration of such a serious stance is supported by the self-evaluation of their own work in the following, "认真查阅了案卷" (review[ing] the case files carefully), "会见了被告人" (interview[ing] the defendant) and "参加了法庭调查活动" (participat[ing] in the court investigation), and a favorable Appreciation of their attitude of the case in Reaction, "比较全面、系统和客观的了解" (a comprehensive, systematic and objective understanding). Intriguingly, these behaviors or characters are demonstrated to be totally consistent with those qualities displayed by the prosecutors. In this case, the defense indirectly constructs themselves as rational and professional speakers like the prosecutors. When the defense lawyer verbally behaves in the manner expected by the tribunal and the public, an alliance can be established between the defense lawyer, the judges, the prosecutors, and the audience all at the same time (see Gaines 2002).

The alignment with their contestants is also observed when lawyers show agreement to the opposing party's arguments that are proved to be based on sufficient evidence.

Excerpt (19) No. X-D-001

被代: 我们认为, 被告人Z某非法剥夺他人生命的事实是清楚的, 其行为已经构成了故意杀人罪。所以, 我们对公诉人指控的罪名不持异议。但是……	DL: We believe that the fact that defendant Z took away another person's life unlawfully is clear and that this action has constituted the crime of intentional homicide. Therefore, we hold no objection to the charge against the defendant. However …

Toward the prosecution's opinion, the defense lawyer holds a positive attitude, which is indicated in "不持异议" (no objection to the charge) and justified by reasons in "事实是清楚的……故意杀人罪" (the fact… is clear and ...the crime of intentional homicide). Naturally, this convergent position shortens the distance between the disputing lawyers and brings the defense closer to their contestants. As a result, a community or an alliance is established.

However, it is important to note that a conversion "但是" (however) follows the positive evaluation in Excerpt (19). With the conversion, a contrastive evaluation is to be presented, which is to be discussed in the subsection on negative evaluations.

6.4.2 *Negative Evaluations*

When lawyers negatively evaluate an argument from the opposing party, it often leads to disagreement and the creation of an *us* versus *them* dynamic in their discourse. Discursively, by highlighting the weaknesses in the opposing arguments, lawyers can undermine the credibility of the statements by the contestants, alienate them, and otherize them into the discursive community of *them* (Duszak 2002; Kuo 2002). The following excerpts provide examples to demonstrate how such critiques can shape the discourse.

Excerpt (20) No. M-D-021

被代: 原告认为第一被告侵害其对域名Iratings.com 享有的民事权益是毫无根据的。理由是: ……	DL: The plaintiff's argument that the first defendant infringed on their civil right to the domain name Iratings.com is **groundless** at all for the following reasons …

In this excerpt, the defense lawyer negatively appreciates the plaintiff's argument in terms of Composition. The lawyer straightforwardly refutes the argument as "毫无根据的" (groundless) and provides some "理由" (reasons) to justify their negation. This apparent Appreciation serves to create and mark the distinction the defense has with the plaintiff. When the lawyer presents their justifications as texts unfold, they may gradually alienate the opposing party in the multi-party talk.

The lawyers' deliberate effort to alienate their contestants is displayed in a refined way when they advance their own arguments.

Excerpt (21) No. M-D-018

被代: 经济电视台没有给原告人署上演唱者的名字, 不仅符合行业操作规范有正当的理由, 也没有违背著作权法的规定, 根本没有什么过错, 原告人完全没有必要 肆意诉讼	DL: The Television Station did not credit the singer's name in the cast. It not only conforms to the industry operating rules, which provide **legitimate reasons** for the said act, but also complies with the regulations of the Copyright Law. Hence, it is not a wrongful act. Therefore, there is utterly no point at all for the plaintiff to have **willfully** filed such a lawsuit

Here in Excerpt (21), the defense lawyer justifies their behavior of "没有给原告人署上演唱者的名字" (not credit[ing] the singer's name in the cast). The lawyer states that their decision has "正当的理由" (legitimate reasons) and is "没有什么过错" (not a wrongful act). With this statement, the lawyer denies the unfavorable propositions that are presumed in the text. Immediately after the negation, the defense makes reinforced negative Appreciations of the plaintiff's complaint. Firstly, the lawsuit is notoriously appreciated as "肆意" (willful); Secondly, it is directly degraded as "完全没有必要" (utterly no point at all). All in all, by justifying their own position and exposing the pitfalls in the opposing position at the same time, the defense pushes the opposing party away from the law and construes them as a party lacking legal professionalism.

Despite the move to alienate their contestants by unequivocal negative evaluations, there are instances where lawyers attempt to convince and align them at most. See Excerpt (22) below.

Excerpt (22) No. X-D-026

被代: 我们认为《起诉书》指控的被告人的犯罪行为, 大部分事实基本上是清楚的, 证据也是确实、充分的, 在此基础上提出的定性意见也是正确的。但是, 我们也坦率地指出, 《起诉书》指控的相当一部分被告人的犯罪行为或者事实还不清楚, 或者证据不够充分, 或者在认定的数额及对行为的定性上不够准确。下面我们分别加以论述, 作为我们对被告人的辩护意见	DL: We acknowledge that a significant portion of the criminal facts alleged in the Indictment are essentially true and that most of the evidence provided is both authentic and sufficient. We also recognize that the legal determination of the facts based on the evidence is correct. However, we must candidly point out that **a significant portion** of the alleged criminal acts or facts in the Indictment remain **slightly unclear**, with evidence related to these facts being **somewhat inadequate**. Moreover, the sum of bribes involved and the nature of the acts are **less accurately determined.** In the following, we will elaborate on these points separately as part of our defense

In this excerpt, negative Appreciations are expressed skillfully and clearly but in a mitigated way. They are shown in several aspects, including the alleged criminal facts "还不清楚" (slightly unclear), evidence "不够充分" (somewhat inadequate), and the sum of bribes "不够准确" (less accurately determined). With a triadic structure of "不" (un/in-), these negative attitudes are accentuated. By these negative evaluations, the defense lawyer has rebutted the propositions from the opposing party and effectively alienated them.

The defense's use of negative evaluations in a mitigated manner reveals their effort to convince and align their contestants. Four mitigated strategies are observed in these negations. Firstly, the negative evaluations are prefaced with an adjunct of interpersonal function "坦率地" (candidly). With the adjunct, the defense not only undermines the threatening effect associated with their evaluations but also invites the prosecution to propose an alternative argument, thereby encouraging further interaction. Secondly, quantifiers are used to modify the evaluated topics, like "相当一部分" (a significant portion) of the criminal facts, and vague descriptions are employed to mitigate the negations, for instance, "不够充分,不够准确" (somewhat inadequate, less accurately) and "还不清楚" (slightly unclear). As the quantifiers and adjectives are both indeterminate in meanings (Channell 1994), the lawyer leaves room for both parties to negotiate meanings. Lastly, the use of the conjunction "或者" (or) between the several negative evaluations also conveys tentativeness in the attitudes (Hunston and Thompson 2000). It reduces the accumulative prosody of critical evaluations, which would appear too aggressive (and face-threatening) when conjunctions such as "并且" (and) were used otherwise. Conjunctions, which are primarily used to convey ideational meanings, can be made to "appraise, even though explicitly evaluative lexis is avoided" (Martin and Rose 2003: 64). Therefore, it can be stated that, when advancing the legal opinions of their side, the lawyer attempts to draw the perspective of the prosecution into consideration. In other words, the lawyer wishes to align their contestants with the validity of their own perspectives.

Con-textually, mitigated negations may enable lawyers to gain empathy from the judges, who typically value the settlement of disagreement in a mild, peaceful way (see Gaines 2002; Li 2004). As shown in Excerpt (22), the defense lawyer seeks to establish an alignment with their competitors when they display their negative evaluations of the opposing viewpoints.

In summary, in the courtroom, lawyers have to evaluate arguments positively or negatively, and discursively, they may align or alienate the audiences into distinct discursive communities accordingly. Positive evaluations may lead to agreement or alignment between disputing lawyers, while negative ones may result in discord between the two opposite sides. The advancement of negative evaluations distances the opposing lawyers and alienates them into the discursive community of *them.*

6.4.3 Graded Evaluations

In the multi-voiced environment where versatile interpretations of an issue in the trial may occur, lawyers may negotiate meanings by encoding their evaluations in graded meanings, which allows enough room for the audiences to choose, accept, or rebut. In this process, lawyers attempt to align or dis-align the audiences differently and establish two allies among them.

Excerpt (23) No. X-D-008

被害人代理: 故意伤害他人的手段很多, 以毁容最为残忍。毁容的方法各有不同 (如香烟烫、 刀划等), 又以用化学液体毁容最 为灭绝人性。解放前, 采用这种方式毁容的往往是那些黑社会的流氓, 在当时杀人也不用偿命的社会条件下, 黑势力为何舍性命而求伤害呢? 道理十分简单, 就是企图用毁容来摧残被害人的肉体和心灵, 使后者永远生活在生不如死的日子中备受煎熬。解放后, 我国每年要发生的无数起故意伤害案件,但以化学液体毁容的,迄今为止并不多见。这种犯罪的手段极端残忍和灭绝人性, 这种犯罪给被害人带来的巨大的悲剧后果, 使这种犯罪为整个人类社会所不齿、所痛恨, 即使罪犯也极少有人敢采用这种犯罪手段	LV: Among the various means of inflicting intentional injury to the physical body of a person, disfigurement is the **most brutal**. Disfigurement with chemical liquids is considered **the most inhumane** compared with other methods, such as cigarette burns or knife scratches**.** Before the liberation of China [in 1949], disfigurement of this kind was mostly used by hooligans in the underworld. Why did they spare a victim's life but choose to **inflict** disfigurement under the social condition where murderers did not have to pay back with their lives? The answer is very simple: they intended to ruin the victim's body and mind, causing them **endless and indescribable suffering**. Since the liberation of China, there have been numerous cases of intentional injury every year, but disfigurement with chemical liquids has been rare so far. As this kind of crime is **extremely barbaric and inhumane**, with **immense tragic consequences** for the victim, it is **bitterly detested and condemned** by society. Even a criminal would hardly dare to resort to it

In this except, using Affect, Appreciation, and Judgement, the lawyer assesses the severity of disfigurement with chemical liquids, with an intention to align and disalign the audiences. First of all, affective attitudes are conveyed through words that carry strong negative connotations, such as "最为残忍" (most brutal), "最为灭绝人性" (most inhumane), "生不如死的日子中备受煎熬" (endless and indescribable sufferings), and "极端残忍和灭绝人性" (extremely barbaric and inhumane). Being very contagious semantically in function, these adjectives serve to align the audiences emotionally. Secondly, Appreciations in terms of Reaction are expressed when the lawyer describes the consequences incurred by the disfigurement. The criminal behavior brings "巨大的悲剧后果" (immense tragic consequences), and is "所不齿、所痛恨" (bitterly detested and condemned). When the consequences are condemned this way, it is easier for the audiences to perceive the severity of the alleged criminal act and, therefore, more likely for the speaker to secure the emotional support from the audiences. In addition, intensifiers and quantifiers, such as "最" (most), "极端" (extremely), and "巨大的" (immense), are employed to magnify and augment the emotional loadings of these evaluations. As a result, alignment with the audiences is more likely to be secured.

The defendant is dis-aligned by means of Judgement. An indirect Judgement of the defendant's character is conveyed through the construction of the images of two transgressive groups, "黑社会的流氓" (hooligans in the underworld), and "罪犯" (criminals). The prototypically lawless images of the two groups can effectively elicit an invited evaluative attitude from the audiences (Martin 2004b). For audiences with background knowledge of Chinese history, life before the liberation was just a hell, where killers did not necessarily receive due punishment, and the brutality of the hooligan deeds in disfigurement with chemical liquids gave those hoodlums more satisfaction than killing did. By analogy, the choice of the same criminal behavior puts the defendant and the hoodlums together in association. In the civilized world, splashing chemical liquids onto a person's body would be the last choice for criminals. Therefore, the association of the defendant with the two images in this context evokes a strong Judgement that the defendant in this case is no better than the worst people in the dark old society. In other words, readers are led to develop a stronger sense of indignation over the defendant's criminal behavior and a negative Judgement of the defendant's character.

In short, in Excerpt (23), by coupling graded Affect, Judgement, and Appreciation in the evaluations of the criminal means, the lawyer emotionally aligns the audiences to their position and dis-aligns the defense. Another instance of effective emotional alignment is offered in Excerpt (24) below.

Excerpt (24) No M-D-019

被代: 我们认为《H公主》的一二部是一个完整的电视剧作品, …… 如果将它分开, 必然会导致因果分离且瞻前而不顾后, 这对原告来讲似乎有利其诉讼的隐秘动因, 而对被告来说, 就是不公平了, 因为这样不能让被告人很好地行使举证、辩论的机会和权利, 抹杀了电视台给原告人的理解、同情和满足。同时, 也会将法庭引入片面的审判歧途, 给全面、公正的审理投上黯然的哑色……	DL: We believe that Part One and Part Two of the TV serial Princess H comprise an integral TV drama…If they are disintegrated, there will be a lack of clarity in the causal relationship between the plot and the case. The disintegration may benefit the plaintiff in the litigation but is definitely **unfair** to the defendant, as it would prevent the defendant from the full exercise of their chances and rights to present evidence and participate in debates and would **undermine** the understanding, sympathy, and satisfaction that the defense offered to the plaintiff. Meanwhile, it could also **mislead the court** in its adjudication and **cast a shadow** on the fair hearing of this case …

In this excerpt, the defense lawyer presents their arguments in response to the alleged disintegration of the two parts in the specific TV drama. The most prevailing feature of their arguments is the technique of "defending my position in your terms", which involves explaining the legitimacy of one's position in terms of the moral standards or cultural traditions of the other party (Liu 1999: 297–315). First of all, the plaintiff's proposal is interpreted "不公平了" (unfair) to the defense. The potential detriments associated with the proposal are encoded in derogatory verbs in the following clauses, "不能让被告人很好地行使…权利" (prevent the defendant from the full exercise of their chances and rights to) and "抹杀了……给原告人的理解、同情和满足" (undermines the understanding, sympathy, and satisfaction… to the plaintiff). Meanwhile, the potentially detrimental effects of the plaintiff's disintegration of the drama are effectively described in "将法庭引入片面的审判歧途, 给全面、公正的审理投上黯然的哑色" (mislead[ing] the court in its adjudication and cast[ing] a shadow on the fair hearing of this case). By exposing the pitfalls in the plaintiff's argument from the perspective of the court, the defense lawyer creates an emotional connection with the court, bringing it to their side and aligning it attitudinally.

In short, standing in the position of the court, the defense makes a negative evaluation of the plaintiff's argument. In this process, the lawyer constructs an alliance with the court as *us* in opposition to the community of *them*, the plaintiff. By proclaiming the common interest that the defense shares with the court, the lawyer has increased the interpersonal cost for their contestants or other persons to advance alternative positions (White 2003: 271). Owing to this, making evaluations on the footing of the court is an effective and "strategic" use of language in the institutional court (Garcia 2000).

In addition to employing attitudinal appeal, lawyers may also achieve alignment when presenting evaluations of the logical relations between various issues in a trial talk (FT). Alignment achieved in this way is typically found where conjunctive adjuncts or links are utilized to convey interpersonal meanings.

To substantiate and naturalize their legal positions, lawyers have to assume the role of a persuader to the immediate addressees, the panel of judges, and others. They may resort to an argumentative style, which is encoded in and signaled by such connectives and conjunctions, *therefore, thus, accordingly, because, for this reason,* and *this is why*. An example is provided below in Excerpt (25), which contains a longer text of the same case compared with Excerpt (6).

Excerpt (25) No X-D-025

被代: 1996年12月Lian公司所送2万元不应认定为被告人受贿	DL: The 20,000 yuan received from the Lian Corporation in December 1996 should not be determined as a bribe for the following reasons:
1. 利用职务上的便利是构成受贿罪的必不可少的条件, 是受贿罪各要件的核心。因为这一条件决定了受贿罪的亵渎性质。如果没有利用职务上的便利, 则不构成受贿罪	1. The use of one's position for personal gain is an essential element of the offense of bribery and forms the core of its various components because this element determines the corrupt nature of the offense. Without the exploitation of one's position, bribery cannot be established
2. 被告人为L某担保不是起诉书所指控的是以Lian 公司的名义担保, 而是以被告人个人名义担保, ……	2. The guarantee that the defendant provided for the debtor L is not in the name of the Lian Company, as is alleged in the bill of indictment, but in his own personal name…
3.根据《担保法》的规定, 个人担保是合法的, 而不论单位还是个人, 不管担保有效与否, 担保都必须要负赔偿责任或连带责任的	3. In accordance with the Security Law, a personal guarantee is legally binding. The guarantor, whether an organization or an individual, is held liable for compensation or joint liability, irrespective of the validity of the guarantee
4.被告人以个人名义担保的行为未利用任何职权, 也未利用职务上的便利, 因为借贷双方和担保人是以平等主体的身份出现的	4. The guarantee that the defendant provided has no relation to his position or any privileges associated with the position. The creditor, debtor, and guarantor are all legal subjects with equal civil rights
因此, 我们认为这2万元应视为被告人以个人名义担保, 承担了担保风险后刘某给的风险费, 不应视为受贿	As a result, we believe that this sum of money should be determined as the profit that the defendant deserved as a return for the risks he bore and should not be determined as a bribe

In this excerpt, the defense lawyer presents several reasons listed in numerals to justify their legal position that the 20,000 yuan received from the company should not be defined as a bribe. Firstly, taking advantage of one's duty is interpreted as an essential condition of bribery according to the regulation of law. This interpretation of the law is justified by the importance of the factor to the crime, "因为这一条件决定了受贿罪的亵渎性质" (because this element determines the corrupt nature of the offense) and "如果没有……, 则不构成……" (without…, bribery cannot be established).

Secondly, in a relational process "不是……; 而是……" (not…but…), the identity of the defendant in the given guarantee is considered irrelevant to the core condition of the crime. Thirdly, the alleged behavior of providing a guarantee is appreciated positively to be lawful, which is supported by the legal regulation which stipulates that "不论单位还是个人……, 担保都必须要……" (the guarantor, whether an organization or individual, is held liable for…). Fourthly, the allegation is negated in terms of Valuation and justified in the clause introduced by "因为" (because).

Interpersonally, by exploring the logical meanings conveyed in the conjunctions and connectives, the lawyer draws the audiences into their perspective and convinces them of their position regarding the legality of the said sum of money. This kind of persuasion and alignment turns out to be the most potent and convincing expression of lawyer evaluation.

In summary, lawyers may express varying degrees of evaluations regarding their contestants' arguments and other issues at hand in a trial, ranging from positive to negative to somewhere in between. By showing graded evaluations, lawyers construct certain relationships with the audiences in the way they perceive to be necessary and appropriate. Initially, the judges stand independently above the disputing lawyers. With the advancement of their legal positions, lawyers may create a new frame of interpersonal relationships. The judges and the audiences may be compelled attitudinally to align with their side, and the opposing party may be alienated.

6.5 Summary

This chapter has discussed in detail how lawyers interpersonally position themselves in relation to the opposing lawyers and the judges. By showing different evaluations, lawyers construct their stances rationally in relation to the others. The discourse of lawyers' stance encompasses three features: equal role relationships, multi-voiced environment, and distinct discursive communities. Firstly, by evaluating the common ground or the "life-world" shared by participants in the court, lawyers build an equal role relationship with the other participants. Secondly, by projecting and acknowledging the various voices of the participants and the audiences in the court, they construct a multi-voiced environment, which is necessary for rational legal communication to be carried out. Thirdly, in the heteroglossic environment, lawyers polarize their attitudes with respect to their contestants' positions and various issues in a trial.

The polarization of attitudes has different effects on communication. In some cases, the lawyer's textual voice harmonizes with opposing voices; in other cases, it sharply contrasts with them. In many instances, the textual voice presents graded attitudes towards various issues in the court. Through the polarization of attitudes, lawyers may align and dis-align the addressees and audiences differently. They may successfully create an affinity with the judges and the auditors, thereby highlighting the "otherness" of their opponents. Consequently, they position themselves in alignment with the judges (and the audiences) in a discursive community of *us* and position themselves in opposition to the opponents who are alienated into a discursive community of *them*.

Repeated close readings of the data have consistently evidenced the following lexico-grammatical resources as being those most exploited in construing lawyer stance: attitudinal lexis, conjunctions and connectives, quantifiers, intensifiers, modality and modulization, polarization, thematic highlighting, grammatical parallelism, nominalization, projection and so on. The order in which the resources are listed is not intended as a quantitative ranking of instances of use. Nor does the order imply functional importance of them in the construction of lawyer evaluation. In discourse, specific choices of linguistic expressions are made coordinately by the context of situation as a whole (Miller 2002, 2004).

The discussion in this chapter is only a rough taxonomy of how lawyers (re)construct interpersonal relationships in the court through lawyer evaluation. Identifying lawyers' stances is a complicated matter situated in context and co-text. Just as Miller (2002) says, identifying the speaker's perspective is a complex process that involves tracing the development of meanings as they unfold in the text. Attitudinal values presented by multiple voices in various ways are not solely dependent on context but also co-textually on how evaluative prosodies position readers gradually through textual interpretation. In other words, understanding speaker orientations requires a close analysis of how meanings are constructed and conveyed through textual expression. Therefore, to fully grasp the prosodic nature of lawyer evaluation in its entirety, it is crucial to examine lawyer evaluation and attitude locally in clauses but also to understand lawyers' interpersonal positioning on the phases of text.

References

Bakhtin, M. 1984. *Problems of Dostoevsky's poetics*, trans. C. Emerson. Minneapolis: University of Minnesota Press.

Channell, J. 1994. *Vague language*. Oxford: Oxford University Press.

Cooke, M. 1998. Introduction. In *On the pragmatics of communication*, ed. M. Cooke, 1–20. Cambridge: MIT Press.

Duszak, A. 2002. Us and others: an introduction. In *Us and others : Social identities across languages, discourses and cultures*, ed. A. Duszak, 1–28. Amsterdam/Philadelphia: John Benjamins.

Gaines, P. 2002. Negotiating power at the bench. *Forensic Linguistics: THe International Journal of Speech, Language and Law* 9 (2): 213–234. https://doi.org/10.1558/sll.2002.9.2.213.

Garcia, A.C. 2000. Negotiating negotiation: The collaborative production of resolution in small claims mediation hearings. *Discourse & Society* 11 (3): 315–343. https://doi.org/10.1177/0957926500011003003.

Goodwin, C., and M. H. Goodwin. 1997. Contested version: The discursive constitution of Rodney King. In *The construction of professional discourse*, ed. Britt-Louise Gunnarsson, P. Linell, et al., 292–316. London and New York: Longman.

Habermas, J. 1996. *Between facts and norms*, trans. William Rehg. Massachusetts: MIT.

Halliday, M.A.K. 1994. *Introduction to functional grammar*. London: Edward Arnold.

Hunston, S., and G. Thompson, eds. 2000. *Evaluation in text*. Oxford: Oxford University Press.

Kangasharju, H. 1996. Aligning as a team in multiparty conversation. *Journal of Pragmatics.* 26: 291–319. https://doi.org/10.1016/0378-2166(95)00051-8.

Kangasharju, H. 2002. Aligning in disagreement: Forming oppositional alliances in committee meetings. *Journal of Pragmatics* 34: 1447–1471. https://doi.org/10.1016/S0378-2166(02)00073-5.

Kšrner, H. 2000. *Negotiating authority : Logogenesis of dialogue in common law judgments*. Unpublished doctoral dissertation, Sydney University, Sydney.
Kuo, Sai-hua. 2002. From solidarity to antagonism: The uses of the second-person singular pronoun in Chinese political discourse. *TEXT* 22 (1): 29–55.https://doi.org/10.1515/text.2002.004
Lakoff, R. 1990. *Talking power: The politics of language*. New York: Basic Books.
Li, Wen-xiang. 2004. 人文主义与中国传统法律文化 [Humanism and traditional Chinese legal culture]. 江海学刊 [*Jianghai Academic Journal*] (10):136–138.
Liu, Ya-ming. 1999. Justifying my position in your terms. *Argumentation* 13: 297–315.https://doi.org/10.1023/A:1007866519621
Martin, J. 2004a. Mourning: How we get aligned. *Discourse & Society* 15 (2–3): 321–343. https://doi.org/10.1177/0957926504041022.
Martin, J. 2004b. Sense and sensibility: Texturing evaluation. In *New Perspectives on Education and Discourse*, ed. J. A. Foley, 65–96. London and New York: Continuum.
Martin, J., and D. Rose. 2003. *Working with discourse*. London, New York: Continuum.
Miller, D. 2002. Multiple judicial opinions as specialized sites of engagement: Conflicting paradigms of valuation and legitimation in *Bush v. Gore 2000*. In *Conflict and negotiation in specialized texts*, ed. M. Gotti, D. Heller, et al., 119–141. Bern: Peter Lang.
Miller, D. 2004. "To meet our common challenge": ENGAGEMENT strategies to alignment and alienation in US international discourse. *Textus XVIII* 1: 39–62.
O'Barr, M. 1982. *Linguistic evidence: Language power and strategy in the courtroom*. New York: Academic Press.
Ostman, J.O. 1981. *You know: A discourse functional approach*. Amsterdam: Benjamins.
Phillips, A. 2003. *Lawyer's language: How and why legal language is different*. London and New York: Routledge.
Simon-vandenbergen, A. 2004. Intersubjective positioning in talk shows: A case study from British TV. *Text* 24 (3): 399–422. https://doi.org/10.1515/text.2004.016.
Simpson, P. 1993. *Language, ideology, and point of view*. London and New York: Routledge.
Stubbs, M. 1996. Towards a modal grammar of English. In *Text and corpus analysis*, ed. M. Stubbs, 196–228. Oxford: Blackwell.
Verschueren, J. 2000. *Understanding pragmatics*. Beijing: Foreign Language Teaching and Research Press.
White, P. 2003. Beyond modality and hedging: A dialogic view of the language of intersubjective stance. *Text* 23 (2): 259–284. https://doi.org/10.1515/text.2003.011.

Chapter 7
Lawyer Evaluation in Action: Negotiating Justice

Abstract This chapter investigates how the rational discourse of lawyer evaluation performs its function in relation to legal dispute resolution or criminal case disposition in the court. As illustrated by data, lawyers argue their cases and negotiate justice in three aspects, the accuracy or clarity of facts, the categorical meanings of a specific charge or claim, and the appropriacy or fairness of legal decisions.

7.1 Introduction

This chapter is dedicated to an analysis of the functions of lawyer evaluation in trial proceedings. It mainly investigates how the rational discourse of lawyer evaluation contributes to legal dispute resolution or criminal case disposition in the trial.

According to the theoretical framework on lawyer evaluation in Chap. 3, the achievement of personal goals in a trial is integrated into the accomplishment of the common goal of the trial, which is the cooperative search for truth or justice in the case at hand. Now that justice is indeterminate by its very nature, what it means in a specific case has to be negotiated intersubjectively. Functionally, lawyer evaluation becomes a very effective way through which to negotiate justice. As a discursive process, negotiating justice in a trial differs from other communicative activities in legal conflict resolution outside the court, including mediation, Alternative Dispute Resolution (ADR), and plea-bargaining in the Western court. Instead, the negotiation is mainly realized through lawyers' evaluations of the various topics classified in accordance with Field (Fig. 3.1).

L. Zhang, *Lawyer Evaluation in Chinese Courtroom*,
https://doi.org/10.1007/978-981-97-1211-3_7

In light of the process of legal reasoning in the Chinese context (Yong et al. 2002), this chapter will conduct data analysis of lawyer evaluation in three stages: presenting facts of a case, deliberating the facts and a specific charge/complaint, and making a legal decision, and explore how lawyers argue the case and negotiate justice in the respective stages.

7.2 The Accuracy or Clarity of Case Facts

To determine the nature of a disputed act or behavior involved in a case, both the plaintiff/prosecution and the defense have to present the "facts" of the case to the court so that what has happened between the two parties can be established before a legal decision is to be made.

Divergence is engendered in the presentation of facts. First of all, the past is irrecoverable. Although supported with the necessary evidence, an account of the past event discursively constructed in court is different from that in the physical world outside the court. On the one hand, the irreversibility of time makes it impossible to know what has happened exactly. The evidence to be presented, no matter how sufficient and adequate, is only a partial, or even worse, twisted reflection of the past event. On the other hand, the totality of the past constructed on the basis of gathered evidence is never the faithful replication or perfect counterpart of the past in the outside world. Doubts occur as to whether the past or "facts" constructed verbally based on evidence are approximate to the objective truth in the case facts that the judges wish to approach (Cheng and Huang 2002: 177; Du 2001).

Secondly, descriptions of past events presented by both parties may be colored by personal preferences. On the one hand, since the burden of proof for credibility is on the parties concerned, they may just present those favorable parts of the story and evade the unfavorable ones (see Simpson 1993; Xue 1996). On the other hand, even though the opposing parties both focus their descriptions on the same part of the event, their reproduction of it may still be divergent due to their opposing perspectives of Judgment and valuation of the past (Chafe 1979). Thus, the "factual indeterminacy" (Posner 1990: 204), which lends its way to confusion in the trial, is the first problem to address when lawyers negotiate justice in a legal dispute. It thus provides a space where lawyers may negotiate graded meanings regarding the case facts.

The main task of this section is to analyze how lawyers discursively negotiate the meaning of the case facts in two aspects: scaling the presentation of facts and grading the evaluations of the facts.

7.2.1 Scaling the Presentation of Facts of a Case

The legally admissible presentation of disputed facts in court usually observes the "Seven *W*s": what action/behavior/matter, when, where, in what manner, why, with what tool/instrument, who(m) (Yong et al. 2002: 179). The seven elements can be paraphrased into a question: when and where, who does what to whom, in what way, with what instrument, and why. These elements roughly correspond to the essential constitutive elements of a charge normalized in the law, which includes, technically, the legal subject, object of a claim/charge, the time and place of the offense/misconduct, motive, consequences, and other factors.

Due to the interests of each party, lawyers emphasize certain aspects of the case facts when presenting them. Data analysis shows that they may scale the presentation of the facts in two ways: by shaping the focus of the facts and by controlling the sources of voices in evidence presentation.

7.2.1.1 Scaling the Focus of the Facts

Driven by competing interests, each party chooses to present the parts of the facts favorable to their side and dodge those unfavorable (Cotterill 2001). In this way, the foci of the case facts are scaled and slanted. By selectively describing the constitutive elements of a claim/charge, for instance, the person/character of an event (Atkinson and Drew 1990), the place (see Drew 1992; Sacks 1972), the activity (see Atkinson and Drew 1990; Goodwin and Goodwin 1997; Sacks 1972), lawyers are able to negotiate meanings in the said case.

Excerpt (1) No X-D-008

被害人代理: …被告人在上诉书中便是以"对爱情忠贞、专一"、"精神与物质都给了她"来标榜自己,称自己是"一时情绪失控"。事实完全不是这样! 被害人的品质是众人皆夸的:其自小学至中学年年被评为三好学生;读大学时又被评为**"优秀团员"**,**奖学金获得者**,**校学生会文娱委员**。踏上工作岗位一年后即被评为助理经济师,单位证明其表现很好。 被害人性格**文静**,**做事稳重**。在与被告人交往的1年零5个月中,从未"脚踏两只船"与其他男青年有过亲密交往。与被告人先后发生两次大的风波以及被告人身上所存在的缺点…,她都及时向父母做了汇报,认真听取父母的意见。被害人曾分别于3月与8月郑重向被告人提出分手,皆因被告人再三保证改正而表示愿意给其机会,**遗憾**的是被告人自己不争气。被害人也不是目前社会上的那种"高价姑娘"	LV: … In his appeal, the defendant praised himself as "loyal to love", and "spiritually and materially devoted to his love" and claimed that he was "temporarily out of control" [during the offense]. Nevertheless, that was not the case at all! The victim has a **well-acclaimed** personality: she was awarded the title of "student with merits" every year from elementary school to middle school; when she was in university, she received the award **"Excellent League Member"**, won **scholarships**, and served as a **member of the student union** in charge of entertainment activities; one year after she started working, she was promoted to an assistant economist, and received a good evaluation from her employer With a **placid disposition**, the victim is **serious** when handling personal relationships. During her one-year-and-five-month relationship with the defendant, she never "had a foot in two camps" or developed a close relationship with any other males. She reported to her parents in time the two conflicts with the defendant and the defendant's shortcomings … and sincerely listened to their suggestions. The victim once proposed breakups sincerely with the defendant in March and August but eventually agreed to give him time to mend his ways as the defendant repeatedly swore that he would rectify his behaviors. **Unfortunately**, the defendant failed to do that as he promised The victim is not the sort of "gold digger" that is very common in society at present

Extracted from a case involving the defendant's serious offense against the female victim, this excerpt contains two contrasting character descriptions of the defendant and the victim. As is read from the surrounding text, the defense lawyer has probably presented the defendant's character in a positive light, which can be found in the quoted testimony from the suspect, "对爱情忠贞、专一"(loyal to love). The presented statement from the defendant was used as a defense strategy to justify the criminal motive and to mitigate potential indignation toward the accused behavior of disfiguring the victim (the defendant's ex-girlfriend).

In response to the positive appraisal of the defendant by the defense, the lawyer for the victim gives a firm denial, exclaiming, "事实完全不是这样!" (that is not the case at all!). Instead, the lawyer presents their version of the stories that focuses on the victim's character in three positive aspects. First, the victim's personality is well-regarded, described as "众人皆夸的" (well-acclaimed), supported by her winning prizes and awards in schools and receiving favorable comments at work. Secondly, her attitudes and behaviors with regard to personal relationships are considered appropriate. During her relationship with the defendant, she "从未与其他男青年有过亲密交往" (did not develop a close relationship with any other males) and showed tolerance to the defendant's weakness by "表示愿意给其机会" (agree[ing] to give him more time to mend his ways). Thirdly, her values are appreciated very positively as free from materialism, "高价姑娘"(gold-digger). With such favorable Judgments of the victim in every aspect, her studies, work, personality, attitude in love and money, and her responses to problems in their relationship, the lawyer portrays the victim as a flawless girl whose behavior provides no clue relevant to the offense against her. Indirectly, such a description of the victim highlights the brutality of the defendant and the wickedness of his desire to control the victim.

In short, while lawyers from both sides scale the case facts in their own descriptions, the representative lawyer for the victim has constructed an image of the victim who behaves in conformity with the moral requirements for a good girl. The character description is meant to rebut the defense's version of the fact.

For more explanations regarding how case facts are scaled in lawyer evaluation, see Excerpt (2), which contains an activity description in a civil case.

Excerpt (2) No. M-D-022

被代: 一个缺乏内在显著性普通的人称称谓,怎样才可能变成具有特别含义的商品名称或者标志呢?方式与知名商标特有名称的形成过程完全相同。第一,靠长时间特有地使用在特定的商品上。第二,就是靠广告, 通过重复性的宣传,在消费者心里建立起特定的心理联系。"老干爹"也不例外。首先,从1997年开始,NY公司和NM公司分别在各自的 "豆豉辣酱"上使用 "老干爹"这个标志。再者,NY公司为在消费者心里建立起 "老干爹"与 "豆豉辣酱"之间的特别联想,一直在作广告宣传。1998年12月到1999年12月NY公司申请商标注册的那一年,广告费开支达数百万元,这个数字对于一个刚刚成立两三年的公司是巨大的。然而,这个广告投资使普通的 "老干爹"变成了一个区别性标志,一个可以注册的商标,在赋予 "老干爹"原来并不具备的显著性,取得特有的第二含义过程当中,这项投资发挥了决定性的作用。 不理解的同志,请回想一下井冈山的革命故事。井冈山本来是…	DL: How can a very ordinary form of address with no inherent distinctive features become a commodity name or symbol with special meanings? It has to undergo the same process as any particular name of a well-known trademark. First, the name is used on a particular product for a significant period; second, advertising is essential. By repetitive publicity, a particular psychological association is to be established in the minds of consumers. "LAO GAN DIE" is no exception. First of all, ever since 1997, the NY Corporation and the NM Corporation both have used the name LAO GAN DIE in their own fermented bean pepper sauce. Furthermore, the NY Corporation has extensively advertised its products on local mass media and successfully established a strong psychological connection between the brand name and the pepper sauce. During the period from December 1998 to December 1999, the time when the NY Corporation applied for the registration of the name as its trademark, it had spent millions of yuan on advertisements, which was a **considerable sum** for the company established just three years ago. Luckily, the investment in the advertisement has transformed the ordinary address LAO GAN DIE into a distinctive symbol eligible for trademark registration. It **played a decisive role** in imbuing the ordinary address LAO GAN DIE with distinctive features and connotative meanings Those who do not understand this may refer to Mount Jinggang in association with those revolutionary stories. Initially, the Mount was…

In this instance, to illustrate the enormous efforts the NY Corporation has made in making the phrase "LAO GAN DIE" become the symbol of its food product, the lawyer employs an activity description. To explain how the brand, which is initially "缺乏内在显著性普通的人称称谓" (an ordinary address with no inherent distinctive features), obtained the special meaning and "变成具有特别含义的商品名称或者标志" (became a commodity name or symbol with special meanings), the lawyer highlights the activity of advertising and evaluates it positively as it **"发挥了决定性的作用"** (played a decisive role). The **"巨大的"** (huge sum of) money, which amounts to about "达数百万元" (millions of yuan), was invested in advertising. Meanwhile, the advertising was invested purposefully, with the aim "为在消费者心里建立起…" (to establish a strong psychological connection…). In addition, to reinforce the "exclusive" contribution of the advertisement in the transformation of the brand name, the lawyer cites the revolutionary stories associated with "井冈山" (Mount Jinggang) as a similar case.

Above all, the description of advertising as an activity strengthens the audience's perception of the special connection between the company as an agent and the popularity of the brand name, thereby making a favorable impression that the company (defendant) should be the substantive (co-)owner of the brand.

In the selective presentation of persons, places, activities, and other factors, the facts of a case are tailored: some parts are scaled up while other parts are scaled down. In this process, judgments are inevitably made on whether descriptions "fit the normative requirement of categorical incumbency" (Matoesian 1993: 26).

7.2.1.2 Scaling Facts Presentation Through the Introduction of Voices

In an adversarial trial, where competing versions of facts need to be checked and verified on the basis of evidence, introducing sources of voices in the witness testimony is another way to scale the facts. The focus of facts may be perceived or scaled differently when two contestant voices are placed in contrast or when the voice of a third party is introduced.

In cases where there are two competing versions of facts in a case, displaying one version of facts in direct contrast to the other tends to elicit more attention (Stiff and Mongeau 2003). In Excerpt (1), two character descriptions are placed in contrast. In the defense's version, the defendant is described as a person who is "对爱情忠贞、专一" (loyal to love) but is compelled by some external factors to be "一时情绪失控" (temporarily out of control) in the criminal behavior. The lawyer representing the victim denies the defense's version and gives their version of the facts in which the victim is not only a well-behaved girl both at work and in school but a patient and cool-headed young woman. As discussed previously, the facts from the victim side have been scaled up.

Lawyers may shape the representation of an event or a fact by introducing an external voice in the form of a witness statement. In Excerpt (3), the defense lawyer presents the external voices of four witnesses involved in the case to refute the accusation against defendant H. In this process, the defense scales up their side of the story in a dialogical manner.

Excerpt (3) No. X-D-026

被代:"被告人H某利用职务之便,...于2002年至2004年先后三次收受..." 根据案件事实,我们认为起诉书这一指控是缺乏事实根据的。 首先,被告人H某并没有利用职务上的便利为经济技术开发中心谋求利益...根据L某2005年向检察人员陈述... G某也证实:2004年12月L某打电话叫我到他办公室,让我给... Z某也提供了与上述人员所说的内容完全一致的证词。... W某也证实了上述过程: 2004年... 从以上证词可以看出,无论是借贷方的W某,Q某,还是贷款方的G某、Z某,以及从中联系协调的Z某,都一致证明,...H某与他们任何人也没谈过或介入过此事。由此可见,在这件事上,根本不存在被告人H某利用职务...	DL: "Defendant H took advantage of his position...took bribes three times from 2002 to 2004..." Based on the facts of this case, we believe that the allegation in the bill of indictment lacks a factual basis First of all, defendant H did not take advantage of his position to seek profits for the Economics and Technological Development Center ... According to the statement made by witness L to the prosecutors in 2005 ... Witness G also testified that: in December 2004, L called me and asked me to go to his office, where he told me ... Witness Z also gave testimony that was completely consistent with what the other witnesses stated ... Witness W confirmed in his statement the afore-mentioned event. In 2004, ... It can be seen from the testimonies mentioned above that all the witnesses, either the creditors W and Q, the debtors G and Z, or the middleman Z, have proved unanimously that ...H did not talk about the matter with them or get involved in it. Therefore, there is definitely no such fact that H took advantage of his position ...

In this excerpt, the lawyer cites voices from four witnesses, surnamed L, G, Z, and W, respectively. As is shown in the speech act verbs or reporting verbs in the following projecting clauses, such as "根据L某...陈述" (statement by Witness L), "G某也证实" (Witness G also testified ...), "Z某也提供.....完全一致的证词" (Witness Z gave testimony that was completely consistent...), "W某也证实了" (Witness W confirmed...), the lawyer manages to frame the evaluative attitudes from the witnesses as consistently in favor of the defense's version of the fact. Through the introduction of these external voices, the defense concludes that the testimonies "都一致证明,...H某与他们任何人也没谈过或介入过此事" (unanimously prove that H did not talk about the matter with them or somewhat got involved ...). The external voices allow the lawyer to rebut the prosecutor's version of the story by conclusively stating that "根本不存在..." (definitely no such a fact that...).

As is illustrated in Excerpt (3), with the assistance of the external voices of the witnesses, lawyers may present a favorable version of the fact and dismiss the opposing version as groundless.

7.2.2 *Grading Judgment of Case Facts*

Facts, which do not exist as a category of neutral or unquestionable knowledge, are subject to an ongoing semiosis of translation between the prosecution and the defense. To be admitted as evidence, the facts can be verified, discussed, and debated. When they are presented and defined in the process of dynamic deliberation, legal professionals may challenge and/or alter their properties and effects. The process of discussion and negotiation could be seen as an evolving dynamic of continuous marking and interpretation or a transitional interaction, which may move between objects, meanings, and interpretations and shift from being objective/fair to being subjective/biased, depending on the practitioner's skill in representation and translation.

The negotiation of meanings in the facts of a case is demonstrated in how lawyers make graded judgments of these facts in terms of their worth and weight and how lawyers evaluate the logical relevance of the facts to the case.

7.2.2.1 Facts and Graded "Values"

In the institutional situations of a courtroom, it is a normative requirement for lawyers to refrain from making purely subjective judgments on individuals, objects, and other evidence based on their personal preferences. Instead, they are expected to present their evaluative attitudes unequivocally on the meanings of the facts within the legal framework. As a matter of fact, lawyers usually implicitly convey their attitudes and evaluations through the use of "objective terms" so as to ensure the admission of their arguments in the trial (Rogers and Erez 1999).

An evaluative Judgement on parties involved in a case, such as the defendant and the victim, in terms of Social Esteem, Social Sanction, or Social Punishment, creates a space of challenge and negotiation between disputing lawyers. Similarly, an Appreciation of various issues of the trial in terms of Valuation, Reaction, or Composition also becomes a subject of contention.

Excerpt (1) serves as a good example to illustrate how the characters of the two parties receive graded Judgement. The defendant is depicted favorably by the defense lawyer as "对爱情忠贞、专一" (loyal to love) and "精神与物质都给了她" (spiritually and materially devoted to his love) in terms of Social Sanction. However, from the perspective of the lawyer representing the victim, the defendant is judged negatively and explicitly to have "缺点" (shortcoming) and "自己不争气" ([have] failed to do that as he promised). The victim is judged explicitly and positively in adjectives like "众人皆夸的" (well-acclaimed), "性格文静" (placid), and "做事稳重" (serious). The explicit positive Judgement is made justifiable and noticeable when the lawyer presents implicit evaluations of her behaviors in a series of polarized ideational meanings, such as "被评为三好学生" ([being] awarded the title of "student with merit") and "从未'脚踏两只船'"(never "have[ing] a foot in both camps"). To audiences with the background of Chinese culture, these descriptions may invite a very positive evaluation of the woman and evoke, at the same time, a deep sympathy for the injury she suffered and, ultimately, an indignation at the defendant's cruelty. By means of Judgment in combination with graded ideational meanings, a rather "objective" judgment of the case facts in relation to the defendant's criminal motive may be construed.

In a similar way, lawyers indicate their graded Appreciation of the singing activity when they present facts in Excerpt (4).

Excerpt (4) No M-D-018

被代:原告人并非电视剧《H公主》主题歌的主唱者,也不是原唱者。... 在刚才的庭审调查中...从中我们可以看到,原告所诉的三首歌,亦非片头或片尾的歌曲,也非贯穿全部剧情的主题歌,只是剧中艳、薇、康等人物在表演时因情节需要,自己边演边唱的几个小段子。原告人在这里只是一个配唱者(为荧屏上画面中的人物配上唱腔)。她不像演唱主题歌或独唱歌曲的演员那样,通过荧屏画面与音乐的结合,用自己的演唱技巧和情绪,体现出歌曲的优美,从而感染听众,她只是在服从荧屏上面人物的表演和剧情需要的前提下恰当地表现自己,也就是说她在剧情和人物的限制下辅助地完成表演。	DL: The plaintiff was neither the **chief singer** nor the **original singer** of the theme songs in the TV series Princess H. ... In the trial investigation conducted just now ...we can see that the three songs the plaintiff sued for were not the title songs or closing credit songs nor the theme songs that recur throughout the play. They were just several **tunes** that the characters like Yan, Wei, and Kang sang when they acted, subject to the needs of the plot. So, the plaintiff was just a **vocal performer** (who provides vocals for the characters on the stage). Unlike actors who perform a theme song or a solo, she did not use her own singing techniques and emotions to express the beauty of the song to influence the audience through the perfect integration of the frames and the music. Instead, the plaintiff just acted properly within the constraints of the character's performance on the screen and the needs of the plot, which means that she finished her acting in an auxiliary manner under the restriction of the plots and the characters

This excerpt shows contested criteria for "原唱者"(original singer), "主唱者"(chief singer), and **"配唱者"** (vocal performer). The defense lawyer manifests their negative Appreciation of the plaintiff's performance in terms of Valuation, **"并非...主唱者,也不是原唱者"** (neither the original singer nor chief singer). To justify this Appreciation, the lawyer expresses graded valuations of the songs in question as not "片头或片尾的歌曲" (title songs or closing credit songs) nor "贯穿全部剧情的主题歌" (the theme songs that recur throughout the plays), but rather just "几个小段子**"** (several tunes). To delimit the Valuation of the singing, the lawyer defines the plaintiff's role as a **"配唱者"** (vocal performer), who is "服从...剧情需要的前提下....." (subject to the needs of the plot) and "在...的限制下辅助地完成表演" (acting in an auxiliary manner under the restriction...). The worth of the plaintiff's performance is toned down when it is placed against the Valuation of "演唱主题歌或独唱歌曲的演员" (the actors who sing a theme song or a solo), who may "用自己的演唱技巧和情绪,体现出歌曲的优美,从而感染听众" (use their own singing techniques and emotions to express the beauty of the song so as to influence the audience). Above all, by providing a graded appraisal of the said singing, the defense lawyer belittles the weight of the plaintiff's work in the play and attempts to strengthen their legal argument.

7.2.2.2 Facts and Graded "Measurement"

Negotiating the determinacy of meaning in case facts emerges when lawyers "measure and weigh" the facts presented as evidence in terms of reliability and sufficiency (Yong et al. 2002: 189–233). Technically, reliability means truthfulness, objectivity, and lawful acquisition, while sufficiency pertains to the logical relation between the evidence and the claim it is meant to support. Although the measurement of evidence in these two regards is mainly a mental activity of inference, semiotically, it is facilitated by and reflected in the use of experiential meanings (such as those related to amount, size, or space) or logical meanings (such as the connection between the described facts and the corresponding claim).

Excerpt (5) No. M-D-003

被代:2001年1月5日,我公司的关联公司YT公司与HX公司签订了"大光路167号项目联建协议"及"补充协议",此两协议的性质和主要内容为联合开发房地产项目。我公司为配合YT公司履行该协议,与HX公司签订了"大光路167号项目贷款及抵押担保协议"。该协议的性质为贷款担保协议...。前述三协议无论从名称上、形式上还是从实质上看,均不是HX公司所说的"融资"协议。因此,HX公司所诉我公司和YT公司应向其提供"融资"是不符合事实的	DL: On Feb. 5, 2001, YT Corporation, an affiliated company of my defendant [Z Corporation], signed a "Joint Development Agreement for No.167 Daguang Road Project" and a "Supplementary Agreement" with HX Corporation. Both agreements were joint development agreements on real estate projects in terms of their nature and content. To assist YT in fulfilling its obligations, my defendant signed with HX Corporation a "Loan and Mortgage Guarantee Agreement Related to the No. 167 Daguang Road Project", which was a loan guarantee agreement by its nature. Regardless of their form, content, or substance, none of the aforementioned three agreements are about "financing" as HX alleged. As a result, the claim by HX that my defendant and YT shall provide "financing" for it is not consistent with the facts

In this excerpt, to appreciate the reliability of the evidence provided by the plaintiff HX, the defense lawyer disembowels the contents of the three agreements and interprets them respectively as belonging to "联合开发房地产项目" (joint development agreement in real estate) and "贷款担保协议" (a loan guarantee agreement). Based on this, the lawyer negatively evaluates the logical relation between the three agreements and the plaintiff's claim, as seen in "均不是HX公司所说的'融资'协议" (none ... about "financing" as HX alleged) in terms of "名称上、形式上还是实质上" (form, content, or substance). By measuring the reliability of evidence, the defense overthrows the validity of the evidence presented by the plaintiff and the opposing argument.

Lawyers may also negotiate meanings when they measure the sufficiency of evidence, as is to be demonstrated in Excerpt (6) below.

Excerpt (6) No. M-D-006

被上诉人代理:J检察院认为,第二家具厂基建科长Z某证明DG公司挂靠劳务公司负责该厂商住楼工程施工。以此认定项目经理部为被诉人分支机构。然而,Z某的说法无一份材料予以印证,也就是说DG公司与被诉人是挂靠关系还是联合经营关系,J省检察院没能举证说明,因此Z某的说法只能是个人主观认识,不能代替客观事实。J省检察院将其判断建立在个人主观认识上,显然该判断不能成立	Representative for the appellee: The Prosecutorial Office of J Province claimed that Z, head of the Infrastructure Section of No 2. Furniture Factory, testified that the DG Corporation, which is attached to a labor service company, was responsible for constructing the commercial building for the factory. Based on that testimony, the Prosecutorial Office determined that the Project Management Department is a branch of the appellee. However, Z's statement was not supported by any material, meaning that the Prosecutorial Office of J Province failed to produce evidence to show whether the DG Corporation had an affiliation relationship or joint operation relationship with the appellee. Therefore, Z's statement was purely personal conjecture and cannot be deemed factual. The Prosecutorial Office of J Province based its judgement on a personal subjective opinion, and as such, it cannot be considered valid

In this excerpt, the appellee's lawyer tries to measure the sufficiency of the evidence related to the opinion made by the Prosecutorial Office. Read in the surrounding text, the Office seemed to have based its argument on the witness statement made by Z. The lawyer attacks the validity of the statement with a negative Appreciation, as seen in "无一份材料予以印证" (was not supported by any material), and then interprets it as a kind of hearsay evidence, being "只能是个人主观认识" (purely personal conjecture). Accordingly, the lawyer appreciates the argument of the Prosecutorial Office in negative terms, "显然该判断不能成立" (as such, it cannot be considered valid). Undermining the credibility of the witness statement and revealing the logical fallacy in the prosecutorial office's inference are meant to shatter the story presented by the appellant and dismount the appeal.

7.3 The Categorical Boundary in Complaints or Alleged Charges

Once the clarity or accuracy of the facts of a case is settled through negotiation, the next step involves categorizing or classifying those facts under a specific legal rule. This process is commonly referred to as "legal subsumption", technically. As a transition between the issue of facts and the issue of law, legal subsumption refers to the process of incorporating something into a broader or more general category. In simple terms, it involves assigning the name of a legal charge or claim to the facts of a case. Unlike categorization, classification, and sorting, which are all processes of arranging various things into classes and categories, it involves evaluating the defined case facts in accordance with legal rules or assessing how the particular instances align with the general categories established by those rules. The process consists of two steps: first, incorporating the case facts into a general category of the legal claim or charge, and second, matching the attributes of the case facts with the conditions specified in the legal rules pertaining to the claim or charge (Yong et al. 2002: 275–279).

As the legal rules and the circumstances contained in them are generally abstract, while the case facts under consideration are always specific, trivial, and disorderly, the process of legal subsumption inherently entails legal agents' evaluation and deliberation regarding the relations between the rules and the facts. The involvement of the legal agents' work in legal subsumption leads to the negotiation of meanings between disputing parties in a court in two regards: interpreting a legal rule and determining the prototypicality of the legal claim/charge. These two aspects roughly correspond to the two steps of legal subsumption.

7.3.1 *Interpreting Applicable Legal Rules*

Given that the meaning of legal rules is presumed to be a shared understanding or "lifeworld" upon which rational agreement among legal professionals is to be sought, lawyers are required to demonstrate their interpretations of these rules in court. Therefore, although the legal rules may be interpreted or explained in a monological manner, they are mediated by language and made to be inherently interactive and negotiable. Lawyers mainly concentrate their interpretation on the legal concepts or terms found in the regulations, placing special emphasis on connotative meanings.

Excerpt (7) No. X-D-024

DL: 根据刑法第397条规定,滥用职权罪,是指国家工作机关工作人员超越法律、法律赋予的职权,擅自处理其无权决定、处理的事项,或者违反规定处理公务,致使公共财产、国家和人民利益遭受重大损失的行为。所谓滥用职权罪主要表现为不正确行使职权或超越职权,或者利用手中的职权随心所欲,胡作非为,违法地处理公务。对不同问题作同样处理或对相同的问题作不同的处理,应这样做而那样做,不应做而做	DL: In line with Article 397 of the Criminal Law, the crime of abuse of power refers to behaviors in which an employee of governmental departments exceeds the authority granted to them by law and regulations and handles matters that they are not entitled to decide on or handles public affairs in violation of relevant regulations, incurring significant damage to the public property, the interests of the state or the people. This crime is mainly characterized by the irregularities that occur when the employee improperly exercises their authority, exceeds their authority, or willfully uses their authority to handle public affairs unlawfully. To put it simply, issues of different kinds are handled uniformly, while those of the same kind are handled differently, or issues are handled in ways prohibited by law or when they shall not be done

The interpretation of the crime of abuse of power in this excerpt is monologically presented. However, rhetorically speaking, the interpretation should be understood as dialogically oriented. In accordance with Bakhtin's (1984) view, the essence of "dialogue" lies in the reciprocal relationship between a speaker and their listener at the individual or social level. Each utterance expresses the author's relation to the other. Because of the reciprocal responsiveness, meanings may be generated in a continuous process of verbal communication, or meanings in a given text may be co-created by the speaker/author and their listener/reader and, therefore, are open to change. In this sense, dialogue may be understood as the speaker's attitude or orientation toward communication. When presenting the rule on "滥用职权罪" (the abuse of power), the defense lawyer assumes that the opposing lawyers, the judges, and other audience share with them the understanding of it, which is provided in the law. The audiences are constructed as a community of legal interpreters who have the same "lifeworld" as the background of the ongoing discussion. Accordingly, the lawyer's authorial voice is in interaction with the audiences.

Meanwhile, by making public the understanding of the rule in an argumentative way, the defense lawyer assumes the role of a persuader and identifies the audiences as persons to be persuaded. Prospectively, the speaker makes the interpretation open to responses from the audiences. Therefore, the lawyer may have created an interpersonal space for the opposite party to negotiate meanings.

The lawyer's interpretation of the concept may also be understood as an attempt to create an interpersonal space for negotiation in line with "reported speech" in the Bakhtianian sense. The "reported speech", which means quoting another speaker's utterance in one's speech, may appear in two types: linear style (citation or repetition) and pictorial style (paraphrase or transformation) (Voloshinov 1973). In the linear style, a strict boundary between the authorial voice and the speech reported is maintained. In the pictorial style, an author infiltrates the reported speech with their authorial voice. The analysis of the two different styles, which are intrinsically related to the issue of dialogue, is relevant to the study of ideological values. Reporting in the linear style indicates the reporter's or speaker's tendency to reject changes and stick to a fixed meaning, namely, monologue. In contrast, by reporting in the pictorial style, the speaker tries to weaken or even eliminate the boundaries of reported utterances and make the contextual factors permeate the reported utterance.

Accordingly, analyzing how the lawyer reports the legal rule in Excerpt (7) reveals their basic tendency to the voice of the law and other interactants. After quoting the regulation of "滥用职权罪" (the abuse of power) in Article 397 of the Criminal Law of the People's Republic of China, which appears to be abstract and general, the defense lawyer interprets the rule in their authorial voice. First of all, the speaker illustrates the term by listing some typical behaviors such as "不正确行事职权或超越职权,或者利用手中的职权随心所欲,胡作非为,违法地处理公务" (to improperly exercise their authority or exceed their authority, or willfully use their authority to handle public affairs unlawfully). Then, the lawyer transcends the boundary of formal and legal jargon and paraphrases the term in plain language: "对不同问题作同样处理或对相同的问题作不同的处理,应这样做而那样做,不应做而做" (issues of different kinds are handled uniformly, while those of the same kind are handled differently, or issues are handled in ways prohibited by law or when they should not be done). The dynamic change of the speech style in the interpretation, from banal quoting to the use of formal legal jargon and then plain language, indicates that, although the authorial voice remains the only one talking as if in a monologue, the lawyer is actually engaged in an interaction with the body of the law and the audiences as well for their (potential) responses. In this sense, the defense lawyer is dialogue-oriented with the aim to apply the said legal rule to the specific case.

In addition to the meanings of legal concepts, interpreting what the legal concepts comprise analytically creates another place for lawyers to deliberate the nature of the behaviors involved in a case and negotiate alternative meanings.

Excerpt (8) No M-D-021

被代:被告NY公司认为,依《反不正当竞争法》第五条之规定,判定被告行为是否侵犯知名商品特有名称、包装、装潢的前提是看原告主张的产品“在一定的市场”上是否享有较高的知名度。判定被告的行为是否构成不正当竞争的第二个法律要件是看诉争商品的名称、包装、装潢是否为原告所特有。第三个要件是看结果是否造成误认	DL: The defendant, NY Corporation, believes that in accordance with regulations in Article 5 of the Unfair Competition Law, the precondition for deciding whether the defendant's behavior has infringed on a well-known product in its specific name, package, and decoration is to assess whether the product that the plaintiff sued for has gained a reasonably high reputation in a specific market. The second condition is to determine whether the plaintiff is the exclusive holder of the name, package, and decoration of the product in question. The third condition is to consider whether the defendant's action results in misidentification of the product in question

A comparison of the original regulations in Article 5 of the Anti-Unfair Competition Law (1993), which is attached in Appendix 3, and the paraphrased regulations presented in Excerpt (8) makes evident that diverging from the original rules, the defense lawyer concentrates their interpretation on certain items among the four scenarios listed in the original regulations. Apparently, the second scenario has been chosen as a focal point of interpretation. The lawyer's preference of choice is indexical of their evaluative Judgment on the weight and value of each constituent of the legal claim in the given case.

More importantly, the lawyer shows an interpersonal orientation in their interpretation of the second scenario of the rules. The speaker disintegrates the normative descriptions of the second scenario specified in Article 5 into three segments according to punctuation. These segments are: (i) *unauthorized use of distinctive names, packaging, or decoration specific to a well-known product*; (ii) *the use of names, packaging, or decoration similar to those of a well-known product;* and (iii) *causing confusion with the well-known products to the effect that consumers may mistakenly believe the products in question are the said well-known products.* Actually, the logical relations between the segments, which are not entirely transparent, may allow for two possible interpretations. In terms of focus or emphasis, the original regulation may be understood with a focus on either "擅自使用" (unauthorized use) or features "知名商品特有的" (specific to a well-known product) within the clause "擅自使用知名商品特有的名称、包装、装璜,或者使用与知名商品近似..." (unauthorized use of the names, packaging or decoration specific to a well-known product). With regard to the logical relations between the components, segment (iii) could be considered a direct consequence of the first two or a POSSIBLE consequence incurred by the enactment of the first two.

In this excerpt, the lawyer has chosen to focus their interpretation solely on the phrase "知名商品特有的" (specific to a well-known product), disregarding another potential interpretation. As a result, the defense establishes the logical relationships between the segments of the clause as follows: the well-known products and their specificity serve as concurrent conditions for the alleged act of unfair competition, and segment (iii) is deemed as a straightforward consequence of the enacted act. According to their interpretation, the act of "unauthorized use of distinctive names, packaging, or decoration" is downplayed, while "a well-known product" and "specific to" are given prominence.

In summary, the defense lawyer negotiates meanings related to the legal concept by offering different interpretations of the components of the concept. When they present their view as the sole perspective in the text, they also engage in a dialogic interaction and anticipate responses from the community of legal interpreters. This dialogical stance is partly supported by the textual evidence, "被告NY公司认为" (the defendant NY Corporation believes), which marks the subjectivity of the defense lawyer and their inclination toward interpersonal negotiation.

7.3.2 Discussing Prototypicality in Legal Claims or Charges

In legal subsumption, it is crucial to assign a legal claim/charge to the case facts and match the attributes of the facts with the prescribed circumstances in the legal claim/charge. However, due to the inherent nature of fuzziness in category names and the limitation of perception (Channell 1994), it is very challenging to determine the boundary between the categories of claims/charges. Similarly, demarcating the boundary between the prescribed circumstances in legal claims/charges and the attributes of facts of a case is equally complicated. According to the prototype theory (Lakoff 1987; Rosch et al. 1976), concepts are composed of sets of prototypical features that necessarily and sufficiently define their instances as distinct from others. The prototypical instances or features are conceived to be the core meanings of the concepts, while those similar but non-typical ones are regarded as peripheral meanings. Cognitively, to achieve maximum differentiation when distinguishing between concepts, we usually take the prototypical instances of a category as the essential and distinctive features to separate it most clearly from all other categories. This cognitive principle is applied in legal subsumption. When legal professionals match the case facts with a legal charge/claim, they attempt to distinguish the core meanings of the claim/charge from the peripheral ones. Hence, by expressing an appropriate evaluative attitude regarding the meanings of the case facts and the legal charge, disputing lawyers are engaged in the negotiation of a specific claim/charge.

A typical illustration is provided in Excerpt (9), where lawyers argue about the semantic relations between the two similar features, *actual intent* and *oblique intent,* of the category *intentional homicide.*

Excerpt (9) No. X-D-001

被代:我们认为,被告人Z某....行为已经构成了故意杀人罪。所以,我们对公诉人指控的罪名不持异议。故意犯罪可以分为直接故意与间接故意两种。直接故意是指行为人知其行为的结果而直接追求该结果的发生;间接故意是指行为人虽知其行为可能发生的结果却放任结果的发生。从主观恶性和对社会的危害性来讲,张某在对曹某实施暴力攻击的时候,主观上并没有希望或追求把曹某杀死的故意;杀人行为的实施是处理矛盾不当,盛怒之下丧失理智所致,是偶发性犯罪,其杀人动机应属间接故意	DL: We believe that defendant Z's…action has constituted the crime of intentional homicide. Therefore, we hold no objection to the charge brought by the prosecution against the defendant. Intentional crimes may be divided into two kinds: those with actual intent and those with oblique intent. The former applies to situations in which an actor knows the consequence(s) of such act and directly pursues the occurrence of such consequence(s); the latter applies to situations where an actor purposefully does nothing to prevent the consequence(s) of their act despite knowing the possible consequence(s) of the act. In terms of subjective wickedness and the potential harm to society, when Z assaulted the victim C by violence, he displayed no intent to anticipate or seek to cause the victim to die; the killing resulted from his loss of reason at the height of his fury over his failure to properly handle his dispute with the victim. Therefore, the defendant's behavior should be considered a sporadic crime, with oblique intent in terms of the criminal intent

In this excerpt, the defense lawyer expresses their agreement to the alleged charge, "故意杀人罪" (intentional homicide). In the counter-argument that follows the agreement, the lawyer concentrates their graded evaluations toward two types of crimes depending on the actor's criminal motive: "直接故意" (those with actual intent), "间接故意" (those with oblique intent). To deliberate the defendant's action in nature, the speaker distinguishes meanings of the two kinds of crimes in terms of motive at the outset: "直接追求" (pursue) versus "放任…发生" (purposefully does nothing to prevent), where differences lie in how the actor responds to the result of the offense. By the comparison, actual intent is highlighted as the prototypical feature of intentional homicide, as presumed in the analysis of the behavior under discussion, where the defendant "主观上并没有希望或追求" (displayed no intent to anticipate or seek). Subsequently, the defense lawyer argues, in terms of the severity of the intent and the potential threat, for subsumption of the defendant's criminal act into a "偶发性" (sporadic) crime, which possesses the periphery feature of intentional homicide. With the classification as a transition, the lawyer re-evaluates and re-classifies the defendant's action of killing under the category of "间接故意" (homicide with oblique intent). In this way, the defense downplays the "focus" of the defendant's violent offense and undermines the severity of the criminal motive. All in all, the defense's negotiation for the semiotic conversion of the facts of the defendant's behavior into legal terms undergoes a process of graded evaluations from the typical instance, "直接故意" (actual intent), to the less typical one, "间接故意" (oblique intent), and to the periphery one, "偶发性" (sporadic).

Another instance where the meanings of a legal category are negotiated is in determining the central features that fall under that category. See Excerpt (10) below.

Excerpt (10) No. X-D-026

被代: 被告人H某并没有利用职务上的便利收受过吴某的财物... W某曾向检察人员陈述,2002年夏季,他...给过H某1万元钱。他说他与H某是朋友关系。H某的家里病人多,他给H某钱是尽点朋友的心意...H某并不否认W某给过他钱,但...送钱的原因是因为他母亲患精神病住院,W某很关心,表示朋友的心意,他才收下,与W某所说完全一致。 除送钱之外,W某、H某都承认,2004年的一天...他俩曾互换了各自戴的手表。当时在场的有朱某,S某以及L某等人。从刚才法庭宣读的证据可以看出,当时W某与H某换戴手表完全是朋友之间开玩笑的背景下发生的,与他们的职务毫无关系。 我们认为,虽然H某收受过W某的钱,互相还换戴手表,但这些完全是朋友之间的正常经济往来,根本不能构成受贿罪	DL: Defendant H did not take bribes by taking advantage of his position... Witness W once testified to the prosecutors that in the summer of 2002, he gave H 10,000 yuan ...He claimed that he and H were friends... and that since H had many patients to care for in his family, he gave H the money to express his goodwill as a friend of H. H did not deny receiving money from W, but stated that... the reason was: when his mother was hospitalized with a kind of mental disease, W was very concerned and offered the money to express his goodwill as a friend. He accepted the money, therefore. H's statement is completely consistent with what W testified. Apart from giving and accepting money, both H and W admitted that one day in 2004, ... they exchanged the watches that they were wearing, in the presence of Z, S, L, and several others. From the testimonies presented in court just now, we learned that the exchange of their watches was purely a playful act between friends and had nothing to do with their positions Above all, we believe that the acceptance of money and the exchange of the watches were merely routine economic practices between friends and did not constitute bribery at all

In this excerpt, contextualizing bribery as a secretive, profit-driven transaction enables the defense lawyer to make two crucial distinctions. Firstly, the defense differentiates between accepting money for the exchange of power versus accepting money for the expression of friendship. Secondly, the lawyer also differentiates between exchanging watches for bribery versus engaging in a playful act in a public setting. These distinctions are exploited to challenge the accusation that H's acceptance of money and the watch was related to his position. The distinctions are shown in the active engagement of witnesses' voices in the speech. According to W's testimony, the money was given as a gesture of friendship because W wanted to "尽点朋友的心意" (express his goodwill as a friend). Similarly, the defendant is quoted to have expressed details of the event in relation to their friendship. Thus, the acceptance of money was successfully contextualized as a behavior between friends during a time of trouble. Likewise, concerning the accusation that H accepted property from W for personal gain, the defense contextualizes the behavior within the framework where a public exchange of watches is "完全是朋友之间开玩笑的背景下发生的" (merely a playful act between friends). Therefore, the acts of accepting money or property have been transformed, from the prosecution's perspective of accepting bribes, to the neutralized and favorable stance taken by the defense, which is re-lexicalized as "完全是朋友之间的正常经济往来" (routine economic practices between friends).

Above all, by exploiting the periphery meaning of exchanging property between two individuals, the lawyer has deconstructed the prototypical context or the main feature of the charge of bribery in this case. Consequently, the characterization of the behavior in question has been subtly altered in an unnoticed way.

There have been numerous reports on how periphery and core meanings of a term are exploited to negotiate meanings in legal subsumption. Typical examples are Danet's (1980) study on the distinction between "fetus" versus "baby", Loftus and Palmer's (1974) work on "crashing" versus "smashing", and Drew's (1990) research on "club" versus "pub".

7.4 The Appropriacy of Legal Decisions

Regarding the issue of the law in a trial, two main steps are involved in the process of reaching a legal decision. One is how to select a specific legal rule applicable and the other is to measure the circumstances of the case against the conditions prescribed in the law. Both steps require lawyers to engage in evaluations (Yong et al. 2002).

The involvement of lawyer evaluation in the law application arises from the complexity of legal principles and rules. Firstly, in law, specific situations often pose challenges that need to be reconciled with more general legal principles. During the application process, rules have to be adjusted in order to accommodate evolving circumstances and exceptions that arise in real life. Furthermore, within the body of the law, there may be overlapping regulations across clauses and acts. Lastly, the revision of legal rules and regulations by legislative organizations further contributes to the complexity of law application, both in selecting the appropriate rules and assessing the conditions in a given case.

It is the complexity in the process of law application that allows for the negotiation of alternative choices in the judgment of a given case. Naturally, the process of reaching a legal decision becomes an arena where rounds of contestation and negotiation take place between disputing parties.

7.4.1 Selecting Specific Rules Applicable to a Case

Choosing a rule that is relevant to a specific case is not a straightforward mathematical calculation that can be performed automatically. It entails the selection of a particular law from a collection of principles or regulations that pertain to the specific subject matter at hand, as well as the selection of a specific clause within that law. The complexity of the selection may be attributed to several factors. Firstly, there may be overlaps or inconsistencies between the laws issued by different law-making bodies at the state, ministerial, provincial, or other organizational levels. Secondly, confusion may arise when determining which edition of a law should be taken as operative, especially if the disputed act occurs during the transitional time between two versions of the law. Lastly, ambiguous expressions resulting from inefficient law-making techniques may lead to potential obstacles for legal professionals to understand and apply the regulations in the judicial process. All of these factors contribute to the contested and negotiable nature of the discursive activity of selecting a legal rule.

Excerpt (11) provides an example to illustrate how negotiation opens up regarding the invocation of regulations on voluntary confession to a specific case.

Excerpt (11) No. X-D-025

被代: S某的自首行为发生在新《刑法》施行前(1997年10月1日前),应根据原来的《刑法》及与原《刑法》相应的司法解释认定(如1994年两高和公安部的规定)。在原来的规定中,只要司法机关未采取强制措施,向其他部门交代的均应认定为自首,即使因形迹可疑被司法机关传讯后,主动交代的也应认定为是自首。新《刑法》颁布后,在本案起诉前,对自首问题也没有明确的司法解释,但从新《刑法》关于自首的规定看,对自首的要求更宽	DL: The defendant S's act of surrender occurred before the revised Criminal Law (prior to October 1, 1997) entered into force. Therefore, it should be determined in accordance with regulations in the original Criminal Law and the relevant judicial interpretations (such as the judicial interpretations issued by the Supreme People's Court, the Supreme People's Prosecutorial Office, and the Ministry of Public Security in 1994). Pursuant to those regulations, as long as no coercive measures were taken by the judicial authorities, presenting oneself voluntarily to an organization other than judicial organs should be recognized as a voluntary surrender; the act of reporting or admitting offenses voluntarily to judicial organs by an offender should also be regarded as voluntary surrender even if the offender was initially brought in for questioning due to suspicious behaviors. Although there has been no specific judicial interpretation issued on surrender after the promulgation of the revised Criminal Law and before the prosecution in this case, the provisions in the revised Criminal Law regarding voluntary surrender suggest broader requirements for such an act

As is co-textually read in this excerpt, the trial of the defendant's case happened after October 1, 1997, the time when the revised Criminal Law came into effect, while the investigation into the case started before that date. The lawyer contends that the defendant's act of cooperating with the prosecutors "应" (should be) determined as voluntary surrender in accordance with the relevant regulations in the original version of the Criminal Law.

Actually, the defense lawyer has presumably taken the defendant's act as a "自首行为" (voluntary surrender), which is indicated in their nominalized packaging of "S某的自首行为" (S's surrender) and explained explicitly in the clause "S某的自首行为发生在新《刑法》施行前" (S's act of surrendering occurred before the revised Criminal Law entered into force). In order to provide a broad definition of the concept, the lawyer uses conditional clauses of concession, in "只要...,即使因..." (so long as ...even if the offender...). Interactively, in order to limit or close down any alternative view to contest their voice or position, the lawyer continues to argue that the scope of the term in the revised Criminal Law should be interpreted more broadly, as seen in "要求更宽" (broader requirements). Meanwhile, the lawyer's negotiation efforts are reflected in their language in lexico-grammar. The coupling of the high-value modal verb "应" (should) and the graded evaluative lexis, "更宽" (broader requirements) conveys the defense's preference for an interpersonal orientation. The argumentative tone enables the lawyer to demonstrate their intention to negotiate meanings.

7.4.2 Measuring Compensations or Penalties

To measure the circumstances in a given case against those prescribed in the selected rule, many factors, such as the severity of the act or offense, consequences of the alleged misconduct, and corresponding liability, have to be considered (Yong et al. 2002). As a general rule, to allow for a more extensive coverage of possibilities in real life, legal descriptions of the circumstances and relevant punishment are vague and abstract. Naturally, lawyer evaluation regarding the penalty or compensation to be imposed in a case becomes a process of negotiation for interpersonal meanings.

Excerpt (12) No. X-D-025

被代:对被告人量刑时可以考虑的其他情节:1.被告人犯罪的主观恶性小,即,罪大恶不极。S某受贿数目特别巨大,但是其犯罪情节并非特别严重。综观S某的整个受贿事实,没有一次是主动索贿,都是人家主动提出给好处,... 与那种卡、要、不给钱不办事...其主观恶性较小。2. 被告人的犯罪行为并没有给Lian公司造成损失。3. 被告人犯罪后能坦白交代自己的罪行。4. 积极配合退赃。5. 被告人曾经对国家、集体做出过突出贡献。综上所述,我们认为被告人...不是不杀不足以平民愤的犯罪分子,也不是不杀不足以防止其继续危害社会的犯罪分子,也就是不是必须判决死刑立即执行的犯罪分子,请求法院根据坦白从宽的政策,对被告人从轻处罚	DL: Other circumstances that should be considered when determining the penalty on the defendant are presented in the following. Firstly, the defendant's subjective evil character **is slight.** Although the defendant is **guilty of a serious crime, it is not the most heinous one**. The bribes that the defendant S took were exceptionally huge in amount, but the circumstances of his crime were not **particularly severe**. A review of the various facts of his bribery makes evident that he never extorted bribes even once and the bribers offered to provide benefits for him each time… Compared with those practices such as setting up improper barriers against beneficiaries out of self-interest, extorting benefits, and making service contingent upon the offer of money… the defendant's behaviors show a comparatively slight subjective evil character. Secondly, the defendant's criminal acts did not cause any loss to the Lian Company, where he worked. Thirdly, the defendant voluntarily confessed to all his wrongdoings. Fourthly, the defendant returned his bribes with full cooperation. Fifthly, the defendant once made outstanding contributions to the state and the organization for which he worked All in all, we believe that the defendant… is not a criminal who must be executed so as to vent public outcry or prevent further harm to society. In other words, the defendant is not a criminal who must be given the death penalty and executed immediately. The defense requests that the court give him a less severe penalty in accordance with the policy of "lenient punishment for voluntary confessors"

To negotiate a less severe penalty for the defendant, the defense lawyer presents their evaluative attitude toward the circumstances in the said case and begs the court to consider them. Their evaluative attitudes are negotiated through linguistic operations in several aspects. Firstly, the four-character phrase, "罪大恶极" (*zui da e ji,* in pinyin), which literally means a heinous crime, is creatively used. As a fixed expression, "罪大"(a serious crime) and "恶极" (the most heinous crime) are used in company or in a paired group to describe the seriousness of the crime. In this context, this idiom is skillfully manipulated to create a graded meaning: the defendant is guilty of the serious crime—the bribes that he took were "特别巨大" (exceptionally large in amount)—but not of the most heinous crime, of which **"**其犯罪情节并非特别严重**"** (the circumstances were not particularly severe).

Secondly, idioms are skillfully exploited to undermine the severity of the defendant's criminal motive. The graded meanings in the evaluative adjectives are modified by adverbs of degree, such as "特别巨大" (exceptionally huge) in amount and "特别严重" (particularly severe) in the circumstances, which reserves some space for interpersonal negotiation. Thirdly, the defendant's action is placed in contrast to the extremely treacherous practices of "主动索贿" (extorting bribes), "卡、要、不给钱不办事" (setting up improper barriers against beneficiaries, extorting benefits, and making service contingent upon the offer of money), thereby mitigating the severity of the defendant's crime. Fourthly, to accelerate the persuasive effect, the several circumstances are skillfully arranged in succession, from the most important to the least important. At last, by way of conclusion, the lawyer employs a unique structure to reinforce their position. The structure composed of two negations "不是" (not) in the last few lines has continuously diminished the severity of the defendant's action to the extent that it is possible for the defendant to receive a less severe punishment.

Above all, the lawyer's evaluations circulate throughout the whole text and form an accelerating piece of attitude, as if in a musical prosody.

7.5 Summary

This chapter has thoroughly analyzed how lawyers employ evaluations in rational discourse to functionally realize the communicative tasks of legal dispute resolution or criminal case disposition in the trial. As revealed in the data, their discursive negotiation of meanings goes through three stages: the construction of the facts of a case, the deliberation of the facts in the legal framework, and the process of reaching a legal decision. When constructing the facts, lawyers argue fiercely for the accuracy or accuracy of the narrated facts. They may scale the focus of the presented events through descriptions or scale specific aspects of the facts through the introduction of external voices. Meanwhile, they may grade their Judgments or Appreciations of the facts of the case, in particular, the characters of the party involved or the quantity or scope related to the specified behaviors in the case. When deliberating the nature of the facts within the legal framework, they contest with each other to negotiate the categorical meanings of the legal concepts. They intensely dig into the definition clause that contains key legal concepts and intensely analyze the prototypical meanings of those concepts. When it comes to making a legal decision, they exert their efforts on the appropriacy of the decision by either discussing the most relevant rule applicable to the case concerned or arguing about the degree of measurement related to the forthcoming penalty or compensation.

In the end, it is worth noting that the division of the three stages is only for analytical purposes in this study. As a matter of fact, the focus of lawyers' negotiation for the scales of justice may be initiated at any point within the three stages in accordance with the characteristics of the case at hand.

References

Atkinson, R.C., and P. Drew. 1990. *Order in Court*. Hampshire and London: Macmillan Academic and Professional Ltd.

Bakhtin, M. 1984. *Problems of Dostoevsky's Poetics*, ed. C. Emerson. Minneapolis: University of Minnesota Press.

Chafe, W. 1979. *The Pear Story: Cognitive, Cultural and Linguistic Aspects of Narrative Production*. Norwood, NJ: Ablex.

Channell, J. 1994. *Vague Language*. Oxford: Oxford University Press.

Cheng, Chun-hua. and Bin Huang. 2002. 试论建立现代自由心证制度 [Tentative thoughts on the establishment of a modern system of free assessment of evidence]. 中国司法审判论坛第二卷[*China Judicial Trial Forum* (vol.2)]. Beijing: Law Press.

Cotterill, J. 2001. Domestic discord, rocky relationships: Semantic prosodies in representations of marital violence in the courtroom. *Discourse & Society* 12 (3): 315–336. https://doi.org/10.1177/0957926501012003002.

Danet, B. 1980. "Baby" or "fetus": Language and the construction of reality in a manslaughter trial. *Semiotica* 32: 187–219. https://doi.org/10.1515/semi.1980.32.3-4.187.

Drew, P. 1990. Strategies in the contest between lawyer and witness in cross-examination. In *Language in the Judicial Process*, eds. Levi, J.N., and A.G. Walker, 39–64. New York and London: Plenum Press. https://doi.org/10.1007/978-1-4899-3719-3_2.

Drew, P. 1992. Contested evidence in courtroom examinations. In *Talk at Work: Interaction in Institutional Settings*, ed. P. Drew and J. Heritage, 470–520. New York: Plenum Press.

Du, Jin-bang. (2001). 从法律语言的模糊性到司法结果的确定性 [From the vagueness of legal language to the definiteness of judicial outcomes]. 现代外语[*Modern Foreign Languages*] (3), 305–310.

Goodwin, C., and M.H. Goodwin. 1997. Contested version: The discursive constitution of Rodney King. In *The Construction of Professional Discourse*, eds. Britt-Louise Gunnarsson, P. Linell et al, 292–316. London and New York: Longman.

Lakoff, G. 1987. Cognitive models and prototype theory. In *Concepts and Conceptual Development: Ecological and Intellectual Factors in Categorization*, ed. U. Neisser, 63–100. Cambridge: Cambridge University Press.

Loftus, E.F., and J.C. Palmer. 1974. Reconstruction of automobile destruction: An example of the interaction between language and memory. *Journal of Verbal Learning and Verbal Behavior.* 13: 585–589. https://doi.org/10.1016/S0022-5371(74)80011-3.

Matoesian, G.M. 1993. *Reproducing Rape: Dominance Through Talk in the Courtroom*. Oxford: Polity Press.

Posner, R.A. 1990. *The Problems of Jurisprudence*. Cambridge: Harvard University Press.

Rogers, L., and E. Erez. 1999. Contextualization of objectivity in sentencing among legal professionals in South Australia. *International Journal of the Sociology of Law* 27: 267–286. https://doi.org/10.1006/ijsl.1999.0092.

Rosch, E., B. Mervis, W.D. Gray, et al. 1976. Basic objects in natural categories. *Cognitive Psychology* 8: 382–439. https://doi.org/10.1016/0010-0285(76)90013-X.

Sacks, H. 1972. On the analyzability of stories by children. In *Directions in Sociolinguistics: The Ethnography of Communication*, eds. Gumperz, J.J., and D.H. Hymes, 325–345. New York: Holt, Rinehart & Winston.

Simpson, P. 1993. *Language, Ideology, and Point of View*. London and New York: Routledge.

Stiff, J., and P. Mongeau. 2003. *Persuasive Communication*, 2nd ed. New York and London: The Guilford Press.

Voloshinov, V.N. 1973. *Marxism and the Philosophy of Language*. Cambridge: Harvard University Press.

Xue, Shao-feng. 1996. 律师论辩学[*Lawyers' Advocacy*]. Beijing: People's Public Security University of China Press.

Yong, Q., Cheng-guang Jin, and Rong-mao Yao. 2002. 法律适用中的逻辑[*Logic in Law Application*]. Beijing: China University of Political Science and Law.

Chapter 8
Conclusion

This chapter concludes the study by providing a brief summary of the preceding chapters. Then, it presents the major findings provided in this study and discusses the potential implications. Lastly, it addresses the limitations of this study and provides suggestions for future studies on lawyer evaluation.

8.1 Summary

To address the legal communication issue between disputing lawyers in China's current trial system, this study focuses on lawyer evaluation as its subject. It aims to examine the discourse of lawyer evaluation in the current legal context. Chapter 1 introduces the research topic, defines the key concept, lawyer evaluation, and then briefly presents the significance of the research topic.

Chapter 2 provides a comprehensive review of previous studies on lawyer evaluation, emphasizing the importance of studying it as a linguistic phenomenon situated within the social context. Adopting the social-semiotic perspective of Systemic Functional Linguistics as the guiding theoretical foundation, this study proposes to incorporate the Habermasian viewpoints of law and legal communication into the analysis of lawyers' speech in the Chinese courtroom.

Chapter 3 presents a theoretical framework for understanding lawyer evaluation in the Chinese courtroom. First of all, three components of lawyer evaluation are categorized and redefined. Then, in line with the Hallidayan view on the mutual determination between context and text, the contextual features of the courtroom in the Chinese context are described, and the impacts of these contextual features on lawyer evaluation are analyzed. The context of situation in the courtroom interaction reveals that confrontation is an essential characteristic of the interpersonal relationship between disputing lawyers; at a broader level of context, the statements of Habermas on the role relationship between participants in legal communication determine that the

L. Zhang, *Lawyer Evaluation in Chinese Courtroom*,
https://doi.org/10.1007/978-981-97-1211-3_8

rational discourse of lawyer evaluation encompasses three features. These features are then realized by and manifested through lawyer evaluation of various topics in trial communication. Lastly, the discursive construction of lawyer evaluation with these features is meant to fulfill the communicative tasks of legal dispute resolution functionally.

To validate and illustrate the theoretical framework of the rational discourse of lawyer evaluation, this study conducts comprehensive discourse analysis in four chapters, spanning from Chaps. 4–7.

8.2 Major Findings

To address the legal issue of how the "rational contest" is verbally organized between disputing lawyers in the court, this study has made a linguistic endeavor to the presentation of lawyer evaluation in the current Chinese courtroom from the Hallidayan socio-semiotic perspective, particularly its framework on interpersonal meanings. The major findings are presented below.

Firstly, since the three kinds of speaker attitudes in Appraisal Theory, AFFECT, JUDGMENT, and APPRECIATION, are present in judicial discourse, lawyer evaluation has been categorized into Affect, Judgement, and Appreciation, all of which are shaped or conditioned by the legal context where objectivity is regarded as a vital principle. The three attitudes, in particular, Judgement and Appreciation, are modified or redefined based on court scenarios. Notably, a sub-variable called Social Punishment is proposed to evaluate the character of an individual within the legal framework. This variable, positioned under Judgement alongside Social Esteem and Social Sanction, allows for more nuanced distinctions to be made among the characters of a person as an individual, a community member, and a legal citizen.

The variable of Social Punishment is designated as such for consideration in two regards. In the first regard, when evaluating the qualities of a person in a trial, it is always necessary to demarcate the boundaries between the ethical and the legal aspects, although the former is intertwined with the latter. Making a strict distinction between the two aspects is not only a legal and cognitive operation in judicial reasoning (see Yong et al. 2002) but also a practice observed in lawyers' arguments when they assess the credibility of a witness statement or the severity of an alleged offense or complaint in terms of motive. In the second regard, in a socio-cognitive sense, the Chinese had developed a particular view of law and morality due to the influence of humanism-centered Confucianism in the Chinese legal tradition, which has impacted language use in trial communication today. As revealed in the coded laws in the traditional legal history of China, the law, written as 刑 in the Chinese character (*xing* in pinyin, which means *penal law*, literally), was typically understood as a means of punishment throughout the imperial societies (before 1911), and given a secondary role to play after the primary and predominant place of the Confucian moral education and cultivation in the regulation of social activities and maintenance of social order (Zhang 2003; Shi 2006). The legal practice of law-making was aligned with the legal ideology characterized by the phrase "德主刑辅" (*de zhu xing fu*, in pinyin), which literally means the rule of virtue (moral cultivation) was primary, and the rule of punishment (penal law) was secondary in social control and management (Qu 1984). Although the modern view of the law as a rule-based system to regulate social life and safeguard the rights and duties of people has been widely adopted in the legal and social world of China today, the traditional view of the law may still remain active in the cultural memory of people to a certain extent.

In the courtroom, where mandatory rules govern the presentation and admission of evidence and legal opinions, the three constituents are distributed and realized differently. Judgment and Appreciation both play a significant role in lawyer evaluation in the court, while Affect plays a minor role. Meanwhile, contrary to everyday settings where evaluations are typically expressed through adjectives or nouns, lawyer evaluation in courtrooms is primarily conveyed by a combination of congruent and incongruent expressions, which means the coordinated use of a variety of structures, including nouns, verbs, other lexis associated with ideational meanings, grammatical structures, and discourse structure in large phases of text.

Secondly, in the exploration of lawyer evaluation during trial proceedings in China, the situational context of the courtroom and the broader context of legal culture both exert their impacts on the regularities of lawyer speech in a trial. Accordingly, lawyers in Chinese courts share similarities with their counterparts in Western courts and also manifest some features typical of Chinese culture.

Similar to situations in Western countries, the essential relationship between disputing lawyers in China is confrontation and competition, as the Chinese courtroom follows an adversary trial system in proceedings, just like the system in Western courts. This relationship is reflected in the three functions of language in text: conflicting conceptions of rights and duties of each party in ideational meanings, competing interests of each party in interpersonal meanings, and contestant information presentation in the thematic structures of the text.

With the mediating role of the legal culture concerning the role relationships between participants in legal communication in China, lawyers may choose to orient their speech to confrontation on the dimension of solidarity, which can be observed in the three meta-functions of language in text.

Thirdly, guided and supported by the higher-level context of the legal culture, lawyer evaluation in the Chinese court manifests particular features of its own, which are in alignment with the Chinese culture regarding the resolution of conflicts and the achievement of peace and harmony in society. The statements on the relationship in roles between participants engaged in legal communication, proposed by Habermas in his theory of law, which has been elaborated to be consistent with the specific situations of China in legal, social, and cultural senses, have provided a solid foundation for analyzing lawyers' stance in the court debate. Therefore, the analysis of lawyer evaluation and its pattern in text is highly motivated both in theory and in practice.

Lawyer evaluation in rational discourse consists of three main features as follows: an equal role relationship, a multi-voiced environment, and discursive communities of *us* versus *them*. The discursive construction of rational discourse is fulfilled through direct or indirect evaluations of the various topics concerned in trial communication. A variety of resources, including modality, graduation, projection, and other linguistic devices, may be employed.

Fourthly, lawyer evaluation has to be understood in close connection with the communicative tasks of legal dispute resolution in the trial. Only in this way can the positioning of lawyers be fully understood in its nature. Lawyer evaluation in rational debating serves as the linguistic process to realize the main task of the trial, which is to negotiate justice in the specified case at hand.

In the two goals of trial communication, the personal goal of winning a case is integrated into the common goal to search for a fair judgment of the case or to seek truth/justice in that case. The linguistic negotiation for justice, which runs throughout the whole process of the trial, encompasses contested evaluations made regarding the following aspects: the accuracy or clarity of the facts of a case, the categorical boundary of specified legal concepts in relation to the facts, and the appropriateness or suitability in the legal decisions to be made.

8.3 Implications

The implications to be drawn from this study are discussed in theoretical and practical aspects, respectively.

8.3.1 Theoretical Implications

The study on the presentation of lawyer evaluation in China provides some insights for judicial discourse studies, institutional discourse analysis, and evaluation studies. First of all, when examining the specific language used by legal professionals in judicial settings of a particular region or country, it is crucial to go beyond the local situational context and consider the role of legal ideology or legal culture. The contextual information in the domain of legal culture may offer interpretations contributing to the analysis of how legal professionals may display particular communicative behaviors in texts of the specific context, which may in turn distinguish them from those in judicial contexts of other cultural patterns.

Similar to Bernstein's (1972) concept of coding orientations (see related discussions in Halliday 1978), social or legal ideology has a significant influence on language use, just as it does in distinguishing the levels of speech used between working-class children and middle-class children. In the context of an adversarial trial, legal ideologies may influence the salient dimensions on which lawyers from the opposing sides interact with each other in the trial talk. As demonstrated in this study, lawyers in Chinese courts operate their communicative activities within the cultural framework influenced by Confucian values that prioritize harmony in interpersonal relationships. These values have become implicit conventions in the moral or ethical sense that are used to regulate people's daily behaviors. Additionally, the construction of a harmonious, modern society has been considered a political agenda. Given all that, Chinese lawyers may choose to prioritize confrontation on the dimension of solidarity, in contrast to their counterparts in English-speaking countries who are more focused on the dimension of power, despite both orientations being potentially operated in the local context of the adversarial trial system.

Since legal ideologies may have different coding orientations (or interpretations of the role relationships between legal agents), it is highly likely that in accordance with the viewpoints of Habermas (1996) on communicative action in law, solidarity would be a prominent feature in the interpersonal relationship between legal professionals; and in places where other legal ideologies, such as formal positivism or critical law, are prominent, power and status would be a more salient feature conveyed through interpersonal meanings in lawyer talk. In this sense, our findings on the cultural positioning of lawyers align with Philips' (1998) observation of the influence of legal ideologies on the language of the trial judge.

However, it should be acknowledged that other factors, for instance, the presence or absence of a jury in court, could act as intervening variables in this relationship. In most adversary trials in common law countries, the presence of a jury puts tremendous pressure on the counsel's use of language (see O'Barr 1982). In contrast, in the adversary trials of China, the role of "people's jurors" has been found to assume a marginal role in most cases (Huang 2011; Niu 2013).

Secondly, this study may be enlightening to research on institutional discourse by addressing the common problem of "unequally distributed access" among participants in institutional settings. Usually, one of the primary goals for institutional discourse studies is to uncover the contextual constraints imposed by institutional settings on language and to explicitly identify the accepted norms of "good discourse" under these constraints. Critical Discourse Analysis, which is centered on the dimension of power and control in language (see, for example, Fairclough 1992, 2003; van Dijk 1996), has the same objective. As commented by Martin and Rose (2003: 264), "the main focus of CDA work has been on hegemony, on exposing power as it naturalizes itself in discourse, and thus feeling in some sense part of the struggle against it." However, if improving the unequal distribution of access to institutional discourse is regarded as the ultimate goal of discourse studies, applying the "existing standards" (Hasan 1996: 405–406) to the participants is not sufficient to eliminate power and control within these institutions. It would be more effective if participants were equipped in a way so that they are able to produce knowledge of their own instead of replicating existing standards. Teaching a person how to fish is better than giving them a fish. By empowering participants in institutional settings to construct their meanings within various constraints, they would not only be able to accomplish communicative tasks but also learn how to work to their advantage. Following this line of reasoning, this study aligns with an alternative approach to institutional discourses, namely, Positive Discourse Analysis (Martin and Rose 2003: 264), which is centered on the dimension of solidarity and provides an instance of effective speech patterns with which people may negotiate meanings rationally or peacefully in conflicting environments.

Lawyer evaluation presented along the dimension of solidarity in this study may be seen as one endeavor to improve communication in institutional settings. In the courtroom, where power and social status are distributed unequally, rational discussions through lawyer evaluation could contribute to changing power relations. Everything being equal, the interpersonal positioning of lawyers as rational debaters could effectively bring changes to interpersonal role relations, both between the lawyer-lawyer relationship and the lawyer-judge relationship. This study argues that the Habermasian viewpoints on communicative action in law that serves as a guiding legal principle on lawyer speech is expected to make trial communication less coercive, compared with the culture that emphasizes control and dominance. As elucidated by distinguished Judge Jiang in recent discussions on the trial practices in China, the lawyers' speech pattern has surpassed the contesting, combative stage where the prosecution and defense competed with each other in court like gladiators on a battlefield. Instead, it is evolving or progressing toward a cooperative stage where lawyers negotiate with each other to ensure that justice and fair judgment are lawfully administered to every party concerned (Zhang et al. 2020: 477). Naturally, the use of positive language or the speech style in a rational manner (Zhang et al. 2020: 17) is instrumental in empowering litigants, defendants, or their legal representatives to effectively enact their legitimate role as active agents engaging in a dialogue for a fair solution to the case, rather than as participants who were passively interrogated in the past. The speech pattern also enables the prosecution to better fulfill their duty and safeguard justice.

Thirdly, this study on the evaluative language in lawyer talk also offers insights into research on evaluation studies. Appraisal Theory has long noticed the sensitivity of evaluation resources to culture and context in terms of distribution (Precht 2003: 240). Many studies, such as those conducted by Miller (2002, 2004), Kšrner (2000), and Hood (2004), have examined the institutionally sensitive evaluations in context and have made refined contributions to their respective fields. However, due to the limitation of space or other factors, these studies often lack exploration into the social motivations underlying their findings. This research on lawyer evaluation not only investigated the distinctive features of speaker attitudes within the legal context and tentatively proposed a new variable, Social Punishment, to accommodate the expression of attitudes regarding the legal aspect of an individual's quality or character in law but also provided systematic explanations for how attitudes and evaluations may be influenced and determined by the institutional and cultural context.

8.3.2 Practical Implications

Pedagogically, this study offers some suggestions on how to educate law students. Technically, it also proposes some linguistic strategies for lawyers to use as references.

8.3.2.1 Pedagogical Discussions

In the current education of law students, instructions provided on how to effectively utilize language are very limited, and there is a lack of emphasis on the multifaceted functions of language (Zhang 2022). Reflections on the teaching curriculum in law schools in current China reveal that law students used to receive solid training in legal theories and practical professional skills, but there is a lack of instruction specifically related to the principles of language use itself (see Li 2022; Tang 2014). It is not surprising, then, that many legal professionals still intuitively use language as a functional tool without being well-informed about how to harness the power of language, particularly in terms of constructing their stance and aligning the readers simultaneously (see also Zhang et al. 2001).

Currently, proper training in language use appears to be of utmost importance for the effective implementation of the latest Criminal Procedure Law (2018) in China. The training in language is particularly relevant as there is an increasing demand for more proficient lawyers to provide defense services for laypersons in order to ensure fair justice in trials, especially as the trial system is now moving into a cooperative pattern. On the one hand, the cross-examination of evidence and witnesses necessitates highly skilled lawyers with solid advocacy skills (Zhang et al. 2020: 251). On the other hand, since the principle of making a confession of one's offenses or misconducts in exchange for leniency in a prospective judgment (similar to plea-bargaining in the Anglo-Saxon law) is practiced in the criminal law of China, striking a proper balance between assisting a defendant in negotiating their case for leniency and avoiding the risk of the defendant self-incriminating themselves poses a challenging task to lawyers both linguistically and cognitively.

Therefore, more attention should be devoted to the education of law students with respect to the potential of language. The positive impact of the coding orientation or principles in legal culture on lawyer evaluation should be acknowledged. Meanwhile, the various kinds of resources in the language system that facilitate the expression of lawyer evaluation should be exploited (Halliday 1996; Hasan 1996).

8.3.2.2 Technical Discussions

To enhance the effectiveness of lawyers' engagement in trial discourse, this study proposes several linguistic strategies. The strategies offered here are not in any sense related to the manipulation of language for power and control in institutional settings. As social actors, lawyers are bound to behave linguistically within the constraints of the communicative situation. However, as individuals, they should also have the awareness and ability to construct their identities appropriately and creatively by employing specific strategies.

First and foremost, since the presentation of the facts of a case is situated in the competitive environment of a court where alternative interpretations or voices exist, when expressing their legal positions or stances, lawyers have to be aware, from the outset, of the presence of alternative voices or potential responses from their contestants and audiences. Active engagement in interactive interactions throughout the trial works better than adhering solely to a monologic speech or a fixed stance.

Second, when presenting legal positions or evaluations in the court, lawyers should be mindful that their speech is to be influenced by various pragmatic factors, which include but are not limited to the following.

A. Conventions within the institutional context of the trial, for instance, the pre-allocated turn-taking system and the legal ideology of procedural justice. Guided by the rational coding orientation of law, lawyers are expected to take justification and criticism as two important principles with which to align the audiences and alienate their opponents.
B. Communicative purposes of the addressees, in particular, the opposing parties, in the immediate context of the courtroom. Given that there are both personal goals and common goals in the trial communication, emphasizing the common goal is crucial to mitigate conflicts.
C. The interactive environment. To make one's speech more appealing and convincing to others, speakers should express evaluative attitudes concerning the case in question properly, ensuring that both the opposing parties, the judges, and the audience may understand them well as potential recipients of the speech.

Third, evaluations of a given case are facilitated, mediated, and consolidated by language resources, particularly the systems of Affect, Judgment, and Appreciation, which have been found to be positively associated with effective communications in various institutional contexts, including judicial situations. A thorough understanding of the potential of the resources in context would surely have significant impacts on the realization of various purposes in legal activities.

Fourth, when the *right* linguistic resources are adopted, such textual factors as the organization of information (the thematic structure), the prosodic overflow of the attitudinal stance as a whole, and the aesthetic impact on the audience should be considered so as to use these resources skillfully in the specific context and text.

8.4 Limitations and Suggestions

This study has three limitations to be clarified. First of all, the discourse of lawyer evaluation is just outlined generally, and the linguistic means examined in this study are far from exhaustive.

Secondly, this study assumes that the interpersonal positioning of lawyers in rational discourse could be conducive to changing the perspective of the judges, the opposing lawyers, and the audience. It is taken for granted that lawyer evaluation has a persuasive effect in aligning and dis-aligning. In line with the statement that "texts can be understood as naturalizing a reading position for an ideal reader" (Martin 2003: 173), it is argued that through the rational speech style, lawyers could establish and naturalize their positions in the given case as the texts unfold and that textually, judges could be aligned and the opponents be alienated.

Thirdly, the scope of this research is delimited in two aspects. First of all, the discussion on the rational discourse of lawyer evaluation assumes that disputing parties are genuinely engaged in the trial to assert their legitimate rights. The effectiveness of rational speech is primarily considered in routine lawsuits. The situation of a fraud lawsuit where one party attempts to take a lawsuit as a way of achieving other strategic purposes is not taken into account here. Because of this, caution is required when discussing the effects of lawyer evaluation in other situations. In addition, as an exploratory study, this research tackles only the substantial wordings used in lawyer speech. The expressions of evaluation at prosodic or nonverbal levels are not considered.

Two suggestions are proposed for research on lawyer evaluation in subsequent studies. Firstly, experimental studies may be conducted on the persuasive effect of the rational discourse of lawyer evaluation. As suggested in the empirical study about the relationship between witnesses' presentational style and the credibility of their evidence (O'Barr 1982), well-designed experiments are needed to investigate whether lawyer evaluation may produce a much better persuasive effect on the audience than the simple, aggressive debating style. In this regard, many inspiring discoveries made in persuasive communications (see Stiff and Mongeau 2003) may serve as a blueprint to guide the design of prospective experimental studies.

Secondly, the examination of rational discourse in lawyer evaluation, including the constituents of lawyer evaluation redefined in this study, particularly the new variable Social Punishment proposed, is limited to adversarial trials in China and constrained by the cultural context of China. Due to the scope of data and the complexity of theoretical abstraction, the framework on the rational stance of lawyers awaits scholarly scrutiny in the future. However, it is hypothesized that this pattern of lawyer evaluation, including the constituents of lawyer evaluation, may also be present in courtrooms of other regions with similar contextual features, particularly in the legal cultural context. Therefore, it is suggested that further research be conducted specifically on lawyer evaluation in East-Asian countries that share a similar legal tradition with Confucianism as its basis.

References

Bernstein, B. 1972. *Class, codes and control*. London, New York: Routledge.
Fairclough, N. 1992. *Discourse and social change*. Cambridge: Polity Press.
Fairclough, N. 2003. *Analyzing discourse*. London: Routledge.
Habermas, J. 1996. *Between facts and norms*, trans. William Rehg. Massachusetts: MIT.
Halliday, M.A.K. 1978. *Language as social semiotic*. London: Edward Arnold.
Halliday, M.A.K. 1996. Literary and linguistics: A functional perspective. In *Literacy in society*, ed. R. Hasan and G. Williams, 339–376. London & New York: Longman.
Hasan, R. 1996. Literary, everyday talk, and society. In *Literacy in society*, ed. R. Hasan and G. Williams, 377–424. London & New York: Longman.
Hood, S. 2004. Managing attitude in undergraduate academic writing: A focus on the introductions to research reports. In *Analyzing academic writing*, ed. L. Ravelli and R. Ellis, 24–44. London & New York: Continuum.

Huang, Bin-bin. 2011. 简论现行人民陪审员制度的完善 [Brief discussions on the improvement of People's Jurors]. 法制与社会 [*Law and Society*] (3): 121–122. https://doi.org/10.19387/j.cnki.1009-0592.2011.08.067

Kšrner, H. 2000. *Negotiating Authority: Logogenesis of dialogue in common law judgments.* Unpublished doctoral dissertation, Sydney University, Sydney.

Li, Xiao. 2022. 创新涉外法治人才培养机制 [Training system for foreign law-related Legal Professionals with creativity]. 中国社会科学报 [*Social Sciences in China*], Dec. 7, 2022.

Martin, J. 2003. Introduction. *TEXT* 23 (2): 171–181. https://doi.org/10.1515/text.2003.007

Martin, J., and D. Rose. 2003. *Working with discourse.* London, New York: Continuum.

Miller, D. 2002. Multiple judicial opinions as specialized sites of engagement: conflicting paradigms of valuation and legitimation in *Bush v. Gore 2000.* In *Conflict and negotiation in specialized texts*, ed. M. Gotti, D. Heller, et al., 119–141. Bern: Peter Lang.

Miller, D. 2004. "To meet our common challenge": ENGAGEMENT strategies to alignment and alienation in US international discourse. *Textus XVIII* (1): 39–62.

Niu, Jian-hua. 2013. 回顾与展望: 人民陪审员制度实践探索之观察思考 [Retrospect and prospect: investigations into the system of people's jurors in practice]. 法律适用 [*Law Application*] (2): 99–102.

O'Barr, M. 1982. *Linguistic Evidence: Language Power and Strategy in the Courtroom.* New York: Academic Press.

Philips, S.U. 1998. *Ideology in the Language of the Judge.* New York: Oxford University Press.

Precht, K. 2003. Stance moods in spoken English: Evidentiality and affect in British and American conversation. *Text* 23 (2): 239–257. https://doi.org/10.1515/text.2003.010.

Qu, Tan-zu. 1984. 中国法律与中国社会 [*Law and society in traditional China*]. Beijing: San Lian Bookstore. 三联书店.

Shi, Guangquan. 2006. *The comprise of li and law and historical changes of Chinese traditional legal culture.* Beijing: Law Press.

Stiff, J., and P. Mongeau. 2003. *Persuasive communication*, 2nd ed. New York, London: The Guilford Press.

Tang, Hai-qing. 2014. 卓越法律人才实践应用能力培养的若干思考 [Some reflections on the cultivation of practical application ability of excellent legal talents]. 教育评论 [*Journal of Education Review*] (4): 75–77.

van Dijk, T.A. 1996. Discourse, power, and access. In *Texts and practices*, ed. Carmen R. Coulthard and Malcolm Coulthard. London and New York: Routledge.

Yong, Q., Cheng-guang Jin, and Rong-mao Yao. 2002. 法律适用中的逻辑 [*Logic in law application*]. Beijing: China University of Political Science and Law.

Zhang, Fa-lian. 2022. 提高涉外法治专业人才培养质量的思考 [Reflections on how to improve the quality of training in foreign law-related legal specialists]. 中国高等教育[*China Higher Education*] (7-2): 57–59.

Zhang, Jinfan. 2003. *中国法制史* [*History of Chinese legal systems*]. Beijing: Higher Education Press.

Zhang, Jun, Wei Jiang, and Wen-chang Tian. 2001. 刑事诉讼: 控、辩、审 [*Criminal trials: Dialogues between the prosecution, defense and tribunal*]. 北京: 法律出版社.

Zhang, J., Wei Jiang, and Wen-chang Tian. 2020. 新控辩审三人谈(增补版) [*Further dialogues between the prosecution, defense and tribunal*] (Supplement Version). Beijing: Law Press.

Appendix A
Transcription Notations

A.1 Aspects of Speech Delivery, Including Aspects of Intonation

Intonation	the punctuation marks are NOT used grammatically, but to indicate intonation.
。	the period in Chinese indicates a falling, or final, intonation contour, not necessarily the end of a sentence.
?	a question mark indicates rising intonation, not necessarily a question.
,	a comma indicates "continuing" intonation, not necessarily a clause boundary.
!	An exclamation mark indicates a falling tone with transparent emotions.

A.2 Other Markings

A.2.1 Transcriber's Comments

(()) A	double parentheses are used to mark transcriber's descriptions of events, rather than representations of them: ((cough)), ((sniff)), ((telephone rings)), ((footsteps)), and the like.
(word) B	when all or part of an utterance is in parentheses, or the speaker identification is, this indicates uncertainty on the transcriber's part, but represents a likely possibility.
[word] C	square brackets are used to mark information provided by transcribers in the translated version of the data to make explicit something retrievable in the context of the data.

L. Zhang, *Lawyer Evaluation in Chinese Courtroom*,
https://doi.org/10.1007/978-981-97-1211-3

A.2.2 Numbering

1-n numbers appearing on the left of the discourse are used to designate the sequence of turns and to facilitate later unambiguous reference to each turn.

A.3 Abbreviations

DL	the defense lawyer
PL	the plaintiff's lawyer
LV	the lawyer representing the victim
AL	the appellant's lawyer
X-D-03	the combined use of letters and numbers with hyphens between them designates the number of the data in the dataset.

Appendix B
Selected Trial Transcripts

The trial transcripts attached below, which involve three civil cases, were retrieved from the teaching materials in CD-ROM released by People's Court Press (Beijing) in 2004. For the sake of privacy protection, all information that may lead to the identification of those concerned was anonymized. The numbers in Arabic form (typed before the designated speakers) indicate the sequence of the speech in turns in the verbal exchange and interaction.

1. The trademark infringement case (No. M-S-Z-09)

Case Background

The plaintiff, YANG FEI Toast Chicken Fastfood Corporation Ltd., registered the brand name YANG FEI as the trademark for its products, pancakes, in 1997, and started to use the name ever since, while the defendant, HW Food Corporation Ltd., registered the name of BIN GE as its trademark in 2003. During the period from January to July in 2003, the defendant produced and sold in many supermarkets its pancakes which were labeled "XIN YANG FEI Pancakes in BIN GE". The package of the defendant's products contained information of three kinds: the characters of 新杨妃 and their corresponding pinyin at the top, the trademark BIN GE, and the Chinese characters 新杨妃烧饼 (literally, XIN YANG FEI PENCAKE) in the middle, and the full name and location of the defendant at the bottom. Upon discovering the sold pancakes produced by the defendant, the plaintiff considered that their ownership of the trademark was infringed and then filed a lawsuit against the defendant. However, the defendant did not think their pancakes with the marks mentioned above violated the trademark law.

L. Zhang, *Lawyer Evaluation in Chinese Courtroom*,
https://doi.org/10.1007/978-981-97-1211-3

Trial Transcript

1. 原代: 原告杨妃快餐有限责任公司, 我们的诉讼请求是: 第一项, 判令被告HW食品有限公司停止侵权。第二项, 判令被告赔偿损失30万元……	1. PL: The plaintiff, YANGFEI Fast Food Co. Ltd., has the following claims: first, the defendant, HW Food Co. Ltd., **shall** be ordered to stop the infringement; second, the defendant **shall** be ordered to pay 300,000 yuan in compensation …
2. 被代: 应杨妃快餐公司诉我单位商标侵权一案, 答辩如下, 我单位不构成对原告商标的侵权。原告诉请赔偿经济损失30万元没有客观依据。……	2. DL: In response to the infringement case filed by YANGFEI Fast Food Co. Ltd. against our company, the defendant replies as follows: Our company does not constitute an act of infringement on the plaintiff's trademark, and the plaintiff's claim for 300,000 yuan in compensation has no factual basis …
3. 原代: 被告他在自己的产品的包装上, 使用新杨妃文字以及拼音。这个事实呢, 经过刚才的法庭调查呢是已经得到确认的。所以我们认为呢, 对方的侵权事实呢, 也是已经成立的	3. PL: The defendant used the characters of "新杨妃" and their corresponding pinyin on the packages of their products. This fact has just been ascertained in the court investigation. As a result, we think the opposing party's **infringement** has already been established
4. 被代: 我单位的商标与原告的商标没有任何的相同或相似之处。因此, 我单位商标不构成对原告的商标侵权	4. DL: The trademark we use has no similarity or resemblance of any kind to that of the plaintiff. Therefore, our trademark does not constitute an infringement on the plaintiff's
5. 原代: 我们认为呢, 本案的事实清楚, 原告自取得注册商标专用权之后, 就开始在自己生产的烧饼上使用了这个杨妃的商标。(在) 被告提供的证据里, 他已经提供了, 而且被告代理人也已经承认了, 他们当时在采用这个新杨妃的这个称呼的时候, 也是考虑到有一个杨妃在先, 所以我们认为他的侵权是属于明知的	5. PL: We think that the facts of the case are clear. The plaintiff has been using "杨妃" (YANGFEI) as the brand name for the pancakes they produced ever since they acquired ownership over the trademark. In the evidence they presented, the defendant has shown (that their brand name was "新杨妃" [XIN YANGFEI]). Besides, the defense lawyer has admitted that, when they decided to use the name XIN YANGFEI, they were aware that the brand name YANGFEI had been in use. As a result, we think that their infringement was deliberate
6. 被代: 我们认为呢, 不构成商标的侵权。对于商标的这个概念和定义, 法律都有明确规定。所谓商标, 也就是图形和文字的组合。那么, 从图形和文字的组合, 从双方的商标对比来看, 它不可能是相同的, 相同不存在	6. DL: We think that our action does not constitute trademark infringement. There are specific regulations regarding the concept and definition of the term *trademark*. A trademark refers to a combination of graphics and words. In a comparison of the two brand names in terms of the combination of graphics and words, it is not possible for the two to be identical, and there is nothing identical between the two

(continued)

(continued)

7. 原代: 被告他在自己的产品的包装上, 使用新杨妃文字以及拼音, 这个事实经过刚才的法庭调查是已经得到确认的。所以我们认为呢, 对方的侵权事实呢, 也是已经成立的	7. PL: The defendant used the characters of "新杨妃" (XIN YANGFEI) and the pinyin on the packaging of their products. This fact has just been ascertained in the court investigation. Therefore, we think that the opposing party's infringement has already been established
8. 被代: 我单位的商标与原告的商标没有任何的相同和相似之处。因此, 我单位商标不构成对原告的商标侵权	8. DL: Our trademark has nothing identical or similar to the plaintiff's. Therefore, our trademark does not constitute an infringement on the plaintiff's trademark
9. 原代: 按照商标法的实施细则第50条的第一项, 在同一种或者是类似的商品上, 我们这属于在同一种商品上, 将与他人注册商标相同或者近似的标志作为商品名称, 或者商品装潢使用, 误导公众的, 这构成侵犯商标专用权	9. PL: In accordance with the first item of Article 50 of the Specified Regulations on the Enforcement of the Trademark Law, where one uses a sign that is identical or similar to a registered trademark of another person on the same or similar products as those covered by the registered trademark—it is the same products in our case—as a commodity name or decoration of the products, and causes confusion or misunderstandings among consumers regarding the two products, it constitutes an infringement of the exclusive right to use a trademark
10. 被代: 对于原告所谓使用商标条例里的这一规定, 但是这一规定呀, 我想, 它首先离不开商标法对于商标侵权的这一定义以及它的标准的概念。就是说, 我觉得, 应该以商标法, 以及最高人民法院所颁布的有关司法解释作为我们审判的依据 ((面向法官))	10. DL: With respect to the plaintiff's argument that the provision in the Trademark Law should be applied, I think, the provision should not be considered in insolation from the definition and criteria for trademark infringement specified in the Trademark Law. What I mean is this: we should take the rules in the Trademark Law and the relevant interpretations issued by the Supreme Court as guidelines for our determination of this case ((turning the head toward the judge))
11. 原代: 本案呢, 我们认为是符合这一规定的, 因为他们在商品上使用了杨妃文字和拼音, 以及在它的发票上, 还有超市的机打小票上, 都注明的是新杨妃烧饼。所以, 他们在这个名称上也是使用了这个商标。所以我们认为它这个侵权事实是客观存在的	11. PL: We think this case does fit in with those regulations because the defendant used the characters and pinyin of YANGFEI on their products. Besides, they specified "XIN YANGFEI pancakes" in their invoices and printed customer receipts. That is to say, they used the registered trademark as the designation of their products. As a result, we think that the fact of the defendant's infringement is objective
……	…

(continued)

(continued)

12. 原代: 关于被告侵权的数量呢, 根据我们调查取证, 就是被告6月28号当天, 在各大超市出售的状况, 大概在2000袋左右。每天2000袋, 一个月呢, 大概是6万袋, 然后, 侵权时间呢, 据我们掌握呢, 是起码有半年了。我们认为这个侵权数量, 应该可以作为本案这种赔偿的定案依据的	12. PL: Regarding the quantity of infringement, based on the evidence that we investigated and collected, on June 28, the defendant sold about 2000 bags in the supermarkets. If there are 2000 bags a day, then it would be about 60,000 bags a month. Then, the infringement time, in accordance with the information we gathered, exceeds half a year at least. We think the infringement quantity calculated this way should be taken as evidence for the determination of compensation
13. 被代: 对于刚才原告方关于三十万损失的证据, 我方表示疑义, 啊 ((面向审判席)), 因为首先, 从原告所出示的证据来反映, 所谓这个三十万元的构成依据不存在。那么, 对于这个每天两千袋, 一个月六万袋这个推算数字来讲, 也不符合情理。啊, ((面向对方)), 即使说是, 一天有两千袋, 也不可能是每天都有两千袋。就是说, ((面向法官)) 如果是六万袋的话, 必须有六万袋的数据	13. DL: As for the evidence the plaintiff has proposed in support of their claim for 300,000 yuan in compensation, we have some doubts. Er, ((turning to face the bench)), because at first, the evidence the plaintiff presented indicates that there is no supportive evidence for their claim for 300,000 yuan in compensation. Moreover, regarding the estimated figures, 2000 bags a day and 60,000 bags a month, the estimation does not align with our common-sense perception. Um, ((turning to face the contestants)) even though there were 2000 bags sold in a single day, it is impossible that there would be 2000 bags every day. What I mean is, ((turning back to face the judge)) if the plaintiff proposes the figure 60,000 bags, there must be evidence to support it

(continued)

(continued)

14. 原代: 被告所提交的证据……是属于虚假的. 所以我们认为呢, 在被告拒不提供确切的销售数量以及销售成本, 以及提供的这个销售数量和销售承本明显虚假的情况下, 法院应该采纳我们这方提供的证据。根据最高法院有关规定, 以及商标法的有关规定, 商标法56条规定, 侵权人因侵权所得, 所得利益或被侵权人因被侵权所得损失难以确定的, 由人民法院根据侵权行为的情节判决给予50万元以下的赔偿。所以我们认为呢, 我们所向法庭主张的三十万元的赔偿数额, 应该是应当的, 而且是有理有据的	14. PL: The evidence the defendant presented … is false. Therefore we think, under the circumstances that the defendant refuses to provide accurate information about the sales figure and sales cost, or the sales figure and sales cost they provided are apparently false, the court should take the information provided by our side as evidence. According to the regulations issued by the Supreme Court and the relevant rules in the Trademark Law, Article 56 of the Trademark Law provides that "if neither the income nor interest obtained by the infringer nor the loss suffered by the infringed party can be calculated, the people's court may award compensation of no more than 500,000 yuan based on the circumstances of the infringement act". Consequently, we think our claim for 300,000 yuan in compensation to the court shall be reasonable and well-founded
15. 被代: ((面向对方)) 那么对损失的计算呢, 现在呢, …	15. DL: ((turning to face the contestants)) Well, as to the calculation of the financial loss, now, the Supreme Court …

2. The tort case related to reputation (No. M-S-Z-08)

Case Background

The plaintiffs, three computer resellers, sued the defendant, the X Consumers Association, on the grounds of reputational damage. In 2012, the defendant, X Consumers Organization, organized an experiment to check the radioactivity status of computers, and the computers produced by the three plaintiffs were chosen as samples. In the experiment report issued later, the said computers of the plaintiffs were rated high in radioactivity, which means these computers may emit harmful waves into the environment. The plaintiffs later claimed in litigation that the defendant's behavior caused harm to the reputation of their products.

Trial Transcript

1. 原代: 既然法律没有明文的授权, **X**消费者协会, 做这个 ((比较实验)), 就是违法的, 很明确, 第一点。第二, 既然你又是起草者, 又是立法者, 你不能既当运动员, 又当裁判员。你既然起草了, 又为什么要去执法?这是法律最基本的原理。……最起码的观点, 你怎么能执行这个法律?我从整个举证中, 所有的证据中看不出哪一点有明确的授权。相反,《消费者权益保护法》《产品质量法》把你们的权利规定的清清楚楚, ……你们的职能就是参与行政部门的协调, 这就是职能。接受消费者投诉, 有了投诉, 你们协调一下, 就这么回事	1. PL: Now that there is no clear authorization in law, it is **illegal** for the **X Consumers Association** to conduct the comparative experiment. It is a very clear fact. This is the first point I make. The second point is that **you** are both the drafter and the law-maker in this case, but **you** can not work as both athletes and referees. Now that you are the drafter of the law, how could you be the executor of the law in practice? This is a basic principle in law. … The simplest question is, how can **you** be the implementer of the law? Reviewing all the evidence you presented, all the evidence, **I** cannot see where you are specifically authorized ((to do the experiments)). On the contrary, the Law on Protecting the Consumer's Rights and Interests and the Product Quality Law have delimited **your duties clearly**, … **Your function** is to assist the relevant administrative departments in supervising and checking commodities and services. This is your function, to accept the complaints from consumers. Upon receiving complaints, you may mediate the negotiation process. That is all you can do
2. 被代: 我不知原告注意到了没有, 最近, 最近这段时间, 已经, 国家工商局已经抽检了多少批次, 我不知道你注意到了没有, 这个不是说, 就只有你一家, 这是一个概念。第二个概念,《消费者权益保护法》《产品质量法》以及很多法律法规, 中消协是, 都参与制订的, 都是提了意见的……所以这个, 跟你说的那个情况, 不是一回事。什么又是裁判员啦, 又是什么这个, 我觉得这个说法是不对的	2. DL: I do not know whether the plaintiff has noticed how many products per time the State Administration of Industry and Commerce has already checked recently, just recently. I do not know whether you have noticed this or not. This is not to say that you are the only one [whose products were checked and examined]. This is the thing we have to make clear here. The second thing to be made clear is that the China Consumers Association did participate and propose suggestions in the drafting and making of many laws and regulations, such as the Law on Protecting Consumers Rights and Interests and the Product Quality Law … Therefore, it is not the same as what you said just now: the referees or whatever. I do not think those viewpoints are correct

(continued)

(continued)

3. 原代: 被告**指使**其工作人员, 以普通工作人员的身份, 购买商品, 违背其工作(原则), 有**陷阱取证**的行为。其抽取的样品, 不具有客观性, 真实性	3. PL: In breach of its duties, the defendant incited its workers to buy the commodity as ordinary consumers. It is an act of "**trapping evidence**". There is no objectivity and authenticity in the sampled commodities
4. 被代: 比如说, 我们在座的所有各位, 你们到商场购买东西的时候, 你们用什么方式?这个问题不就是你看到了商品, 你选嘛?!你选择, 选好你付钱么, 对吧!我们就是用这个方式, 消费者是怎么买商品, 我们就用什么方式去做, 完全是按照模拟消费	4. DL: I would like to ask people at present a question. How do you typically buy commodities when you go shopping? Don't you just select the item you like among many and then pay for it when you get your selection? Right? That is precisely what we did when we sampled the computers. We conducted the sampling the way consumers do their shopping, using what is called simulated consumption
5. 原代: 这种鉴定无法保证其公正性, 而且就不排除国家电子检测中心为了这个产品进行处理, 打击大部分企业, 同时为了收取费用。……那就表明了这里面有一些**不属于合法的手段**, **也不属于正当的手段**。被告应当**心知肚明**	5. PL: That testing cannot guarantee the impartiality of its result. Additionally, it cannot rule out the possibility that the National Electronic Radiation Test Center may have engaged in some misconduct against these computers with a view to pressing a majority of other enterprises and also gaining profits out of the testing … This suggests the involvement of **some illegal and illegitimate means**. The defendant should **have been aware of this**
6. 被代: 消费者协会开展商品比较实验, 完全是公益的	6. DL: It is utterly **non-profitable** that the Consumers Association conducts comparative experiments on commodities
7. 原代: 被告口口声声声称自己是公益事业。我们承认被告是公益事业, 但是任何公益事业都必须在遵守法律的前途下进行。否则, 就会破坏国家法制的健全	7. PL: The defendant **has claimed** their work is **non-profitable**. We may acknowledge that it is non-profitable. However, any non-profitable work has to be conducted in accordance with the law. Otherwise, it would do harm to the integrity of the law

3. Tort case related to personal injury (No. M-S-Z-10)

Case Background

The plaintiff, Miss T, had a cosmetic surgery performed by the defendant, KUN Hospital. A few days later, she found red spots emerged on her nose, for which she had to seek extra medical treatments. Then, attributing the red spots to misconduct associated with the surgery, the plaintiff filed a lawsuit against the defendant and claimed compensation related to the injury in her nose. The defendant denied such a claim, arguing that the surgery caused no injury.

Trial Transcript

1. 原代: 根据我国民法通则的规定, …… 被告的行为构成了美容损害, 应当承担损害赔偿责任	1. PL: In accordance with the General Principles of Civil Law of the People's Republic of China, … The defendant's act constituted medical malpractice in the cosmetic surgery, and they should be held liable for the injury compensation
2. 被代: 手术效果, 我刚见到T女士, 啊, 我认为看的很细, 鼻梁的造型比照片还要美的多, 美的多!鼻梁非常好, 立体感!啊, 我们认为, 手术是成功的。既不存在伤害问题, 也不存在手术不成功的问题。这对于原告方提出的各种赔偿补助, 我们不予接受	2. DL: The clinical effect, when I met Miss T just now, er, I think I observed her nose very closely. The shape of her nose looks more beautiful than in the photo, more beautiful! The bridge of the nose is very nicely done. How upright it is! Ah, we think, the operation was **successful**. There was neither any injury nor failure in the operation. Therefore, we would not accept the plaintiff's claim for injury compensation
3. 原代: 被告说, 手术效果是成功的, 那我们可以看一看, 原告现在就坐在法庭上, 那这一个是鼻尖, 鼻梁歪斜, 这, 我觉得常人都可以观察的到, 嗯, 这个, 可以进一步的观察。第二, 鼻尖发红, 这个已经为HS美容外科医院它的医疗鉴定, 出的是医疗证明, 它是由于假体大小不合适所造成的, 这个, 我觉得是不容置疑的事实。所以说, ……	3. PL: The defense argues that the operation was successful. Er, we may have a closer look at the plaintiff, who is seated over there in the court. Er, first of all, the nasal apex and the bridge of the nose are deviated, which, I think, may be noticeable to every person. Um, the deviation may be checked further. Secondly, there are red spots in the nasal apex, which have been diagnosed by the HS Cosmetology Surgery Hospital. According to the medical report made by the Surgery Hospital, the red spots were caused by improper implants. This, I think, is **an undeniable fact**. Therefore …
4. 被代: 我们认为手术成功的, HS美容医院不是医疗事故签定权威单位, 它也是个美容医院, 啊, 它如果说有医疗事故鉴定权力, 请它出示相关的证明和批文	4. DL: We believe that the operation was successful. The HS Cosmetology Surgery Hospital is not an authorized organ for appraising medical malpractice. It is a cosmetology hospital, too. Er, if the Hospital claims that it has the authorized right to appraise medical malpractice, we would request that it present relevant certificates and official documents
……	…
5. 原代: 证据一, 广告信息一份, 所要证明的事项是, 一, 证明被告于2003年4月1日在《现代女报》上刊登广告, 宣称其为正规的医疗机构, 并承诺……, 第二, 证明……	5. PL: Exhibit No. 1, one copy of the advertisement, proves two points. Firstly, the defendant put up an advertisement in the newspaper of Modern Women on April 1, 2003, claiming that it is a medical institute with professional qualifications and offering guarantees of … Secondly, it proves that …

(continued)

(continued)

6. 被代: 证据一, 按复印件来看, 没有我KUN医院的名字, 这我看了看, 这都不是	6. DL: Exhibit No. 1, as observed in the photocopy of it, has no information of the defendant's name in it. I have read it all over. There is no reference to the QIAN KUN Hospital in it
7. 原代: 证据二, KUN医院治疗单和X市门诊收费专业收据各一份, 证明事项, 一, 证明原, 被告双方之间存在美容服务法律关系的事实, 第二, 证明 原告向被告缴纳的手术费650元, 与被告广告宣传的收费标准不符	7. PL: Exhibit No. 2, one medical treatment record of KUN Hospital, and one official medical examination receipt in X City prove two points. Firstly, there is a legal relationship between the plaintiff and the defendant as per the beauty contract. Secondly, the plaintiff paid the defendant 650 yuan for the surgery fee, which was not consistent with the charge standards specified in the advertisement
8. 被代: 隆鼻术确实收了650元, 这个没有争议, 啊。如果这个广告是KUN医院的, 600元与650元, 这个没有根本的很大的冲突	8. DL: The nose augmentation operation did charge the defendant 650 yuan, which is indisputable. Ah, if the advertisement is indeed from the KUN Hospital, 600 yuan or 650 yuan, there is no substantial difference between them
9. 原代: 证据三, HS美容医院诊断证明书一份, 证明事项: 一, 证明原告笔尖发红的原因是由于隆鼻手术所用的假体大小不合适所致。第二, ……	9. PL: Exhibit No. 3, one diagnosis record from HS Cosmetology Hospital. It proves two things. Firstly, the red spots in the nose apex of the plaintiff were caused by the improper implant in the nose augmentation operation. Secondly …
10. 被代: HS美容医院是一所部队美容医院, 啊, 跟其他美容医院一样, 都是美容医院和美容科, 啊, 它在美容的鉴定上, 没有权威性, 没有法律性	10. DL: The HS Cosmetology Hospital is an aesthetic hospital run by the military. Um, like other aesthetic hospitals, it is an aesthetic hospital or aesthetic department without any authoritative power or legal authorization in the appraisal of beauty operations

Appendix C
Article 5 of Anti-Unfair Competition Law of China (1993)

第五条 经营者不得采用下列不正当手段从事市场交易, 损害竞争对手	Article 5 When engaging in market transactions, business operators shall not adopt any of the following unfair means, which may cause damage to their competitors
(一) 假冒他人的注册商标	(1) Counterfeiting registered trademarks of others
(二) 擅自使用知名商品特有的名称, 包装, 装璜, 或者使用与知名商品近似的名称, 包装, 装璜, 造成和他人的知名商品相混淆, 使购买者误认为是该知名商品	(2) Unauthorized use of distinctive names, packaging, or decoration specific to a well-known product, or the use of names, packaging, or decoration similar to those of a well-known product, causing confusion with the well-known product to the effect that consumers may mistakenly believe that the products in question are the said well-known products
(三) 擅自使用他人的企业名称或者姓名, 引人误认为是他人的商品	(3) Unauthorized use of another person's enterprise name or personal name on their own goods, creating the mistaken impression that their products in question are the goods of another person
(四) 在商品上伪造或者冒用认证标志, 名优标志等质量标志, 伪造产地, 对商品质量作引人误解的虚假表示	(4) Falsifying or using counterfeit symbols of product quality such as authentication marks, famous brand or quality brand indicators, fabricating the place of origin, or making misleading or false representations regarding the quality of their products

L. Zhang, *Lawyer Evaluation in Chinese Courtroom*,
https://doi.org/10.1007/978-981-97-1211-3

MIX
Papier aus verantwortungsvollen Quellen
Paper from responsible sources
FSC® C105338

If you have any concerns about our products,
you can contact us on
ProductSafety@springernature.com

In case Publisher is established outside the EU,
the EU authorized representative is:
Springer Nature Customer Service Center GmbH
Europaplatz 3, 69115 Heidelberg, Germany

Printed by Libri Plureos GmbH
in Hamburg, Germany